The Split-Level Cookbook

The Split-Level
COOKBOOK

Family Meals to Cook Once and Serve Twice

LouAnn Gaeddert

THOMAS Y. CROWELL COMPANY

New York   Established 1834

For Esther and Orlan

Acknowledgments

My special thanks go to Glenna McGinnis and Eleanor Haugh. I never could have written the book without Mrs. McGinnis' encouragement and cheerful criticism. Mrs. Haugh helped me test the recipes.

Designed by Joan Becker

Manufactured in the United States of America

L.C. Card 67-23675

First Printing

Contents

Introduction

The leisurely family dinner with Father presiding at the head of the table has, for millions of families in this country, become a sometime —even a rare—thing. Blame Father's commuter train, his business duties which often keep him at his desk long after his secretary has gone home, or his huge business lunches. Blame the early hunger pangs and bedtimes of young children. Blame the Scouts, band practice, and other early-evening activities of older children.

Wherever the blame lies, the result is the same. Mother has become a short-order cook. Her "dinner hour" may begin as early as five o'clock when she feeds the children. What does she feed them? Too often it is the hamburgers and canned peas that all children are supposed to love, and they may. This kind of unimaginative meal planning, however, hardly helps children learn to enjoy a wide variety of foods.

Then, while Mother is cleaning up after the children, supervising baths and homework, and rushing the older children off to their activities, she must turn right around and prepare another dinner for the adults. If she weren't exhausted, this later dinner with adult conversation could be the delight of her day. But in practice, the hours of preparation for both dinners are apt to leave her in a state of collapse.

This book is designed to cut your dinner preparation time in half. It offers menus and recipes for dishes that can be prepared either just before the children's dinner hour or earlier in the afternoon. The adults' portions can be held until the later dinner hour and served with no more than a few minutes of additional kitchen time. Obviously, these menus will also be useful when you entertain.

Right now, I would like to make one thing clear. Though it is often necessary for children and adults to eat separately, it is essential for the members of the family to eat together whenever possible. One has only to listen to the dinner-table conversation of two or three young children to see that they need to learn to dine graciously. This is almost impossible to learn in the exclusive presence of other, equally uncivilized, children. So do join your children in the dining room whenever possible.

When it is impossible, I hope that the children will eat well and that the adults will enjoy their later meals—perhaps even find them romantic!

WHAT IS IN THE BOOK?

The first part of this book is devoted to main dishes and menus. There are chapters devoted to whole-meal soups, beef, veal, lamb, pork, variety meats, poultry, seafood, and egg and cheese dishes. A menu accompanies each main-dish recipe. An asterisk (*) beside an item means that a recipe appears elsewhere in the book; you can turn to the index and find recipes for these vegetables, salads, breads, and desserts.

This is a family cookbook. You will find no suggestions for seven-course meals or elegant dishes that take hours of preparation. All of the ingredients can be found in any good supermarket.

Many of the recipes and menus would be delightful company fare. To mention just a few: Boeuf Bourguignonne, Blanquette de Veau, Duck in Orange Sauce, Scallop-Lobster Casserole, and Crab Crêpes.

Because it is a family cookbook, economy has been considered. Most of the recipes are relatively inexpensive, and a number of them will be particularly welcome any time you face a pocketbook crisis. On such occasions, turn to recipes for soup, and those using hamburger, tuna, and egg and cheese. See also the recipes for Breast of Veal with Potatoes and Carrots, Lamb Patties and Peaches, Lamb Loaves, Hodge Podge, and Lazy Liz's Sausage 'n Rice.

If you are like me, your greatest problem may be lack of time. There is no reason to spurn shortcuts and convenience foods. Many of the recipes in this book can be prepared in thirty minutes. For half a dozen examples of these, see Beef-Bean Shortcake, Veal Scallops, Canadian Bacon with Apricots and Stuffing Balls, Festive Chicken Livers and Mushrooms, Quick Shrimp Jambalaya, and Clam Bunny.

Ingredients for an emergency meal are like money in the bank. You never know when you'll need them. You may not be able to get to the store on your regular shopping day. Friends or relatives may drop in unexpectedly. The following recipes and menus may save your day: Supper Waffles, Ham or Luncheon Meat with Sweet Potatoes and Pineapple, Luncheon Meat with Apples, Crabby Shrimp, and any of the egg and cheese dishes.

A WORD ABOUT MEAL PLANNING

The menus in this book are meant as suggestions, not laws. You should feel free to substitute whatever you and your family prefer for any of the items in the menus. Your menus should, however, contain variety—variety in texture, color, and flavor. If, for example, the main dish is a stew, you will want to serve a colorful and crispy salad with it. Try always to have something green on your menu and something yellow or red. If the main dish is bland, you will want to serve something spicy or tart with it.

Go easy on the sauces. The cook-now-serve-later cook is apt to overdo sauces since they make reheating very easy. But one sauce or gravy is plenty. One combination dish is enough too. If the main dish is hash, the salad should not be mixed up little bits of many different vegetables but should be made of very distinct and separate vegetables—slices of tomato on greens, for example. The "rule of one" also holds true for seasonings—one dish flavored with onion, one cheese-flavored dish, one lemon-flavored dish, etc.

Vary your main dishes during the week. Beef and chicken are by far the most popular meats—and good. But don't serve either of them more than twice a week. It isn't necessary when you have lamb, veal, pork, variety meats, seafood, cheese and egg dishes to choose from.

A WORD ABOUT UTENSILS

Happy surprise: you really don't need anything special! I assume, however, that you are going to do a lot of cooking now and serving later. You may want to add a few items to your kitchen inventory to make meal preparation easier.

Remember that cooking ware that can go directly to the table cuts down on the dish washing.

In writing this book, I have frequently referred to au gratin dishes. I have two that can be put directly over heat, in the oven, under the broiler, and in the freezer. Frankly, I don't believe I could cook without them. They are both attractively colored enamel over cast iron. One is about 8" x 6" x 2". The other is larger. However, if you don't have au gratin dishes you can usually use pie plates or shallow casseroles. Just remember not to put them directly on heat or under the broiler unless the directions that come with them say that they can be used this way.

Shallow casseroles are frequently more satisfactory than deep ones because food bakes quicker in them and more crust forms. Remember that you can always use foil on your casseroles if they don't have covers. Individual casseroles or 12-ounce custard cups are also useful.

At least one double broiler is essential and you may want to have two, a large one for main dishes and a small one for sauces.

FOR DIETERS ONLY

In preparing this book, I have not been counting calories. Few of these recipes are delicate, however, and you can reduce the calorie count by eliminating some of the butter, substituting skim milk for whole milk, and using dietetic fruit, etc. With the new instant-type flour you can even make a white sauce with *no* butter. Since many of the main dishes are prepared in individual casseroles, you can easily cut the calories for one person in the family and not for the other members of the family.

HOW MANY WILL EACH RECIPE SERVE?

These recipes are for four hungry people except where otherwise noted. They will also serve two adults and three little children. Who knows if any of them will be adequate if you have a teen-age boy? You'll just have to try a few recipes and see how they fit your family. But again, few of these recipes are so sensitive that you cannot easily reduce or increase them to fit your needs.

WHEN IN DOUBT, REFRIGERATE

The question arises as to what to do with dishes between the time they are cooked and the time they are to be reheated for the later meal. In a relatively cool kitchen, most dishes will be safe at

[x]

room temperature for at least two hours. It seems to me, however, that any dish that is cool enough to go into the refrigerator might just as well be put there. Then you can forget it until you are ready to reheat it.

A NOTE ABOUT GRAVY

Whenever you cook a large piece of meat or poultry from which you expect to have leftovers, make twice as much gravy as you think you will need. Gravy costs practically nothing to make, and it is frequently handy when it comes time to cope with the leftovers. You will also want to keep a supply of canned gravies or packages of gravy mix on hand for glorifying leftovers.

Soups

Sing a song in praise of soup!

We've been neglecting it lately. Perhaps we should blame our affluence, in which we have turned to fancier foods. Or perhaps we should blame prepared soups, which are convenient and tasty but just not as satisfying as the kinds we make ourselves.

You will find delicious whole-meal soup recipes here, which can be served with bread and crackers, a hearty dessert and nothing else. I have even included a recipe for Knife and Fork Soup, which has been designed to convert husbands to the soup-for-dinner idea. It contains big slices of beef and whole potatoes, surrounded by rich broth and vegetables—a complete meal if there ever was one.

It is true that many soups take hours to make, but they are hours when you can do something else while sniffing the delicious aroma that the simmering soup sends through the house. Try it. It will make you feel like the best kind of *Hausfrau.*

For those of you who don't *want* to feel like *Hausfraus,* I have also included a number of jiffy—but hearty—soups and some that are suitable for a first course.

A warning to soup makers: Grandma may have kept the soup pot simmering on the back of the range for hours, even days, but don't you try it. If your kitchen is fairly cool, and you expect to serve the adults within two hours after the children have eaten, you may simply set the soup aside to be reheated. But, if your kitchen is warm or the adult dinner hour is uncertain, cool the soup and refrigerate until just before serving time.

Soups freeze well and can easily be thawed by heating in a covered saucepan.

CREATIVE VEGETABLE SOUP

*French Bread with Garlic Butter**
Cherry Pie à la Mode

CREATIVE VEGETABLE SOUP

Housewives are miserable because their lives are so dull and un-demanding. That's what a group of militant authors have been writing about lately. Frankly, I'm fed up with their sermons. Furthermore, I am convinced that making delicious vegetable soup is a lot more "creative" than typing someone else's letters.

It's impossible to write formal recipes for vegetable soup, because what goes into the soup depends on what is in the refrigerator. I'll tell you instead about the soup that's in my kettle right now.

Yesterday I bought a chicken for last night's dinner and a big soup bone that I asked the butcher to saw into pieces. Late in the afternoon I put the bones in a large (4-quart) kettle with an onion, a stalk of celery with leaves on, a carrot and some salt and pepper. Then I poured in about 2 quarts of water, covered the kettle and kept it simmering for about 3 hours. My house was filled with the most delicious scent.

When I prepared the chicken for dinner, I threw the neck, gizzard, and back into the soup pot. Several weeks ago, I bought a rolled roast beef that was a most peculiar shape. In order to even it up, I had cut one end off before I roasted the rest of the meat. This end was in the freezer, so I added it to my soup pot. As soon as the piece of beef was tender, I took it out and let it cool.

I drained the liquid from the boiled potatoes for last night's dinner into the soup pot, too. And I added some liquid from canned vegetables that I had stored in a jar in the refrigerator.

After the three hours of simmering, I drained the soup in a col-lander and threw away everything that didn't go through the holes. The flavor and vitamins were all in the broth after the cooking anyway. I cut the beef in bite-size pieces and added it to the broth, along with some corn that was left over from dinner. When the broth was cool, I covered and refrigerated it.

Today, there was a thick layer of solid grease on the top; this I lifted off. Underneath was a lovely thick gelatin, which I put back into the soup kettle with a box of frozen vegetables, ¼ cup raw rice and an 8-ounce can of stewed tomatoes, another onion (cut up), and more salt and pepper. This mixture will be cooked for about 15 minutes, until the rice and vegetables are tender. That's it. It will be delicious and can be reheated easily.

But that's only one way to make vegetable soup.

Every good vegetable soup needs a rich broth. You may, of course, buy canned consommé. Personally, I think it is much more sporting to make your own broth using bones—a soup bone that you buy, bones left over from a lamb, beef, pork, or veal roast, or a turkey carcass.

Every good soup also needs bites of meat—a 1-pound piece of chuck, or meaty pieces of chicken which you add while you are making the broth. Be sure to remove the meat when it is tender. If you are using chicken, take the meat from the bones and put the bones and skin back in the kettle to continue simmering. Or you may add already cooked meat with the vegetables during the last 15 minutes of cooking. This could be leftovers cut in bite-size pieces or canned meat or meat balls.

As for vegetables, almost anything goes. Leftover vegetables, canned vegetables, or frozen ones. Fresh vegetables in season are the very best. If you use fresh vegetables, time everything carefully so they will be done at the same time. The traditional soup vegetables are carrots, string beans, peas, turnips, lima beans, corn, cabbage, onions, celery, tomatoes, and okra.

Then you will probably want to add something starchy. Potatoes don't reheat very well, so, because I expect to eat my soup for several days, I usually use rice, macaroni, or noodles.

That's it. Just remember that all you need to make delicious vegetable soup are bones to make broth, pieces of meat, vegetables, and a starchy food.

KNIFE AND FORK SOUP

Bread Sticks
Sherbet or Fruit with Cookies

KNIFE AND FORK SOUP

One or several days before you wish to serve this soup, put the following items in a large pot—one that holds at least 4 quarts:

1 marrow bone, sawed into pieces
1½-pound piece of beef chuck,
  tied into a compact form
1 small white turnip, halved ⎫
1 parsnip, quartered   ⎪ Any one
1 leek, split   ⎬ of these
1 large onion, halved   ⎪ can
1 large carrot, quartered   ⎪ be
1 stalk celery with leaves   ⎭ omitted.
1 clove garlic
2 tablespoons tomato catsup
½ teaspoon dried rosemary
2 teaspoons salt
Water to cover other ingredients

Simmer about 2 hours, or until meat is tender, skimming the top once or twice if scum forms. Remove the meat, and cool and refrigerate it. Continue simmering the other ingredients, adding more water if necessary, for as long as is convenient—at least an hour. (This is a wonderful rainy-day project. The simmering soup will make you feel so domestic that you can lie on the couch and read a novel without feeling guilty.) Turn the heat off and allow the soup to cool a little. Then strain the broth into another container and throw away everything that doesn't go through the sieve—the flavor is out of the vegetables and in the broth by now. Cool and refrigerate the broth.

The next day or several days later, remove the fat, which will have solidified on the top of the soup, and discard it. Put the broth back into the large pot with the following ingredients:

3 carrots, sliced into circles
2 stalks celery, sliced, with leaves
  removed
1 turnip, diced
1 onion, diced
Whole potatoes

Simmer for 30 minutes and then add:

1 package frozen cross-cut green beans, thawed
¼ green cabbage, shredded

The children's portion of chuck
Salt
Pepper

Watch the potatoes and remove them when they are done—before they begin to fall apart. When the beans are done, return the potatoes the children will eat to the pot for a minute or two. Then put a potato and a slice of beef in each soup plate and pour the vegetables and broth over them.

When the children are through eating, put the rest of the meat and the potatoes into the soup. Just before you and your husband are ready to eat, bring the soup to a boil and simmer for a few minutes.

If you have any leftover potatoes, save them for another purpose. Dice any leftover meat and add to the soup to be heated up a day or two later with noodles or rice. In fact, you can add canned beef broth or bouillon and vegetables, and this one pot of soup can go on indefinitely. It's magic!

HAM HOCKS AND PEA BEAN SOUP

*Apple Cider Salad on Greens**
Assorted Crackers
*Spice Cake with Maple Frosting**

HAM HOCKS AND PEA BEAN SOUP

2 pounds smoked ham hocks
1 pound dried pea or lima beans
1 large onion, sliced
1 carrot, sliced

1 teaspoon dry mustard
1 tablespoon Worcestershire
2 quarts water
1 can condensed tomato soup

Combine all ingredients except tomato soup in a large kettle and simmer 1 hour. (The beans need not be soaked in advance.) Add the tomato soup and continue to cook until the ham and beans are tender —another 1 or 2 hours. Remove the ham. Discard the skin and fat. Cut the ham into bite-size pieces and return to the soup. Taste for seasoning. Make when convenient and refrigerate. Reheat on top of the stove, adding more water if necessary. Serve in large soup bowls.

HAM AND SPLIT PEA SOUP

Waldorf Salad*
Corn Muffins
Pumpkin Pie

You may have gathered that I like to make soup. I do. And I especially like to make split pea soup because I enjoy eating it and because it is so inexpensive. You can buy a pound of split peas for a few cents. There is one problem you may encounter. If the soup gets too thick, it may stick to the bottom of the kettle. When it cools the stuck part comes loose, but then you have little brown flecks all through the soup. If you should scorch the soup, quickly pour off the unstuck part and transfer to another kettle. Soak the scorched kettle in cold water and detergent.

If you aren't quite as enthusiastic about soup as I am, you may want to try canned or packaged split pea soup. It is good, too, and you can jazz it up with additional meat and sliced carrots and an onion.

HAM AND SPLIT PEA SOUP

1 pound green or yellow split peas	1 large onion, chopped
Water	2 carrots, sliced
Ham bone with some ham but no fat	Salt
	Pepper

Put the split peas and 8 cups of water in a 4-quart kettle. Boil for 2 minutes and then let stand for 1 hour. Add the remaining ingredients. Cover, bring to a boil, lower heat, and simmer until the peas have disintegrated and the soup is thick and smooth. Stir frequently and add more water if necessary. This will take about 2 hours. *Instead of ham,* you may substitute sausage, a thick slice of ham cut in cubes, or cubed canned luncheon meat.

There is nothing delicate about split pea soup. You can cook it at your convenience, 1 or 2 days before you wish to serve it if you like. When the soup is done, remove the bone. Cut off any lean pieces of ham and return the pieces to the kettle. Cool and refrigerate any portion of the soup that will not be eaten within an hour or so.

CHICKEN-CORN SOUP

Assorted Crackers
Assorted Relishes
Apple Pie*

CHICKEN-CORN SOUP

3–4-pound broiler-fryer chicken, whole or cut up
1 large onion, sliced
1 carrot, sliced
1 stalk celery with leaves
1 teaspoon salt
Dash nutmeg
Water
1 cup uncooked noodles
10-ounce can whole-kernel corn

Put chicken, onion, carrot, celery, salt, and nutmeg in pot and cover with boiling water. Simmer from 40 minutes to 1 hour until chicken is tender. Turn off the heat and place chicken in a large sieve or collander. Drain until cool enough to handle. Remove all the chicken from the bones. Save the best pieces for another meal—salad, sandwiches, or casserole. Set aside 2 cups of chicken pieces to be returned to the soup later. In the meantime, return all of the bones and vegetables to the cooking pot and simmer them another hour or so. Strain the broth. The broth may be refrigerated and the soup made the next day. Or you may return the broth to the pan, add the soup chicken, noodles and corn, and simmer for 15 minutes—until the noodles are tender but not mushy. Serve the children. Just before the adult meal, reheat the soup to the boiling point.

Quick Soups

With all of the canned, frozen, and dehydrated soups on the market you may never want to completely create your own soup. Following are some easy, hearty soups made simple with prepared ingredients.

BAKED BEAN SOUP

*Lettuce Wedges with Blue Cheese Dressing**
Cornsticks and Crackers
*Dessert Salad**

This is a good meatless dish. After the beans have gone through the food mill, you could add canned or precooked meat balls, diced ham, or luncheon meat.

BAKED BEAN SOUP

1-pound can baked beans
¼ cup chopped onion
¼ cup sliced celery
¼ cup sliced carrot
2 cups water

8-ounce can stewed tomatoes
1 can condensed consommé
¼ cup chili sauce
2 hard-boiled eggs, thinly sliced
1 lemon, thinly sliced

Simmer beans, onion, celery, carrot, and water for 20 minutes. Add tomatoes and cool slightly. Put in a blender or run through a sieve or food mill. Add the consommé and chili sauce and taste for seasoning. You may want to add salt and pepper. Reheat and serve to the children. Garnish with half of the egg and lemon slices. Cool and refrigerate the remainder to be reheated just before the adults' meal. Garnish with egg and lemon.

LOBSTER-MUSHROOM BISQUE

*Salad with Cooked Vegetables and Greens***
Assorted Crackers
Raspberry Ice and Ginger Cookies

LOBSTER-MUSHROOM BISQUE

1 can lobster bisque
1 can cream of mushroom soup
7-ounce can lobster meat

2 cups milk or light cream
2 tablespoons sherry

Combine all ingredients except the sherry and heat well. Serve the children. Add the sherry and reheat for the adults.

HEARTY POTATO-CORN CHOWDER

Hamburgers or Hot Dogs and Buns
Canned or Stewed Apricots in Orange Juice or
    Orange Liqueur

HEARTY POTATO-CORN CHOWDER

3 slices bacon
1 onion, chopped
1 can frozen cream of potato soup
1-pound can cream-style corn

2 cups milk, cream, or evaporated
    milk, or a combination of any
    of the three
Salt
Pepper

Fry the bacon in a saucepan until crisp. Remove and drain on paper towels. Sauté the onion in the bacon fat and add the rest of the ingredients. Heat well and serve with the bacon crumbled on top.

A FINE KETTLE OF FISH

*Greens with Tomato Slices, Green Pepper Rings, and
   Raw Cauliflower Slices**
Bread Sticks or Crisp Crackers
Peach Shortcake

A FINE KETTLE OF FISH

7-ounce can minced clams
7-ounce can tuna or crab
Water
1 1/2 cups diced potatoes
1 onion, sliced
1/2 cup finely diced celery
1/4 cup finely diced carrots

1/2 teaspoon salt
1 can frozen oyster stew, slightly
   thawed
3/4 cup milk, cream, or evaporated
   milk
1 teaspoon Worcestershire
Dash hot pepper sauce

Drain the liquid from the clams and tuna or crab into a measuring cup. Add enough water to make 2 cups. Pour this liquid into a saucepan with the potatoes, onion, celery, carrots, and salt. Simmer about 15 minutes until the potatoes are soft. Add the clams, tuna, oyster stew, milk, Worcestershire sauce, and pepper sauce. Heat until steamy and serve the children. Cool and refrigerate the rest of the soup to be reheated just before the adults' meal.

And here are more quick soups. Some of them are almost meals in themselves; others should be served as a first course or with a sandwich for lunch.

Make *vichyssoise* by combining 1 can frozen potato soup, thawed, with 1 can chicken broth and 1 can light cream. Beat with an egg beater or blender until smooth. Chill and serve with chopped chives or scallions.

If you don't like plain canned *vegetable soup,* you can cook 1 package frozen mixed vegetables in 1 can beef consommé. Add 1 can tomato soup and 1 can water. Season with instant onion if you like.

Quick *pea soup* may be made by cutting 4 frankfurters or a can of Vienna sausages into thin rounds. Brown in oil or bacon fat and set aside. Combine and heat 1 can pea soup, 1 can tomato soup, and 2 cans of water. Add the frankfurters and serve.

Refrigerate *jellied madrilene* or *consommé* and serve with sour cream or with chopped avocado and lemon juice.

For *curried chicken soup* combine 2 cans cream of chicken soup with 2 cups light cream or milk and ½ to 1 teaspoon curry powder. Serve hot or cold, depending on the weather and your mood. Garnish with slivered almonds or shredded coconut.

For 5-minute *borsch,* combine 2 cans consommé or bouillon, 1 tablespoon instant onions, and 2 jars chopped "junior food" beets. Heat or serve cold with juice of 1 lemon and sour cream topping.

Creamed mushroom and chicken soup may be made by combining 1 can cream of mushroom soup with 1 can chicken with noodles or rice soup, 2 cans of milk, and ½ teaspoon crumbled leaf sage. Heat and serve with onion or bacon-flavored crackers.

One can *Cheddar cheese soup* may be heated with 1 can tomato soup and 2 cans of milk. Serve topped with heated canned French-fried onions.

For a *delicious fish soup,* heat together 1 can frozen New England-style clam chowder, 1 can frozen oyster stew, 1 can frozen cream of shrimp soup (all thawed), and 2 cups milk. Season with a dash of mace.

Another *fish soup* can be concocted in a jiffy by combining canned salmon, frozen cream of potato soup, and milk. Add cooked peas or celery if you like.

Golden mushroom soup can be topped with cheese croutons.

Beef

Cuts of beef vary from one part of the country to another, as do the names of the various cuts. It isn't difficult, however, to figure out the cut that is best for a recipe if you set your mind to it. Just remember that the less expensive cuts, a pot roast for example, require long cooking with moist heat. Some of the less tender cuts may, of course, be cubed or tenderized and cooked like expensive cuts.

PANNED, CUBED, OR MINUTE STEAK

Carrot Mélange*
Escarole Salad*
Hard Rolls
Pound Cake with Blueberry Sauce*

PANNED, CUBED, OR MINUTE STEAK

Cubed steak is round steak or some other boneless, less tender cut which has been put through a machine to make it extremely tender. It cooks so quickly that it can easily be cooked at the last minute. Buy as much steak as will satisfy your family. Five minutes before serving time, melt 1 tablespoon butter and 1 tablespoon oil in a skillet large enough to hold the children's steaks without any overlapping. When the fat is sizzling, put the steaks in the skillet and brown for no more than 2 minutes on each side. Spread with butter and sprinkle with salt, pepper and chopped parsley. Serve immediately. Repeat for the later meal. If you like really rare meat, reduce the cooking time.

RARE ROAST BEEF OR THICK STEAK

Mashed Yellow Turnips and Potatoes*
Braised Celery*
Mother's Green Salad Mold*
Cherry Crisp*

RARE ROAST BEEF OR THICK STEAK

If, and only if, you have excellent controls on your oven, you can reheat rare roast beef or rare thick steak (at least 2 inches thick) with no loss of flavor and moisture. You must, however, be able to hold the oven temperature at 200° F. (If you are not sure of the accuracy of your oven at that temperature—and many ovens that are accurate at one temperature may not be accurate at another—use an oven thermometer to test it or ask your service man to test it for you.)

Cook your roast or thick steak to any desired doneness. Serve the children. One hour before the adults are to eat, return their portion of the meat to a 200° F. oven.

Lamb may be reheated the same way.

This method is also useful if you wish to buy a large piece of meat and serve it on two different days. Roast or broil the large piece of meat, serve it one day, refrigerate the remainder and reheat it two days later for an hour in a 200° F. oven.

Vichyssoise*

COLD ROAST BEEF SLICES

Tomatoes, Cold Asparagus, and Wilted Cucumbers
   on Lettuce*
Hot French Bread with Green Onion and Butter*
Meringues with Strawberries*

This is one of those easy menus that take only a little preparation time and can be brought to the table in the time it takes to heat the French bread. The beef can be left over from a roast served earlier in the week, or it may be purchased at the delicatessen.

BROILED BEEF PATTIES

Broiled Tomato Halves*
Zucchini and Sour Cream Casserole*
Toasted Bread Fingers*
Rhubarb-Strawberry Compote

PAN-BROILED BEEF PATTIES

Potato Salad*
Assorted Cold Vegetables*
Toasted Buns
Pears with Ice Cream and Chocolate Sauce*

BEEF PATTIES

Ground beef is a staple of most American family diets, a favorite of children and adults alike. The best hamburgers are treated with the care given to a steak. Buy good—not necessarily the most expensive—beef. Chuck is a good choice; so are the ends of a flank or skirt steak. Plain ground beef is apt to be too fatty, and ground round, besides being expensive, is usually too dry. Shape the patties *lightly* with your hands. The patties may be thick or thin, large or small. Generally speaking, a pound of ground beef will make 2 adult-size and 2 small patties for very young children. If your children have adult-size appetites, you will need 1½ pounds of beef.

They may be broiled or pan-broiled to any degree of doneness, but they must be cooked at the last minute. They should be seasoned after they have been cooked, as salt tends to draw out the moisture.

To broil, place patties on a greased rack, 3 inches below the heat in a preheated broiler. When well browned, turn and broil on the other side. Total broiling time will vary from 5 to 15 minutes, depending on the size and shape of the patties and the desired doneness. Sprinkle patties with salt and pepper and serve immediately.

To pan-broil, melt just enough oil and butter to coat the skillet. When the fat is sizzling, add the patties. Brown well on both sides. Sprinkle with salt and pepper and serve immediately.

One pound of ground beef may be stretched by adding ½ cup soft bread crumbs soaked for 5 minutes in ⅓ cup milk or evaporated milk, or by adding ½ cup grated raw carrot or potato moistened with 2 tablespoons milk or tomato sauce. Some women like to add an egg to their ground beef. However, if you add *anything* to the ground beef you will have something that resembles meat balls or small meat loaves more than true hamburger.

To vary ground beef patties: Mix chili sauce, chopped onion, chopped green pepper, garlic powder, thyme, or orégano with the meat before you shape it into patties. Hide a small piece of blue cheese in the patty.

After the patties have cooked, mix the de-fatted pan juices with chili sauce, catsup, horseradish, or a few sautéed onion slices or mushrooms, and pour over the patties.

Lay slices of Swiss, American, or Cheddar cheese over the cooked patties and run them under the broiler briefly.

Garnish the cooked patties with very thin slices of raw onion, slices of tomato, or rings of green pepper.

Top the cooked patties with mustard or pickle relish.

BEEF PACKAGES

Green Salad with Croutons and Parmesan Cheese*
French Bread*
Strawberry Sundaes*

BEEF PACKAGES

1½–2 pounds chuck steak, 1 inch thick	Carrots, cut in narrow strips
Meat tenderizer, unseasoned	1 large onion, sliced
2 tablespoons oil	4 green pepper rings
Potatoes, cut in ¼-inch slices	Salt
	Pepper

Cut the steak into 4 servings and prepare with tenderizer, according to package directions. Brown the pieces on both sides in the hot oil. Drain on paper towels. In the meantime, lay out 4 double-thick 12-inch squares of foil. Put a piece of steak on each square. Top with potato slices and carrots (amounts to depend on appetites), onions, and green pepper rings. Sprinkle lightly with salt and pepper. Bring the sides of the foil up and wrap loosely with druggist's folds. Crumple the foil so that the steam cannot escape. Lay the packages in a shallow baking pan and bake in a 350° F. oven for 1 hour. Serve the children their packages. Cool, but do not open, the adults' packages. Reheat the adults' packages for 20 minutes in a 350° F. oven.

BROILED STEAK AND TOMATO-MUSHROOM KABOBS

Stuffed Baked Potatoes*
Lettuce, Mandarin Orange, and Red Onion Salad*
Cheese Cake

Since steak (unless it is at least 2 inches thick—see preceding recipe) must be broiled at the last minute, it is not ideal for a cook-now-serve-later meal. However, if everything else is ready to go, this menu can be prepared with only 10–15 minutes' kitchen time.

BROILED STEAK AND TOMATO-MUSHROOM KABOBS

12–16 fresh mushroom caps	Steak, 1 inch thick
Butter or margarine	Salt
12 cherry tomatoes	Pepper

Wipe the mushroom caps with a damp cloth. Melt butter or margarine in a heavy skillet. Add the mushrooms. Cover and cook over low heat for about 5 minutes or until the mushrooms are tender. Cool until you can handle them. Then put the mushrooms and tomatoes alternately onto 4 small skewers.

In the meantime, prepare the steaks. Preheat the broiler. Slash any fat on the outside of the steak so that it will not curl up. Refrigerate the adults' steak with 2 of the kabobs. Place the children's steak on the broiler rack, which has been rubbed with fat. Put the rack 2 to 3 inches from the heat and broil until the meat is well browned on one side. Turn and broil the other side. The broiling time will vary from a total of 8 minutes for a very rare steak to 18 minutes for a well-done one.

Five minutes before the steak will be done, brush butter over 2 of the kabobs and place them on the broiler rack beside the steak. Broil 3 minutes and turn the kabobs. Brush with more butter and broil an additional 2 minutes. Remove the rack from the broiler and, if you like, spread butter on the steak. Sprinkle both the steak and vegetables with salt and pepper.

The adults' steak will be broiled in the same way.

BEEF STROGANOFF

Brown Rice*
Chilled Brussels Sprouts and Tomatoes with
  Vinaigrette Sauce*
Peach Crisp*

Traditional stroganoff is made with the finest steak, cut very thin, browned briefly, and served with sour cream. I think the recipe here is comparably good. Furthermore, it can be cooked in advance and is much easier on the budget.

BEEF STROGANOFF

1½ pounds round or chuck steak
Flour
1 teaspoon salt
Few grinds pepper
Oil or bacon drippings
1 cup water

1 beef bouillon cube
1 teaspoon dry mustard
4-ounce can mushrooms
1 onion, sliced
1 cup sour cream

Cut the steak in very thin slices across the grain. Toss the beef with ¼ cup flour, salt, and pepper. Heat the oil and brown the beef well on both sides. Add the water, bouillon cube, mustard, mushrooms with liquid, and onion. Cover and simmer until tender, about 40 minutes. Stir 2 tablespoons flour (preferably instant-type) into ¼ cup water and add to the beef, stirring until the sauce thickens. Remove some of the gravy and stir in a few tablespoons of sour cream. Lift out the children's slices of beef and pour the sour-cream gravy over them. Set the rest of the beef and gravy aside. Just before the adults' meal, reheat and add the rest of the sour cream. Heat but do not boil.

BOEUF BOURGUIGNON

*Boiled Potatoes**
*Green Salad**
Pumpernickel
*Lemon Sherbet with Mint Sauce**

Since boeuf bourguignon is one of the most flavorsome dishes ever created, and since it is just as good reheated the second day, I have included a double recipe here. Remember that this is an especially good dinner dish for company; the recipe below will serve 8 adults.

BOEUF BOURGUIGNON

6 slices bacon, cut in fourths
4 pounds lean boneless stewing
  beef, cut in 1-inch cubes
Flour
1 carrot, sliced
1 onion, sliced
1½ teaspoons salt
Few grinds pepper
2 cloves garlic, pressed or minced

Pinch thyme leaves
1 bay leaf, crumbled
8-ounce can tomato sauce
2 cups dry red wine
1–2 cups beef stock or bouillon
20–24 small white onions
2 tablespoons butter or oil
½ cup beef bouillon
1 pound mushrooms, sliced

Fry the bacon until brown in a large flameproof casserole or Dutch oven. Remove with a slotted spoon. Dredge the meat in flour and brown well, a few pieces at a time, removing each piece when it is well browned on all sides. If necessary, add oil to the bacon fat. In the same fat, brown the sliced vegetables slightly.

Return the bacon and beef to the pot. Stir in salt, pepper, garlic, thyme, bay leaf, and tomato sauce. Add enough wine and stock to just cover the meat. Bring to the simmering point on the top of the stove, cover, and place in a preheated, 325° F. oven. The meat should bake slowly for about 2½ hours, or until tender.

In the meantime, peel the onions and pierce the stem ends with the point of a knife. Put in a skillet with a tight-fitting cover. The skillet should be large enough to hold the onions in 1 layer. Add 2 tablespoons butter or oil and the ½ cup bouillon. Simmer about 40 minutes, or until tender. Then add the sliced mushrooms and simmer another 5 minutes. There should be very little liquid left in the pan. Remove cover and set aside.

When the meat is tender, pour the contents of the casserole or Dutch oven into a sieve over a saucepan. Wash the casserole and return the beef and bacon to it. Distribute the onions and mushrooms over the meat. Skim the fat off the sauce, which should be just thick enough to coat a spoon. Taste for seasoning. If too thin, boil down rapidly. If too thick, add a little water. Remove any additional fat that has accumulated at the top. Pour over the meat, making sure that all of the meat and vegetables are well coated with sauce.

The bourguignon is done. You may feed the children now and let the rest of the dish cool. Be sure to baste the meat and vegetables well with the sauce. When cool, refrigerate all that will not be served within an hour. If it has been refrigerated, allow 20–30 minutes to reheat on the top of the stove, basting 2 or 3 times.

You may cook the entire dish on the top of the stove if you can keep the heat low; the sauce should just simmer.

BOILED BEEF

*Parsley Potatoes**
*Buttered Tiny Peas**
Carrot Sticks
*Fruit Cup with Sherbet and Mint Sauce**

BOILED BEEF

2 pounds beef brisket	1 teaspoon salt
Water	½ bay leaf
1 onion	Few grinds pepper
1 carrot	

Put the beef in a saucepan which will hold it snugly. Cover with water. Bring to a boil and skim off the scum. Add the remaining ingredients and simmer slowly for about 3 hours or until the meat is tender when pierced with a fork. Remove the beef and slice off pieces for the children. Return the rest of the meat to the broth and refrigerate to be reheated by simmering for about 20 minutes before the adult meal.

Serve with horseradish sauce made by combining and heating sour cream, a little broth and prepared horseradish.

TARRAGON-FLAVORED BEEF

*Noodles**

*Zucchini Vinaigrette**

*Cherry Gelatin (Brandied for Adults)**

This is stew with a difference, and one of my great favorites. I came across this recipe soon after I was married and clung to it with such tenacity that some of our friends must have thought I couldn't cook anything else—which was almost the case.

TARRAGON-FLAVORED BEEF

2 pounds boneless chuck, cut in
   1-inch cubes
Flour
2 tablespoons oil
1 teaspoon salt
1 teaspoon Worcestershire
1 tablespoon sugar
1 clove garlic

2 teaspoons dried tarragon leaves
1 onion, chopped
1/4 cup wine vinegar
1 cup consommé or bouillon
4-ounce can sliced mushrooms,
   undrained
8-ounce can tiny white onions,
   drained

Dredge the meat in flour and brown in the oil. When the meat is well browned on all sides, add other ingredients except the mushrooms and onions. Cover and simmer slowly for about 2 hours, or until meat is tender. Add more bouillon if necessary. Add the mushrooms and onions and simmer 10 minutes more. Remove the garlic.

Serve the children's beef on noodles. You may put the adults' portion of the cooked noodles in a shallow casserole and pour the beef over it. Cover with foil and bake in a 350° F. oven for 20–30 minutes before serving. Or you may reheat the beef and the noodles on the top of the stove just before serving.

SWEETISH STEW

*Rice**
*Green Beans**
*Pudding and Cookies**

SWEETISH STEW

2 pounds beef (chuck is fine), cut
  in 1-inch cubes
3 tablespoons flour, mixed with
  1 teaspoon salt
1/4 cup margarine or oil
1 medium onion, sliced
1 cup apple juice or cider

2 tablespoons sugar
1/4 teaspoon cinnamon
1/4 teaspoon ginger
2 cloves
3/4 cup mixed dried fruits (raisins
  may be added)
Boiling water

Dredge each piece of meat in flour and salt, and brown well in hot oil. Pour off any extra fat and add the onion, juice, sugar, and spices. Cover and simmer for 1 hour.

In the meantime, put the fruits in a measuring cup. Do not pack down. Fill the cup with boiling water. Add the fruits and water to the stew and continue simmering another 1/2 hour or until the beef is tender. You may need more liquid. If so, use water or juice.

This dish may be made early in the day, refrigerated, and reheated, or it may be made just before the children's dinner and reheated for the adults.

One cup syrup from canned fruit and 2 teaspoons vinegar may be substituted for the apple juice and sugar.

SWISS STEAK I

Mashed or Baked Potatoes*
Corn*
Slaw with Pineapple, Apple, and Dates*
Coconut Cream Pie*

SWISS STEAK I

Flour
1 teaspoon salt
Few grinds pepper
2-pound piece of chuck, about 1
   inch thick
3 tablespoons oil
2 onions, sliced

1 carrot, sliced
1 stalk celery, sliced
½ green pepper, sliced
2 teaspoons Worcestershire
1 tablespoon brown sugar
1-pound can tomatoes

Mix ½ cup flour, salt, and pepper and pound into steak with a meat tenderizer or the edge of a heavy saucer. Cut into serving-size pieces. Heat oil in a large skillet or Dutch oven. Add the steak and brown well. Pour off any excess fat. Add the rest of the ingredients. Cover and simmer until the meat is tender, about 1½ hours, or bake, covered, in a 325° F. oven for the same amount of time. Remove the steak, skim off the fat, and thicken the gravy with 1 tablespoon flour mixed with a little cold water. Serve the children. Return the adults' steak to the remaining gravy. Cool and refrigerate, to be reheated just before the later dinner.

SWISS STEAK II

Mashed Potatoes* or Buttered Noodles*
Wax Beans*
Cherries in Gelatin Salad*
Chocolate Brownies

SWISS STEAK II

Flour
1 teaspoon salt
Few grinds pepper
1 teaspoon dry mustard
2-pound piece of chuck, about 1
   inch thick
3 tablespoons oil

4-ounce can mushrooms
8-ounce can small white onions
1 beef bouillon cube dissolved in
   ¾ cup water
1 large bay leaf
1 cup commercial sour cream
   (optional)

Mix ¼ cup flour, salt, pepper, and mustard and pound into the meat. Cut in serving-size pieces and brown in the oil in a large skillet or Dutch oven. Pour off fat. Drain the mushrooms and onions and add only the liquid to the meat with the bouillon and bay leaf. Simmer 1 hour and add the mushrooms and onions. Continue to simmer until the meat is tender—about 30 minutes.

Now you can thicken the gravy with 2 tablespoons flour mixed with ½ cup cold water and serve. Or you can thicken the gravy and add ½ cup sour cream into the children's portion of the gravy as you serve it to them. Then you can cool the adults' portion and add the rest of the sour cream after the meat has been reheated.

BEEF POT ROAST AND VEGETABLES

*Sunshine Salad**
Pumpernickel
*Coco Mocho**

BEEF POT ROAST AND VEGETABLES

2 pounds chuck, boned and tied
2 tablespoons oil
1 small onion, chopped
½ carrot, chopped
1 beef bouillon cube
1 cup water
½ teaspoon salt

1 teaspoon Worcestershire
Few drops hot red pepper sauce
Medium-size whole potatoes
Carrots, halved lengthwise
White onions with crosses pierced
   in the stem ends

Dry roast with paper towels and brown on all sides in hot oil in Dutch oven. When well browned, remove the roast and add the chopped onion and carrot. Brown slightly in the oil. Pour off any excess oil and add the roast with the bouillon cube, water, salt, Worcestershire, and hot pepper sauce. Cover. Simmer slowly over low heat or put in a 325° F. oven until barely tender, about 2 hours. Add the potatoes, carrots, and onions and continue cooking until the vegetables are tender. Lift the vegetables and meat out. Strain the gravy and return to the Dutch oven. To thicken the gravy, stir in 2 tablespoons flour mixed with ¼ cup cold water. Serve the children's slices of the roast with the vegetables and gravy. Return the rest of the meat and vegetables to the gravy. Cool and refrigerate to be reheated on top of the stove about 20 minutes before the later dinner.

Increase the amount of beef and add a few extra potatoes if you wish to have leftovers for hash. (See recipe on page 26.)

To vary: Substitute a 1-pound can of tomatoes or 1 cup of dry red wine for the water and bouillon. Add sour cream to the gravy. Add garlic, catsup, orégano, bay leaf, thyme, or basil to the cooking liquid.

CORNED BEEF AND CABBAGE

*Sliced Beets or Beet Pickles**
Dry English Mustard
Rye Bread
*Apple Pie**

CORNED BEEF AND CABBAGE

2½ pounds corned beef
Water
Carrots, whole or halved
Potatoes, whole or halved

1 small or ½ large cabbage, cut in 4 wedges
Salt (optional)

If possible, buy a piece of corned beef that says "mild brine" on the package.

Put corned beef into a fairly deep kettle and add water to almost cover. Cover and simmer for 2–3 hours until the meat is tender when it is pierced with a fork. Add the number of carrots and potatoes that your family will eat and continue cooking until the vegetables are tender. While the vegetables are cooking, pour about 1½ cups liquid from the large kettle into a small saucepan. Bring to a boil and add the children's cabbage wedges. Simmer about 10 minutes until cabbage is tender but crisp. With a slotted spoon, remove to children's plates. Taste for salt. If the corned beef is fairly salty, you may not need any. Remove the meat from the kettle and cut off slices for the children. Also remove their carrots and potatoes. Return the meat to the kettle and set aside or refrigerate.

Twenty minutes before the adults' meal, reheat the meat, carrots, and potatoes, and bring the cabbage water to a boil in its saucepan. Add the remaining cabbage wedges and cook until tender but crisp.

PANNED BEEF HASH (WITH POACHED EGGS)

Tossed Salad*
Hard Rolls
Merry Berry*

PANNED BEEF HASH (WITH POACHED EGGS)

Leftover corned beef, beef pot
  roast, or tongue
Boiled potatoes
1 small onion
2 tablespoons catsup

¼ cup gravy or milk
Salt
Pepper
1 tablespoon oil
4 eggs

Using a coarse blade, grind equal portions of meat and potatoes, and the onion. Or, you may chop them finely with a knife. Proportions are not very important. If you don't have enough meat, add more potatoes. If you have a few leftover cooked carrots, add them. The important thing is to end up with at least 4 cups of meat and vegetables. Add the other ingredients except oil and eggs. If you are using corned beef, you may not need salt. Put the oil in an 8-inch skillet. When it is sputtering hot, add the hash. Turn the heat down and brown over low heat for approximately 30 minutes, stirring occasionally. A Teflon-lined pan is a great hash-making utensil. (Be sure to use the proper stirring utensil if using Teflon.) Poach an egg for each child. Serve the hash with eggs on top. Set aside or refrigerate the adults' portion to be reheated on top of the stove. Poach the eggs for the adults while you heat their hash.

The Mix

Basically, this is meat loaf. It can also be meat balls. The variations on the two themes are infinite, so I always make enough mix for three meals. We eat one and I freeze the other two to be served later in some other form. If you have enough freezer space, you'll find it convenient to do likewise. So, the recipe below is for 3 meals of 4 servings each.

THE MIX

2 eggs
6-ounce can evaporated milk, undiluted, or ¾ cup from a large can
1 cup quick-cooking rolled oats
2 pounds ground beef

½ pound ground veal
½ pound ground pork
1 small onion, chopped
1 teaspoon salt
Few grinds pepper
1 teaspoon Worcestershire

Beat the eggs slightly in a large bowl and add the milk and oats. Stir. Add all of the other ingredients and mix together. Use your hands to do the job quickly and thoroughly. Divide into 3 equal portions.

What you do with the 3 portions depends on your future plans. You will prepare 1 portion according to one of the following recipes and serve. The other 2 may be frozen. If you are serving the first portion as a loaf, you may want to bake a "future" portion in a loaf at the same time. It can then be cooled, wrapped, and frozen to be thawed and reheated for a future meal. If you don't want to bake it before you freeze it, just shape it into a loaf and wrap in foil. When you want to use it, you have only to unwrap from the top, place in a baking pan on the foil, thaw, and bake; this saves washing a pan.

You can shape one portion into balls and then freeze. These can be browned without thawing.

To vary: Substitute fine dry bread crumbs for rolled oats or tomato sauce for evaporated milk. You may also add chopped green pepper, garlic powder, thyme, savory, orégano, or basil.

MEAT LOAF

*Baked Potatoes**
*Scalloped Cabbage**
*Greens with Tomato and Cucumber Slices**
*Fruit Cup**

MEAT LOAF

Shape 1 portion (⅓) of The Mix into a loaf. Put in a baking pan or pie plate and bake in a 350° F. oven for 1 hour. Serve the children. Reheat the adult portion just before the later meal.

ITALIAN MEAT BALLS WITH SPAGHETTI TWISTS

*Green Salad**
Apples and Candy Bars

ITALIAN MEAT BALLS WITH SPAGHETTI TWISTS

1 portion The Mix	2 cups meatless spaghetti sauce
Flour	Spaghetti twists
1 tablespoon oil	Parmesan cheese

Shape The Mix into meat balls about 1 inch in diameter. Roll each one in flour and brown in hot oil. When all of them are browned on all sides, add the spaghetti sauce and simmer, covered, about 15 minutes. You may use sauce that is homemade, canned, or prepared according to package directions from a dry mix.

In the meantime, prepare the spaghetti twists according to package directions. Serve the children their meat balls and sauce over the twists and sprinkle with Parmesan cheese. Add a few tablespoons of the sauce to the rest of the spaghetti twists and toss with a fork. This will facilitate reheating. Just before serving the adults' dinner, reheat the meat balls and the twists and serve. Pass the Parmesan cheese.

CRANBERRY MEAT LOAF

Rice*
Buttered Peas*
Carrot Sticks*
Two-Layer Pie*

CRANBERRY MEAT LOAF

1 portion The Mix
1 cup whole cranberry sauce

3 tablespoons brown sugar
1 tablespoon lemon juice

Shape The Mix into 4 individual loaves, sized to suit the appetites of the various members of the family. Place the children's loaves in one shallow baking dish and the adults' in another. Heat the cranberry sauce and combine with the sugar and lemon juice. Pour the sauce over the loaves and bake in a 350° F. oven for 1 hour. Baste 2 or 3 times during baking. Serve children and reheat adults' loaves at serving time.

DANISH MEAT BALLS

Buttered Noodles*
Carrots Diable*
Cold Asparagus Spears and Tomato Slices on Greens*
Fresh or Canned Pears and Crunchies*

DANISH MEAT BALLS

1 portion The Mix
Flour
1 tablespoon oil

¾ cup beef bouillon
Water
½ cup sour cream

Shape The Mix into meat balls about 1 inch in diameter. Coat each one with flour and brown in hot oil. When all the meat balls are well browned on all sides, add the beef bouillon and simmer, covered, for 30 minutes. Thicken the gravy with 1 tablespoon flour mixed with about ¼ cup cold water. Bring to a boil. Add the sour cream and heat, but do not allow to boil. Serve the children. When the adults are ready to eat, reheat the meat balls in the sauce in the top of a double boiler.

BEEF-BEAN SHORTCAKE

Cole Slaw*
Pickles
Berries and Ice Cream*

This is one of those not very elegant but terribly speedy dishes that are a godsend on days when you don't get home until everyone has already slipped into the decline toward starvation. It also makes a good Saturday lunch or a fine, inexpensive filler-up for a crowd of teen-agers.

BEEF-BEAN SHORTCAKE

1 pound ground beef
1 onion, chopped
¼ cup chopped green pepper
1 tablespoon oil
1 teaspoon chili powder (more if you like it "hot")
1 teaspoon instant coffee
½ teaspoon orégano
½ teaspoon salt
Few grinds pepper
8-ounce can tomato sauce
1-pound can kidney beans, undrained
Slices of sharp processed American cheese (optional)
Toaster-type corn muffins

Brown the meat, onion, and green pepper in the oil. Pour off any excess fat and add all of the other ingredients except the cheese and muffins. Cover and simmer for about 10 minutes. Taste for seasoning. Lay 2 slices of cheese on top of the meat mixture. Simmer for just a minute, until the cheese begins to melt. While the cheese is melting, pop 2 of the muffins into the toaster. Serve the meat mixture over the muffins, lifting the cheese carefully with a spoon so that most of it lands on the top. The rest of the meat mixture may be refrigerated and reheated on top of the stove whenever you like. Naturally, you will add only the cheese that is to be served at each sitting.

"MORE"

French Bread*
Carrot Sticks and Sour Pickles
Bananas with Ice Cream and Chocolate Sauce*

Almost every cook I know makes a baked hamburger and spaghetti dish similar to this. Whatever it is called or whatever its variations, it is a children's favorite. Leftovers make a good luncheon dish.

"MORE"

1 clove garlic, minced
1 large onion, chopped
1 tablespoon oil
1 pound ground beef
¼ cup chopped green pepper
1 teaspoon salt
Few grinds pepper
½ teaspoon orégano
1 teaspoon chili powder

1 teaspoon instant coffee (optional)
10½-ounce can tomato soup
8-ounce can tomato sauce
1½ cups uncooked macaroni or spaghetti (broken)
About 2 cups mixed vegetables (peas, beans, limas, corn), fresh-cooked, canned, or leftover
Sliced American cheese

Brown garlic and onion lightly in oil. Add meat and green pepper and continue to brown. Add all of the seasonings, coffee, soup, and sauce and simmer, covered, while you cook the macaroni (according to package directions) and the vegetables. Combine all of the ingredients and divide into 2 casseroles. Top each with slices of cheese. Cover and bake the children's casserole in a 350° F. oven for 20 minutes. Remove cover and bake 10 more minutes, or until cheese is lightly browned. Refrigerate adults' casserole until 30 minutes before dinner and then bake as children's casserole was baked.

MEAT CUPS WITH MASHED POTATOES AND MUSHROOM GRAVY

*Baked Tomatoes**
*Waldorf Salad**
*Nut Ice Cream with Maple Syrup**

MEAT CUPS WITH MASHED POTATOES AND MUSHROOM GRAVY

MEAT CUPS:

1 pound ground beef
1 egg, slightly beaten
¼ cup rolled oats ("quick" or "old-fashioned")
2 tablespoons catsup

1 teaspoon instant onion
⅛ teaspoon garlic powder
1 teaspoon salt
Few grinds pepper

4 servings well-seasoned mashed potatoes (use instant if you like)
Melted butter

GRAVY:

⅓ cup chopped onion
2 tablespoons chopped green pepper
2 tablespoons butter, oil, or margarine
2 tablespoons flour

2½-ounce can mushroom stems and pieces
Liquid from the mushrooms, with water added to make ¾ cup
1 teaspoon gravy coloring
Juice from meat cups
½ cup sour cream

Mix all of the meat cup ingredients and press against the sides and bottoms of 4 well-oiled 12-ounce ovenproof custard cups. (Or use 6 8-ounce cups.) Do not try to make the meat mixture come to the tops of the cups, as the meat cups must be sturdy and shallow. Bake in a 400° F. oven for 20 minutes. During the baking, the meat will pull away from the sides of the custard cups. Drain the juice from the cups into the gravy.

Remove the meat cups from the custard cups and place the children's servings in one baking dish and the adults' in another. Heap the mashed potatoes lightly into the cups. Brush with butter. Sprinkle with paprika, if you like. Return the children's cups to the oven for a few minutes to reheat. Set the adults' servings aside or refrigerate and bake for an additional 15 minutes just before their meal.

In the meantime, make the gravy. Sauté the onions and pepper in the butter. Add the flour, brown lightly, and then add the liquid, stirring until it is smooth and thick. Add the gravy coloring, meat juices, mushrooms, and sour cream. Heat but do not boil. Serve over the children's meat cups.

Reheat the gravy for the adults' serving. Again, watch it to be sure that it does not boil.

BAKED BURGER BALLS

*Oven-Baked Potato Sticks**
*Spinach**
*Jellied Fruit Salad**
*Cereal Crunch Cookies**

BAKED BURGER BALLS

1½ pounds ground beef
1 cup seasoned stuffing mix, prepared according to package directions

2 tablespoons chopped onion
1 can cream of mushroom soup
Few grinds pepper

Preheat oven to 350° F. Shape beef into 8 flat patties. Add chopped onion to prepared stuffing. Put ⅛ of the stuffing on each patty and bring up edges and mold into balls. Put 4 for the children in one flat casserole and 4 for the adults in another. Spoon soup and pepper over the balls.

Bake the children's portion, uncovered, for 40 minutes. Refrigerate the adults' portion, to be baked 45 minutes before serving; or, bake with the children's and reheat.

STUFFED CABBAGE

Carrot and Celery Sticks
French Bread*
Apricot Pudding Delights*

The first time I stuffed cabbage leaves, I vowed it would be the last. The leaves tore, the rolls fell apart, the sauce burned. But good stuffed cabbage is so good! Do try this. Parboil the cabbage leaves before removing them from the head, which vastly simplifies the process. Double-wrap the meat and pack the rolls tightly so that they stay intact. Bake the dish in the oven, to remove the danger of burning. You will find that white winter cabbage is easier to manage than new green cabbage.

STUFFED CABBAGE

1 large head cabbage
1 clove garlic, minced
1 small onion, chopped
1 pound ground beef
1 tablespoon oil
½ teaspoon salt
Few grinds pepper

½ cup raw rice, cooked in 1 cup
  beef bouillon
About 2 cups tomato juice
⅔ cup broken ginger snaps
2 tablespoons brown sugar
1 tablespoon lemon juice

Cut the core out of the cabbage to a depth of about 1 inch. Place cabbage in a large kettle, cover with boiling water, boil 5 minutes, and drain. When the cabbage is cool enough to handle, carefully remove about 16 outer leaves. Put each one on a paper towel to dry. (The rest of the cabbage will be only slightly cooked. Wrap it in a plastic bag, refrigerate, and use later in any cooked-cabbage recipe.)

While you are cooking the cabbage, lightly brown the garlic, onion, and beef in the oil. Add the salt, pepper, and cooked rice.

Pour 1 cup of the tomato juice in a well-greased 2-quart casserole. Sprinkle half of the ginger snaps, half of the brown sugar, and all of the lemon juice into the tomato juice.

Now it's time to stuff the cabbage leaves. Cut out the white hard rib part of each leaf in a small V. Spread out one of the smaller leaves of cabbage so that it curls upward. Place approximately 3 tablespoons of the meat mixture in the center of the leaf. The amount of stuffing will depend on the size of the leaf. Wrap the sides of the leaf around the mixture as tightly as possible. Then place the wrapped cabbage leaf, fold side down, on a slightly larger upturned leaf of cabbage. Wrap the first leaf in the second leaf and place in the casserole with the second fold side down. Continue to make rolls until you have used up all of the meat mixture—you may need a few more cabbage leaves. Pack the rolls *tightly* into the casserole. You will probably have 2 layers.

When all of the cabbage rolls are in the casserole, top with the rest of the ginger snaps, and brown sugar. Pour enough tomato juice to cover the rolls. (The ginger snaps will thicken the tomato juice to make a delicious sauce.) Cover tightly and bake in a 350° F. oven for at least 1½ hours—longer, if possible. Check occasionally to see that there is enough liquid, and add more tomato juice if necessary.

This dish may be prepared a day in advance, in the morning of the day you expect to serve it, or just before the children's dinner. When the children are ready to eat, remove their rolls with a little of the sauce. You may continue to cook the adults' portion in a low oven, or you may cool and refrigerate the adults' portion to be reheated for 30 minutes before their meal.

BEEF, MACARONI, AND CHEESE BAKE

*Lettuce, Mandarin Orange, and Avocado Salad**
Italian Bread
*Melon Cubes with Sherbet**

BEEF, MACARONI, AND CHEESE BAKE

2 cups uncooked elbow macaroni	Few grinds pepper
2 tablespoons oil	¾ cup cottage cheese
1 clove garlic, minced	¾ cup sour cream
1 small onion, chopped	10-ounce package frozen chopped
1 pound ground beef	spinach
8-ounce can tomato sauce	½ cup shredded sharp Cheddar
½ teaspoon salt	cheese

Cook macaroni according to package directions. Drain. Heat oil in a medium-size skillet and add the garlic, onion, and beef. When the beef is lightly browned, add the tomato sauce, salt, and pepper and simmer 5 minutes. Stir the cottage cheese and sour cream into the macaroni. Cook spinach according to package directions and drain.

Butter 2 1-quart casseroles. Alternate layers of macaroni mixture, spinach, and meat mixture, ending with the meat. Sprinkle with the Cheddar cheese. Bake each casserole in a 350° F. oven 20–30 minutes before serving time.

EGGPLANT PARMIGIANA

Green Salad*
French Bread or Hard Rolls*
Mandarin Orange and Grape Cup

EGGPLANT PARMIGIANA

1 pound ground beef
1 clove garlic, minced
1 medium onion, chopped
6 tablespoons olive or salad oil
2 8-ounce cans tomato sauce
1 cup water
1 teaspoon salt
1 teaspoon orégano

Dash cayenne
1 eggplant (1–1½ pounds)
2 eggs
1 tablespoon water
½ cup fine dry bread crumbs
1 cup grated Parmesan cheese
8-ounce package thinly sliced
    mozzarella cheese

The sauce is made like any other Italian tomato sauce. Lightly brown the meat, garlic, and onion in 2 tablespoons of the oil. Add the tomato sauce and water, salt, orégano, and cayenne. Simmer, uncovered, while you prepare the eggplant.

In a flattish bowl (like a cereal bowl) beat the eggs with 1 tablespoon water until well mixed. In another bowl or plate combine the crumbs with ½ cup Parmesan cheese. Heat 4 tablespoons of the oil in a large skillet. Slice the eggplant rather thinly (¼ inch)—do not peel— and dip each slice first in the egg mixture, then in the crumb mixture, and brown in the hot oil until crisp on both sides. When done, remove each slice.

In the meantime, oil 2 shallow baking dishes—8-inch-square baking dishes will do, or you can use au gratin pans. Put a layer of eggplant in each casserole, top with ¼ cup Parmesan cheese (2 tablespoons in each casserole), half of the meat sauce and half of the mozzarella cheese. Repeat the layers using the remaining eggplant, Parmesan, meat sauce, and mozzarella.

You may put this dish together early in the afternoon and refrigerate both casseroles, or you may prepare it just before the children's dinner and refrigerate the adults' casserole. An unrefrigerated casserole should bake about 25 minutes in a 350° F. oven until the cheese begins to brown and the sauce to bubble. A refrigerated casserole will take about 10 minutes longer.

RAVIOLI PLUS

*Escarole or Chicory Salad**
Italian Bread Sticks
*Fresh Fruit and Lazy Daisy Cake**

RAVIOLI PLUS

2 15-ounce cans ravioli with cheese and tomato sauce
1 tablespoon oil
1 large onion, chopped
1 clove garlic, minced
1 pound ground beef
1 can cream of mushroom soup
2 teaspoons Worcestershire
Few drops hot red pepper sauce
1/4 cup sherry or water
2 tablespoons butter or margarine, melted
1/4 cup grated Parmesan cheese
1/2 cup dry bread crumbs

Any time during the day, butter 2 casseroles or 4 individual ones. Empty the cans of ravioli into the casseroles. Heat the oil in a large skillet and sauté the onion and garlic until the onion is limp. Add the ground beef and brown well. Pour off any drippings. Stir the soup, Worcestershire, hot pepper sauce, and sherry or water into the meat. Pour the meat mixture into the casseroles and toss lightly with a fork to mix the ravioli with the meat.

Combine the butter with the cheese and crumbs and sprinkle on top of the casseroles. Bake, or refrigerate and bake, for 20 minutes in a 350° F. oven until the crumbs are brown and the sauce is bubbly.

SUPPER WAFFLES WITH CREAMED CHIPPED BEEF

Asparagus, Tomato Salad*
Waffle Strawberry Shortcake

SUPPER WAFFLES WITH CREAMED CHIPPED BEEF

¼ cup butter or margarine
¼ cup chopped onion
2 tablespoons flour
1 cup milk

¼–½ pound chipped beef
1 cup sour cream
Waffles, frozen or made from your
   favorite recipe or mix

In the top of a double boiler, melt the butter and sauté the chopped onion, stirring until limp but not brown. Stir in the flour and add the milk, stirring until thick with a wire whisk. Break the chipped beef into small pieces and add to the sauce with the sour cream. Put over hot water and stir until smooth and hot. Serve over the waffles to the children. Refrigerate the rest and reheat over boiling water just before the later dinner. You may bake the adults' waffles when you are baking the children's. Cool them. Reheat and crisp by dropping into the toaster just before serving.

Veal

Back in the early 1930's, when a large can of salmon cost a dime and butter was 15 cents a pound, thrifty housewives used veal as a substitute for chicken, a luxury meat in those days. The tables have turned. Today, veal is not only expensive, it is also chic.

Among the modern American women who have turned to gourmet cooking as an outlet for their artistic energies, veal is a great favorite. This, no doubt, is a reflection of veal's centuries-old popularity in Europe.

In communities with large Italian or French populations, veal is usually plentiful. In other communities, where the demand for veal is low, it may be scarce. This is a pity, for veal is relatively low in fat and calories and it adds variety to the tired old beef–ham–pork chop–chicken routine.

Some cuts of veal—cutlets, scallops, and chops—are usually expensive, but stew meat and breast of veal are good buys. Select young veal that is a very pale pinkish-beige color, not the deep pink meat that looks almost like beef.

OVEN POT ROAST OF VEAL WITH POTATOES

*Green Salad with Raw Cauliflower and Radishes**
*Pudding Delights**

OVEN POT ROAST OF VEAL WITH POTATOES

3½–4 pound shoulder veal roast,
   boned and tied
1 tablespoon oil
1 small carrot, chopped

1 medium onion, chopped
¼ cup white wine
1½ teaspoons salt
Halved potatoes

This will serve 8. See following menu.

In a Dutch oven, slowly brown the veal on all sides in the oil. Add the rest of the ingredients, except the potatoes. Bring to a simmer on top of the stove, cover, and bake in a 325° F. oven for 1½ hours. Add the potatoes and continue to cook, covered, until they are tender. Remove from the oven and slice half of the meat. Serve the children their meat with the potatoes.

Put the sliced meat and potatoes for the adults' meal on an oven-proof serving platter. Put a spoonful of juice on each slice of meat and each potato. Cover with foil. Return to the oven for about 15 minutes before serving. Cool and refrigerate the other half of the meat and the rest of the juice for the following meal.

VEAL AND SOUBISE

Buttered Carrots*
Spinach Salad*
Fruit and Cookies

VEAL AND SOUBISE

Cooked veal (see preceding recipe)
½ cup uncooked white rice
1 cup water
Butter or margarine
3 medium onions, sliced
4 tablespoons flour
1 cup milk

1 cup juice (see preceding recipe),
   or 1 cup chicken broth, or a
   combination of the two
Dash nutmeg
Few grinds pepper
½ teaspoon salt
¼ cup grated Swiss cheese

Slice the cold veal about ¼ inch thick. In the meantime, boil the rice for 5 minutes in the water. Drain well. In a skillet, melt 3 tablespoons of the butter and add the onions. Stir them around just until the onions are well coated, then add the partially cooked rice. Cover tightly and cook over a very low heat for 15 minutes. The onions and butter should give off enough moisture to cook the rice. If necessary, add a little of the juice from the veal.

While the rice is cooking, make a sauce by melting 3 tablespoons of the butter, adding the flour, letting it bubble a moment, and stirring in the juice and milk, nutmeg, pepper, and salt. Stir until thick. Stir about ½ cup of this mixture into the rice and onion.

Now it is time to put the dish together. Put a slice of veal in the bottom of a buttered au gratin dish. Top with several spoons of the Soubise. Overlap another slice of veal, more rice and onion, and continue this until you have used half of each. Then make the second casserole in the same way. Put any leftover rice and onion on top and around the edges. Pour half of the sauce over each casserole and top with grated Swiss cheese and dot with 1 tablespoon butter. Bake each casserole in a 350° F. oven until hot and bubbly, about 20 minutes for the first casserole, 30 minutes for the refrigerated one. If the cheese is not melted and brown, run it under the broiler for just a moment.

Veal Scallops

Veal scallops—very thinly sliced veal cutlets—can be prepared in an incredibly short time, and are absolutely delicious. Unfortunately, they are also expensive.

Select veal that is a very delicate pinkish-beige. If you are lucky, your meat man will cut the scallops thinly for you and then flatten them with the side of his cleaver. If you are not lucky, buy thinly sliced veal, take it home, and pound it with a meat tenderizer (a square, hammerlike object), a rolling pin, or the edge of a heavy old saucer. After you have pounded the scallops (they should be no more than ¼ inch thick), wrap them in wax paper and refrigerate until 10 minutes before serving time. Since they cook so quickly, there is no need to cook all the meat at once.

Cubed veal steaks, which are often economical, may be substituted for veal scallops in any of the following recipes.

BASIC VEAL SCALLOPS   For 2 servings—4 scallops (about ½ pound). In a large skillet, melt 1 tablespoon butter and 1 tablespoon oil, or 2 tablespoons of oil. Wipe the scallops with paper towels so they will brown nicely and add them to the sizzling fat. Keep the fat hot but not burning—about 350° F. in an electric skillet. Sauté 3–4 minutes on one side, turn and sauté another 3–4 minutes, adding more oil as necessary. Sprinkle with salt and pepper and serve. When the adults are ready to eat, repeat the process.

Easy? Yes. And that's all you need to do. However, if you wish to be fancy, a few variations on the scallop theme follow.

LEMON VEAL SCALLOPS

*Baked Acorn Squash**
*Oriental Celery Casserole**
Hot Rolls
*Pears and Chocolate Crunchies**

LEMON VEAL SCALLOPS

Prepare Basic Veal Scallops. Remove scallops and drain off any excess fat. Then add the juice of ½ lemon to the skillet, stir to deglaze the pan, and pour over the scallops. It's even easier just to serve the scallops with wedges of fresh lemon, which each person may squeeze for himself. *Serves 2.*

TARRAGON VEAL SCALLOPS

*Potato-Mushroom-Onion Casserole**
*Green Bean Salad**
Bread Sticks
*Lemon Pie**

TARRAGON VEAL SCALLOPS

Prepare Basic Veal Scallops. Remove scallops and add 1 table-spoon finely chopped green onions. Sauté about 1 minute and add ¼ cup dry white wine and 1 teaspoon dried tarragon. Bring to the boiling point, stirring constantly, and pour over the scallops. *Serves 2.*

MUSHROOM VEAL SCALLOPS

*Brown Rice**
*Brussels Sprouts**
*Sliced Tomatoes and Cucumbers**
*Grandma's Cracker Dessert**

MUSHROOM VEAL SCALLOPS

Prepare Basic Veal Scallops. When tender, add half of a 5-ounce can sliced mushrooms, drained, and ¼ cup heavy cream or commercial sour cream. Heat—but do not boil—and serve garnished with parsley. *Serves 2.*

CHEESE-TOPPED SCALLOPS

*Boiled Potatoes with Dill Weed**
*Buttered Onions**
*Spinach Salad**
Gingerbread and Applesauce

CHEESE-TOPPED SCALLOPS

Prepare Basic Veal Scallops. After browning on one side, turn and top with thin slices of mozzarella or Swiss cheese. Sprinkle with orégano. Continue to brown. If necessary, cover the pan for a few minutes until the cheese melts. *Serves 2.*

[43]

VEAL PARMIGIANA WITH SPAGHETTI TWISTS

Cold Zucchini in Vinaigrette Sauce*
French Bread*
Fruit Cup with Sherbet*

VEAL PARMIGIANA WITH SPAGHETTI TWISTS

½ cup dry bread crumbs
Parmesan cheese
½ teaspoon salt
1½ pounds thin veal cutlets, cut
   in 8 pieces
1 egg, beaten with 1 tablespoon
   cold water
3 tablespoons vegetable or olive oil
1-pound can stewed tomatoes
6-ounce can tomato paste

1½-ounce package spaghetti sauce
   mix
½ teaspoon orégano
½ cup water
8-ounce package spaghetti twists,
   cooked according to package
   directions
8 slices mozzarella cheese, from a
   6- to 8-ounce package

Mix crumbs, 2 tablespoons of the Parmesan cheese, and salt in a shallow plate. Dip the veal pieces in the egg and then in the crumbs. Place on a plate and refrigerate for 30 minutes to set the crumb mixture.

Heat the oil in a large skillet and brown the veal on both sides. Unless the scallops are quite thick, they will be tender by the time they are brown. If not, cover and continue to cook in the oil, adding more oil if necessary. When the scallops are brown and tender, remove them from the skillet. Add tomatoes, tomato paste, sauce mix, orégano, and water. Simmer until thick. You may substitute canned or homemade spaghetti sauce—2 or 3 cups if you like. Mix about half of the sauce into the spaghetti twists and divide between 2 greased casseroles. Lay 4 pieces of the veal, alternated with 4 of the mozzarella cheese slices, across the top of each casserole. Top with rest of sauce and ¼ cup Parmesan cheese. Bake the children's casserole for 20 minutes in a 350° F. oven. Refrigerate the adults' casserole and bake 25 minutes.

VEAL ROLLS AND NOODLES

Green Beans*
Cherry Tomatoes*
Fruit Gelatin and Cookies*

VEAL ROLLS AND NOODLES

8 thin veal scallops (about 1 pound)
¼ pound boiled ham, thinly sliced
Swiss cheese
¼ cup vegetable oil
2 tablespoons chopped onion
2 tablespoons chopped celery
2 tablespoons chopped carrot
¾ cup dry white wine (or chicken broth)
½ teaspoon salt
Few grinds pepper
2 cups uncooked fine noodles
1 tablespoon butter

Lay out the scallops, which have been pounded very thin. Cut the ham to fit the veal. You don't need to fuss much. Two or 3 little pieces of ham will be just as satisfactory as 1. Just lay it on the veal evenly. (You may have a little ham left over.) If you can buy unsliced Swiss cheese, do so. If not, buy cheese that does not have paper between the slices and cut through several layers of cheese to make strips about ¼ inch by ¼ inch and just slightly shorter than the width of the scallops. Save the scraps of cheese, to be chopped and added to the noodles. Put a strip of cheese at one end of each ham-topped scallop and roll up, securing the ends with toothpicks.

Brown the rolls on all sides in the oil in a large skillet. (Choose one with a tight-fitting cover for later use.) When brown, remove the rolls and add the onion, celery, and carrot to the oil and sauté briefly. Return the rolls with the wine, salt, and pepper. Cover and simmer until the rolls are tender when pierced with a fork—about 45 minutes—adding more wine if necessary.

In the meantime, cook the noodles according to package directions. Drain and toss with butter and ¼ cup chopped Swiss cheese. When the rolls are tender, serve them to the children on a bed of noodles with a little of the sauce spooned on top. Put the rest of the noodles in a buttered au gratin pan or pie plate. Lay the rolls on top of the noodles and spoon the rest of the sauce over the rolls. Cool, then cover tightly with foil, and refrigerate, to be reheated for 20 minutes in a 350° F. oven.

BREAST OF VEAL WITH POTATOES AND CARROTS

*Mother's Green Salad Mold**
Cheese Biscuits
*Coco Mocho**

BREAST OF VEAL WITH POTATOES AND CARROTS

4 slices bacon
1/2 cup chopped onion
1/2 cup chopped celery
1 cup packaged stuffing mix
1/4 teaspoon dried savory
1/4 teaspoon dried thyme
1/2 teaspoon salt
Few grinds pepper

2 tablespoons boiling water
4 pounds breast of veal with a
   pocket (this may be whole or
   half of a larger breast)
3 tablespoons salad oil
1 cup chicken broth or bouillon
Medium-size whole potatoes
Carrots, quartered crosswise

Make the stuffing by cooking the bacon in a Dutch oven until crisp. Remove with a slotted spoon, drain, and crumble. Add the onions and celery to the fat and sauté briefly. Stir in the bacon, stuffing mix, savory, thyme, salt, pepper, and water. Pack lightly into the pocket in the veal. Close opening with skewers.

Wipe the Dutch oven with a paper towel. Then add the salad oil and heat. Brown the veal well on all sides. When well browned, pour off any fat, and add the broth. Cover tightly and simmer about 2 hours. Add the potatoes and carrots and a little more broth if necessary, and continue to simmer until the vegetables are tender.

Remove the breast and cut off the children's portion. Also remove their carrots and potatoes. Spoon a little of the liquid over their meat and vegetables and serve. There should be about 1/2 cup liquid left in the Dutch oven. Cool and refrigerate. Twenty minutes before the adults' meal, baste meat and vegetables with the liquid. Cover and simmer until heated through.

VEAL PAPRIKA

Rice*
Lettuce and Cucumber Salad*
Meringues and Raspberries

VEAL PAPRIKA

1½ pounds boneless stewing veal, cut in 1-inch cubes
4 slices bacon, quartered
1 onion, sliced

2 cups chicken broth
Paprika
1 teaspoon salt
Sour cream

Brown veal, bacon, and onion together in a large skillet with a tight-fitting cover. Add broth, 1 teaspoon paprika, and salt. Cover and simmer until meat is tender—1–1½ hours. Add water if the skillet threatens to run dry.

Some children are not fond of sour cream, so give them just a little until they develop a taste for it. In this case, serve their meat on a bed of rice. Put their portion of the sauce in a cup and stir in just a little sour cream and paprika to make the sauce look pink. Pour over the meat.

Refrigerate the adults' portion of the veal, unless you expect to serve it within an hour or two. Reheat in the same skillet before serving time. Let it boil a few minutes and add ½ cup sour cream and enough paprika to make the sauce look pink. Heat, but do not boil.

MAGIC VEAL

Crumbed Broccoli*
Baked Potatoes*
Cranberry Crunch Salad*
Gingerbread

This really is magic! The sauce and meat brown beautifully to make a handsome dish that could hardly be easier or tastier—and it is inexpensive, too.

MAGIC VEAL

2 pounds boneless stewing veal, cubed, or 3 pounds breast of veal, cut up
Few grinds pepper

1 can condensed cream of mushroom soup
1 can condensed onion soup

Put all of the ingredients in a large casserole and bake, *uncovered,* in a 350° F. oven until the veal is tender—about 2 hours. Serve the children and reheat in the oven before the adults' meal.

BREADED VEAL CHOPS

Red Cabbage*
Potato Sticks*
Green Salad*
Banana, Grape, and Grenadine Cup and Cookies

BREADED VEAL CHOPS

4–8 veal chops
Salt
Fresh-ground pepper

1 egg, beaten with 1 tablespoon water (or 2 eggs, if required)
Fine dry bread crumbs
Vegetable oil

Dry chops on paper towel. Sprinkle with salt and pepper. Dip each chop in egg and then in crumbs. Refrigerate chops for at least ½ hour, longer if convenient. Heat enough oil to cover bottom of skillet and brown the chops, adding more oil if necessary. Turn chops carefully with tongs or pancake turner so as not to disturb the crumb coating and brown on the other side. This will take about 10 minutes.

When the chops are brown, place those for the adult meal in a shallow baking dish, cool, cover with foil, and refrigerate. Put the children's chops in a shallow baking dish and bake, uncovered, at 350° F. until tender, about 30 minutes. Bake the adults' chops in the same way, 40 minutes before serving.

VEAL CHOP AND VEGETABLE PLATTER

*Sunshine Salad**
Chocolate Fudge Cake

VEAL CHOP AND VEGETABLE PLATTER

2 slices bacon, cut in 1-inch pieces
4 large veal chops
1 can condensed cream of chicken soup
½ cup milk
10-ounce package frozen peas

Cooked new potatoes or canned potatoes
8-ounce can small white onions, drained
Salt
Pepper

In a large skillet with a tight-fitting cover, fry the bacon. Remove with a slotted spoon and drain on paper towels. Brown chops in the bacon fat. Add the soup and milk. Cover and simmer until the chops are tender—about 40 minutes.

In the meantime, bring the frozen peas to a boil. Remove the adults' portion with a slotted spoon. Continue to cook the children's portion a few minutes or until tender.

When the chops are tender, add the children's potatoes and onions to the chops. Salt and pepper lightly. Cook just until heated through. Serve the children's chops, potatoes, onions, and peas and spoon some of the gravy over the chops and potatoes. Top with half of the bacon pieces.

Arrange the adults' chops and lightly salted and peppered potatoes and onions on an ovenproof platter. Cover with gravy and arrange the peas along the sides or ends of the platter. Cover with foil and refrigerate, to be baked, covered, in a 350° F. oven for 15 minutes. Garnish with bacon just before serving.

BLANQUETTE DE VEAU

Noodles*
Peas*
Lettuce and Tomato Salad*
Peach Pie

BLANQUETTE DE VEAU

2 pounds boneless stewing veal,
   cut in 1-inch cubes
Water
4 chicken bouillon cubes, or
   envelopes of instant chicken-
   flavored broth
1 large onion, stuck with 2 cloves
1 large carrot, cut in fourths
   crosswise
2 celery stalks

1 bay leaf
1 teaspoon salt
12 small fresh white onions
12 fresh mushrooms, quartered
1/4 cup butter or margarine
1/4 cup flour
Heavy cream
2 tablespoons lemon juice
Paprika (optional)

Put the veal in a large Dutch oven and barely cover with water.
Bring to a boil, simmer 20 minutes, and skim. Add the bouillon cubes,
clove-studded onion, carrot, celery, bay leaf, and salt. Cover and simmer
until meat is fork-tender—about 1 hour.

In the meantime, peel the small onions and pierce crossed slits in
the stem ends with the point of a paring knife. Add to the veal and continue to simmer until the onions are almost tender—about 15 minutes.
Add the mushrooms and simmer an additional 5 minutes.

Drain, saving the stock. Return the meat, onions, and mushrooms
to the Dutch oven.

In a small saucepan, melt the butter, stir in the flour, allow to bubble for a moment, and stir in 2 cups of reserved veal stock. Stir with a
wire whisk until smooth and thick. Stir in 1/2 cup heavy cream and
lemon juice and pour over the veal and vegetables. Return to the simmering point and serve the children. Put a tablespoon of cream over the
top to prevent a skin from forming, and cool and refrigerate. Reheat 15
minutes before the adults' meal. Sprinkle with paprika.

Canned onions and mushrooms may be substituted for the fresh.
Add after the meat has been drained.

Lamb

Many Americans insist that they do not like lamb. When questioned more closely, they will tell you that, not only do they not like it, they have not even tasted it for years. A shame, because the lamb they remember was probably not lamb at all, but mutton. Today mutton is extremely scarce. Mild, young lamb is readily available wherever there is a market for it. As with other types of meat, the cost of lamb varies with the cut and the season. What we used to call "spring lamb," however, is now available throughout the year.

POT ROASTED LAMB AND VEGETABLES

Broccoli Spears*
Pineapple Slices on Greens*
Cream Puffs*

This is a "twofer" recipe—two meals from one piece of meat. You may, of course, prepare only the first dish, in which case you would halve the recipe. Read *both* recipes before you begin. And may I suggest that you cook the beans for the second recipe while you are preparing the first recipe? It will save you time.

POT ROASTED LAMB AND VEGETABLES

1 boned and tied shoulder or leg of lamb—about 5 pounds (8 servings—see following recipe)
2 tablespoons oil
1 carrot, chopped
1 onion, chopped
2 cups liquid—red wine, tomato juice, or beef bouillon
1 bay leaf
1 teaspoon dried rosemary
1 clove garlic
1 teaspoon salt
Potatoes
Small white onions
2 tablespoons flour
½ cup water

Dry the roast with paper towels and brown in the oil in a Dutch oven. When well browned on all sides, remove the roast and drain off most of the fat. Sauté the carrots and onion for 2 or 3 minutes in the remaining fat. Return the roast to the Dutch oven with the liquid, bay leaf, rosemary, garlic, and salt. Bring to a simmer, cover tightly and bake in a preheated 350° F. oven for 2 hours. (Or, you may cook on top of the stove over a very low heat for 2 hours.)

Peel the number of potatoes your family will eat in 1 meal and leave whole, unless they are very large. Peel onions for 1 meal and cut crosses in the stem ends with the point of your paring knife. After the roast has cooked for 2 hours, add the potatoes and onions and continue to cook until the vegetables are tender, about 30 minutes.

Remove the meat, potatoes and onions. Strain and degrease the cooking liquid and return 1 cup of it to the Dutch oven. Stir or shake the flour into the water—or use instant flour—and add to the liquid in the Dutch oven. Bring to a boil, stirring constantly with a wire whisk.

In the meantime, slice the portion of the roast you expect the children and adults to eat in 1 meal. Serve the children their meat, potatoes and onions with some of the gravy. Return the adults' lamb slices, potatoes and onions to the Dutch oven. Cool and refrigerate to be reheated just before the adults' meal.

In a separate bowl, cool and refrigerate the rest of the meat and any remaining, unthickened liquid to be used in the following recipe.

LAMB AND BEANS

*Buttered Carrots**
*Mixed Green Salad**
*Lemon Pie**

LAMB AND BEANS

1¼ cups dried lima, pinto or pea beans
2½ cups water
1 teaspoon salt
½ cup chopped onion

1 cup liquid—cooking broth from preceding recipe, tomato juice, or bouillon
Leftover lamb, cubed

Put dried beans and water in a large saucepan. Bring to a boil, boil 2 minutes, turn off heat and allow to sit for 1 hour. Then add salt, onion, and 1 cup liquid and simmer until the beans are tender—about 2 hours. This may all be done on the same day that you are preparing the preceding recipe.

Just before serving time, add the children's share of the lamb cubes and reheat. The reheating may be done in the oven or on top of the stove. If you cook the beans in advance, you may want to stir in the lamb cubes and refrigerate in 2 casseroles, each one to be heated in the oven just before serving time.

LAMB CHOP PLATTER

Bean Casserole*
Whole Wheat Rolls
Strawberry Sundaes

LAMB CHOP PLATTER

Loin lamb chops, 1 inch thick	Melted butter or oil
1 medium-size eggplant, cut in ½-inch slices—do not peel	Grated Parmesan cheese
Salt	Fine bread crumbs
Pepper	16 cherry tomatoes, or 8 tomato halves

Arrange the children's lamb chops and eggplant slices on a greased broiler rack. Sprinkle with salt and pepper and brush the eggplant with melted butter or oil. Place 3 inches below the heat in a preheated broiler. Broil 5 minutes. Remove and turn the chops and eggplant. Brush the eggplant with a generous amount of butter and sprinkle with salt and pepper. Spoon about 1 teaspoon cheese on each slice and shake bread crumbs on top of the cheese. Add the tomatoes to the broiler rack, sprinkling with salt and pepper and brushing with butter. Broil an additional 5 minutes.

Repeat the process for the adults' later meal.

MIXED GRILL

Creamed New Potatoes and Peas*
Bread Fingers with Poppy Seeds*
Pears with Pineapple Sherbet and Mint Sauce*

MIXED GRILL

4 shoulder lamb chops	1 cup Italian dressing
3 or 4 lamb kidneys, split	4 or 8 sausage links
½ pound large fresh mushroom caps	2 tomatoes, thickly sliced

Marinate lamb chops, kidney slices and mushroom caps in salad dressing for at least 1 hour. Fry the sausage links until lightly browned on all sides.

Drain the children's chops and kidney slices and place on a rack in a preheated broiler for about 5 minutes. If the chops are thick or if you prefer well-done lamb, increase the time. Remove and turn. Drain half of the mushrooms and place stem side up on the rack with the tomatoes and sausages. Broil another 5 minutes. Serve.

Leave the adults' chops, kidneys, and mushrooms in the marinade to be broiled in the same way just before their dinner.

LAMB STEW

Cucumbers in Vinegar with Fresh or Dried Mint*
Hard Rolls
Melon with Sherbet and Mint Sauce*

LAMB STEW

2–3 pounds lamb stew meat, cut in pieces (use neck or shank meat with bones)
1 tablespoon oil
2 teaspoons sugar
2 cups water
1 beef bouillon cube
1/4 teaspoon dried thyme

1 clove garlic on a toothpick
1/2 bay leaf
1 teaspoon salt
4 carrots, cut in 1-inch pieces
4 medium-size potatoes, quartered
8-ounce can white onions, drained
1 cup frozen peas

Early in the day or the day before, brown lamb in oil in Dutch oven; add sugar, shaking over the flame for a few minutes until the sugar melts and browns. The sugar makes the stew a rich brown color. Add water and seasonings. Cover and simmer for 2 hours or until the meat is tender and begins to fall off the bones. Strain the broth and remove the garlic, bay leaf, and any loose bones. Return the meat to the broth and cool. Refrigerate until 30 minutes before the children's dinner hour. Remove all of the fat from the top of the broth and reheat the broth. Add the carrots and potatoes and more water if necessary. Cover and simmer until the vegetables are tender. Add the onions and peas. Simmer 5 minutes. Taste for seasoning. If you wish, you may thicken the broth by adding a smooth paste made of 1 tablespoon flour stirred into 3 tablespoons water. Turn off the heat and serve the children. Ten minutes before the adults' meal, reheat the stew.

"BARBECUED" LAMB RIBLETS

*Parsley Potatoes**
*Creamed Peas**
Raw Carrot and Celery Sticks
*Fruit Cup and Cookies**

"BARBECUED" LAMB RIBLETS

4 pounds breast of lamb, cut into riblets (serving-size pieces)
1 teaspoon salt
1 lemon, thinly sliced
1 onion, thinly sliced
8 thin strips green pepper

8-ounce can tomato sauce
1/2 cup water
1/4 cup brown sugar
2 tablespoons vinegar
1 teaspoon dry mustard
1 tablespoon Worcestershire

Early in the day, brown riblets slowly in a large skillet or Dutch oven. The riblets are fatty, so there is no need to add oil. When brown, drain off the fat. Sprinkle with salt and add lemon, onion, and green pepper. Mix the other ingredients and pour over the meat. Cover and simmer slowly for 1½ hours. Cool and refrigerate. Fifteen minutes before the children's dinner, remove the layer of fat from the riblets and heat the children's portion with half of the sauce in a small skillet or heavy saucepan on top of the stove. Reheat the rest of the riblets and sauce 15 minutes before the adults' meal.

BRAISED LAMB SHANKS

*Brown Rice**
*Cucumber and Tomato Salad**
Peach Pie

BRAISED LAMB SHANKS

4 lamb shanks
2 tablespoons oil
1 medium-size onion, chopped
1 carrot, sliced
1 stalk celery, sliced
1 clove garlic, minced

1 teaspoon salt
Few grinds pepper
1 bay leaf
Juice of 1/2 lemon
1 cup dry red wine
1 cup beef bouillon or broth

Brown the lamb shanks in the oil in a Dutch oven or large skillet. Remove and add the onion, carrot, celery, and garlic to the Dutch oven. Sauté lightly and return the lamb shanks with the rest of the ingredients. Cover and simmer slowly until the shanks are tender—about 2 hours. Skim off the fat. An additional cup of bouillon may be substituted for the wine.

If you like, thicken the gravy by stirring 2 tablespoons flour into ¼ cup cold water until smooth, and then stirring into the gravy.

Serve the children. Cool the remainder to be reheated in the sauce or gravy just before the adults' meal.

Clam Juice Cocktail

STUFFED EGGPLANT

*Lettuce Wedges with Cucumbers**
French Bread
Cherry Pie

STUFFED EGGPLANT

2 eggplants, each weighing about ¾ pound
1 pound raw ground lamb (or beef)
1 clove garlic, minced

1 small onion, chopped
¾ teaspoon salt
Few grinds pepper
¾ cup Grape-Nuts
1 can condensed tomato soup

Cut eggplants in half lengthwise. Scoop out the centers, leaving shells about ½ inch thick. Put the shells in a saucepan, cover with boiling water, and simmer for 5 minutes. Drain well.

In the meantime, chop the eggplant centers finely. Put the lamb in a large skillet. Add the chopped eggplant, garlic, and onion and sauté until the lamb is lightly browned. Pour off any excess fat. Add the salt, pepper, ½ cup of the Grape-Nuts and soup. Mix well and spoon into the eggplant shells. Sprinkle with the remaining ¼ cup cereal.

Refrigerate the shells for the adult meal and bake the children's shells for 30 minutes in a 375° F. oven. Bake the adult shells for 35 minutes before the later meal. Or, you may bake together and reheat the adults' portion.

MUSAKA

Green Salad*
Poppy Seed Rolls
Blueberries and Ice Cream*

There seem to be as many different recipes for Musaka as there are cookbooks. Most have eggplant, some don't. Most have lamb, some don't. All may be prepared in advance—even a day or two—and reheated easily. I think you'll like this recipe.

MUSAKA

Eggplant, about 1¼ pounds
Oil
1 large onion, chopped
1 clove garlic, minced
1 pound ground raw lamb (or
   beef, which is also excellent)
8-ounce can tomato sauce
2 eggs, separated

¼ cup dry bread crumbs
Salt
¼ teaspoon orégano
2 tablespoons butter or margarine
2 tablespoons flour
1½ cups milk
Dash nutmeg

Slice the unpeeled eggplant lengthwise, so that you have ovals about ¼ inch thick instead of rounds. Brown lightly in hot oil. Drain on paper towels. When you have finished browning the eggplant, add the onion and garlic and sauté until the onion is limp. Add the lamb and brown lightly. *Cool* and stir in the tomato sauce, unbeaten egg *whites,* crumbs, salt, and orégano.

In a saucepan, melt the butter, stir in the flour and salt, bubble for a second or two, and add the milk, stirring with a whisk until the sauce is smooth and thick. Beat the egg yolks and stir in a little of the sauce to heat the yolks. Then add the yolk mixture to the sauce in the saucepan. Add the nutmeg.

To assemble the musaka, oil 2 1½-quart casseroles or 9-inch-square pans. Put a layer of eggplant on the bottom of each, top with part of the meat mixture. Continue making layers of eggplant and meat until both have been used up. The top layer should be eggplant. Pour the sauce over the top layer and bake both casseroles in a 350° F. oven for 1 hour. Serve the children. Cool and refrigerate the adults' musaka, to be reheated in a 350° F. oven 20 minutes before the later dinner.

The musaka may be assembled at any time during the day, or the day before, and refrigerated until baking time.

LAMB LOAVES

Ratatouille*
French Bread
Grandma's Cracker Dessert*

LAMB LOAVES

1 pound ground lamb	Few grinds pepper
½ cup fine bread crumbs	½ cup chopped onion
1 teaspoon salt	1 egg
¼ teaspoon garlic powder (optional)	¼ cup tomato sauce, from an 8-ounce can

Mix all of the above ingredients and shape into 4 small loaves. Spoon an additional tablespoon tomato sauce over each loaf. Put loaves in a shallow pan and bake in a 350° F. oven for 40 minutes. Serve the children. Reheat the other 2 loaves a few minutes before the adults' meal.

LAMB PATTIES AND PEACHES

Tomato, Corn, and Onion Casserole*
Lettuce Wedges and Dressing*
Lime Pie

LAMB PATTIES AND PEACHES

4 ready-shaped lamb patties, or 1 pound ground lamb, shaped into 4 patties	Salt
	Pepper
4 peach halves	Mint jelly

The children's lamb patties may be broiled for a total of 10 minutes in a preheated oven, or they may be pan-broiled in a heavy skillet or an electric skillet. Add 2 peach halves during the last 2 minutes, just to heat through. Sprinkle the patties with salt and pepper. Just before serving, spoon mint jelly into the peach halves.

Repeat the process for the adults' later meal.

LEFTOVER LAMB AND CURRIED FRUIT BAKE

Brown Rice*
Buttered Celery*
Carrot Sticks
Custard and Brownies

This is delicious as a side dish served with roasted poultry, lamb, ham, or pork.

Or, it may be converted into a main dish. To do so, prepare and bake the fruit any time during the day. Just before each meal, place large slices of leftover roasted lamb (or ham, pork, or poultry) on top of the fruits. Spoon some of the sauce over the meat and heat, covered, until the sauce begins to bubble—about 20 minutes in a 350° F. oven.

CURRIED FRUIT BAKE

3 tablespoons butter or margarine
½ cup packed brown sugar
1½ teaspoons curry powder
8 canned apricot halves, drained

8 slices pineapple, drained
4–8 peach halves, drained
4–8 pear halves, drained
8 maraschino cherries, drained

Melt butter in a small saucepan and stir in brown sugar and curry powder. In the meantime, dry the fruits well on paper towels and layer them in 2 casseroles. Pour the butter mixture over the fruits. Cover and bake 30 minutes in the 325° F. oven. Remove the cover and bake another 30 minutes. This may be done any time during the day. If not to be served immediately, refrigerate and reheat, uncovered, in 350° F. oven until bubbly—about 20 minutes.

LEFTOVER LAMB CURRY

Condiments—Coconut, Peanuts, Chutney, and
  Fried and Crumbled Bacon
*Rice**
Bread Sticks
*Fruit Gelatin and Cookies**

LEFTOVER LAMB CURRY

3 cups cooked-lamb cubes (from a
  roast leg of lamb)
1 cup lamb gravy or canned beef
  gravy
½ cup water
1 beef bouillon cube
1 onion, chopped
2 apples, peeled and chopped

1–3 teaspoons curry powder
1 teaspoon salt
Few grinds pepper
1 teaspoon cracked ginger
1 stick cinnamon
2 inch-long strips lemon peel
¼ cup raisins
½–1 cup yogurt

Combine all of the ingredients except the yogurt in a large saucepan. Bring to a boil and simmer about 10 minutes. Add more water if necessary. Add the yogurt and serve on rice with condiments. Reheat just before the adults' meal.

Pork

It is a mystery why smoked pork is so much more popular than fresh pork. For our purposes, all pork is ideal since it must always be served well done and can, therefore, be reheated easily.

As you know, it is essential to cook pork thoroughly to avoid a sometimes fatal disease called trichinosis. Cook your pork to an internal temperature of 185° F. or until the juices run clear when the meat is pierced with a fork. Well-done pork is white with no trace of pink.

This chapter contains recipes for fresh pork, smoked ham, Canadian bacon, and sausage.

ROAST FRESH PORK

*Scalloped Potatoes**
*Three-Bean Salad**
Chocolate Cake

ROAST FRESH PORK

Pork shoulder, loin, or fresh ham
—about 4 pounds with bone,
less without bone

Apple cider or apple juice
(optional)

Place fat side up on a rack in an open pan in a 350° F. oven. Allow about 40 minutes per pound. I spoon a little cider—about 2 tablespoons—over my roast from time to time during the roasting, but this step is not necessary. When the internal temperature reaches 185° F. on a meat thermometer and the juices are clear when the meat is pierced with a fork, the roast is done. Slice the children's portion. Return the roast to the oven and bake about ½ hour before the adults' dinner.

You may have some leftovers. If desired, you may cook an even larger piece and reheat for another meal.

SIMPLE CHOPS

Mashed Potatoes*
Broccoli*
Cranberry Crunch Mold*
Angel Food Cake

SIMPLE CHOPS

4 shoulder pork chops (about 2 pounds)
½ cup milk

1 can condensed cream of chicken soup

Trim the pork chops and fry the fat in a hot skillet until about 1 tablespoon of liquid fat has accumulated. Remove the pieces of fat, add the pork chops, and brown well on both sides. Add the soup and milk. Cover and simmer slowly for 45 minutes, or until the chops are tender. Serve the children.

The chops for the adults' dinner may be reheated in the gravy just before the meal, or they may be placed in a small casserole with gravy and baked, covered, in a 350° F. oven for 20 minutes. You may reheat the mashed potatoes by mounding them on top of the chops during the last 10 minutes of cooking.

PORK CHOP POTATO CASSEROLE

*Spiced Apple Ring Salad on Shredded Cabbage**
Toasted Corn Muffins
Lemon Sherbet and Cookies (pour Crème de Menthe
on adults' sherbet)

PORK CHOP POTATO CASSEROLE

4–8 lean shoulder or center cut
   pork chops
Potatoes
1 medium-size onion

1 can cream of mushroom soup
½ soup-can milk
Salt
Pepper

Brown chops in large skillet. While chops are browning, peel and slice potatoes. Put potatoes for the children in one shallow casserole and potatoes for adults in another. Peel and slice the onion and divide between the 2 casseroles. Put the browned chops on top of the vegetables. Sprinkle with salt and pepper. (Remember that the soup is salted, so apply seasoning with a light hand.) Pour fat from skillet. Mix soup and milk in skillet, scraping all of the brown goodness left in the pan from the chops. Pour soup over the chops in both casseroles and cover tightly. (Foil may be used.) Bake in 400° F. oven until potatoes are tender—about 45 minutes. Reheat the adults' casserole 20 minutes before serving.

PORK AND MANDARIN ORANGES

*Rice**
*Buttered Broccoli**
*Carrot Sticks**
*Banana Cream Pie**

PORK AND MANDARIN ORANGES

2 pounds end pork chops
2 cups water
2 chicken bouillon cubes
1 teaspoon salt
11-ounce can mandarin oranges

¼ cup dark molasses
¼ cup vinegar
2 tablespoons cornstarch
1 teaspoon soy sauce
¼ cup sliced green onions

Cut meat from bones and cube. Heat a large skillet or Dutch oven and rub with fat from the pork. Brown the pork cubes in their own fat. Drain off fat. Add water, bouillon cubes, and salt. Simmer, covered, until pork is tender—about 1 hour. Drain oranges and mix liquid with molasses, vinegar, cornstarch, and soy sauce. Add to pork, stirring until sauce is thick. Add oranges and green onions and simmer about 5 minutes. Serve over rice to the children. Cool and refrigerate the remaining pork, to be reheated over low heat just before the adults' meal.

PORK CHOPS AND RICE

*Buttered Carrots**
*Green Salad**
*Individual Baked Alaskas**

PORK CHOPS AND RICE

Shoulder pork chops
1 cup raw white rice
1 envelope onion soup mix
Green pepper rings

Prepared mustard
Chili sauce
Thin lemon slices
2¼ cups water

Trim excess fat from chops. Brown in large skillet. Spread rice in the bottom of 2 baking dishes. Each dish should be at least 2 inches deep, and large enough to hold the chops. Sprinkle the soup mix evenly over the rice. Lay browned chops on top of the mix. Put a ring of pepper on each chop and ½ teaspoon mustard and 1 tablespoon chili sauce in the center of each ring. Put a lemon slice on top of each ring. Pour grease from the frying pan. Add water, stirring well. Then pour water into the corner of each baking dish, trying not to disturb the rice too much. Cover each dish tightly. (Foil may be used.) Bake the casseroles in a 350° F. oven for 1 hour. The adults' servings may be reheated in the oven for 15–20 minutes before the adults' meal.

INDONESIAN PORK

*Rice***
*Peas and Water Chestnuts***
*Fruit Salad on Greens***
Cookies

INDONESIAN PORK

1½–2 pounds lean pork cut into
   1-inch cubes
½ cup chunky peanut butter
10-ounce can onion soup

1 clove garlic
2 tablespoons soy sauce
2 tablespoons lemon juice
2 tablespoons brown sugar

Put pork cubes in a casserole. Combine the rest of the ingredients and pour over the pork. Bake, uncovered, for 2 hours in a 350° F. oven, turning the pork several times to brown evenly. Remove garlic. (This will be easier if you put a toothpick through the garlic before you add it to the casserole.) Serve the children. Reheat the adults' portion for 20 minutes in a 350° F. oven.

SWEET AND SOUR PORK

*Rice***
*Cold Asparagus, Cucumber, and Tomato on Greens***
Bread Sticks
Butter Pecan Ice Cream

SWEET AND SOUR PORK

1½ pounds lean boneless pork,
   cut in bite-size pieces
Flour
Approximately 2 tablespoons oil
3 carrots, sliced
½ cup liquid (pineapple or apple
   juice, cider, and/or water)
¼ cup vinegar
¼ cup dark brown sugar, packed

1 tablespoon soy sauce
½ teaspoon salt
1 tablespoon cornstarch
1 tablespoon water
13-ounce can pineapple tidbits,
   drained
¼ cup sliced green onions
1 small green pepper, thinly sliced

Dip the pork in flour and brown quickly and well in hot oil, allowing each piece plenty of room to become crispy. Remove the meat as it browns, and when all the meat is brown pour off any excess oil. Return the meat to the skillet with carrots, liquid, vinegar, sugar, soy sauce, and salt. Cover and simmer 30 minutes until meat is tender. Make a paste of the cornstarch and 1 tablespoon cold water and add to the meat, stirring until liquid begins to thicken. Add pineapple, onions, and green pepper. Cover and simmer 5 minutes until vegetables are crisp-tender. Serve on rice.

The adults' portion may be kept in the skillet or refrigerated and reheated.

ORIENTAL PORK

Green Salad with Mandarin Oranges*
Fortune Cookies

ORIENTAL PORK

1½ pounds lean boneless pork, cut into small cubes or strips
¼ cup vegetable oil
1 cup sliced celery
1 cup chopped onion
2 tablespoons soy sauce
2 tablespoons sugar
½ teaspoon salt
8-ounce can mushrooms, with liquid

1 chicken bouillon cube, mixed with ½ cup boiling water
2 tablespoons cornstarch, mixed with ½ cup cold water
5-ounce can bamboo shoots, drained
5-ounce can water chestnuts, drained and sliced
Cooked rice
3-ounce can Chinese noodles

Brown the pork in the vegetable oil in a large skillet. When well browned on all sides, remove and add the celery and onion. Sauté until golden in color and return the pork to the skillet with the soy sauce, sugar, salt, mushrooms, water, and bouillon cube. Simmer 15 minutes. Add the cornstarch and water to thicken the sauce slightly. Bring to a boil and add the bamboo shoots and water chestnuts. Bring to a boil again and serve the children their pork mixture over rice and topped with the noodles. Refrigerate the adults' portion, to be reheated on top of the stove just before their meal. Be careful not to overcook, as the "crunch" is important to this dish.

HERBED PORK BALLS AND MASHED POTATO CASSEROLE

Buttered Green Cabbage*
Carrot-Raisin Relish Salad*
Cottage Pudding*

HERBED PORK BALLS AND MASHED POTATO CASSEROLE

1 pound lean ground pork
1 egg
½ cup dry bread crumbs
Milk
2 tablespoons finely chopped
   onion
1 teaspoon salt
½ teaspoon dried marjoram

½ teaspoon orégano
Flour
Oil
1 can cream of mushroom soup
4 servings mashed potatoes
Melted butter
Paprika

Combine pork, egg, bread crumbs, ¼ cup of the milk, onion, salt, marjoram, and orégano. Shape mixture into balls the size of large walnuts. Chill or freeze. Remove from the refrigerator and roll each ball in flour and then brown in a large skillet in a small amount of oil. When the pork balls are well browned, place in 2 casseroles. Add the soup and ¼ cup of the milk to the skillet. Mix and pour over the balls. Spoon the mashed potatoes around the edges of the casseroles. Brush butter on the tops of the mashed potatoes and sprinkle with paprika. Bake each casserole 30 minutes in a 350° F. oven.

MANDARIN SPARERIBS

Potato Sticks*
Mixed Vegetable Salad*
Pudding Delights*

MANDARIN SPARERIBS

4–5 pounds meaty spareribs, cut in
   serving-size pieces
1 cup soy sauce
1 cup orange marmalade

3 cloves garlic, minced
1 teaspoon dried ginger
Few grinds pepper

Marinate the spareribs overnight in a sauce made by combining all of the rest of the ingredients. Drain the ribs and arrange on the rack of a roasting pan. Bake in a 350° F. oven for 80 minutes, basting frequently with the marinade. Remove the adults' portion of the ribs and continue to bake the children's portion for another 20 minutes until ribs are glazed golden brown and the meat is tender. Cool the adults' portion and bake an additional 30 minutes before serving time.

BONELESS SMOKED BUTT WITH CRAB APPLES

*Baked Potatoes**
*Creamed Spinach**
Celery Sticks
*Cake with Mint Topping**

BONELESS SMOKED BUTT WITH CRAB APPLES

1 precooked boneless smoked pork butt, about 2 pounds
Cloves
½ cup syrup from jar of spiced crab apples
½ cup apple or currant jelly
1 teaspoon dry mustard
Spiced crab apples

Remove any knit or plastic covering from the butt. Score the fat and stud with cloves. Put on a rack in an open baking pan. Combine the syrup, jelly, and mustard and bring to a boil. Spoon some of the glaze over the meat and bake 45 minutes in a preheated 325° F. oven, basting several times with the glaze. Five minutes before the baking is complete, add the crab apples for the children's dinner. Remove the meat from the oven and slice off the children's portions. Fifteen minutes before the adults' dinner, pour the rest of the glaze over the meat and return to the oven to reheat. Add their crab apples and serve.

If the boneless butt has not been precooked, put it in a saucepan. Cover with boiling water and simmer for 45 minutes or until fork-tender. Then drain, cool, and proceed with the recipe.

ROLLED OR DAISY HAM

Creamed Potatoes and Peas*
Molded Fruit Salad on Greens*
Yellow Cake with Mocha Frosting*

ROLLED OR DAISY HAM

1 rolled or daisy ham
1 cup brown sugar
1 teaspoon dry mustard

½ cup maple syrup, cider, or
  sherry

Place ham on a rack in an open pan. Mix the sugar, mustard, and liquid together and spoon a little of this mixture over the ham. Bake in a 350° F. oven for 1 hour, basting with the brown-sugar mixture from time to time. Slice the children's portion. The rest of the ham may be returned to the oven for about 30 minutes before the adults' meal, or their portion may be sliced and then reheated for about 15 minutes. However you do it, spoon the rest of the glaze over the ham before returning it to the oven.

ORANGE GLAZED HAM BALLS

Brown Rice*
Buttered Green Beans with Thyme*
Carrot Strips
Custard and Brownies

ORANGE GLAZED HAM BALLS

3 cups ground fully cooked ham
½ cup milk
½ cup cracker crumbs
1½ cups orange juice

⅓ cup brown sugar, packed
⅓ cup orange marmalade
3 tablespoons vinegar

Mix ham, milk, and cracker crumbs. Shape into about 12 balls 2 inches in diameter. Place in 2 buttered baking pans. Bring remaining ingredients to a boil and pour over the ham balls. Bake, uncovered, in a 350° F. oven for 40 minutes, basting occasionally with the sauce. If the ham balls are not browned, run the children's portion under the broiler briefly and serve. Cool and refrigerate the adults' portion. Baste and reheat in the oven for about 20 minutes, and run under the broiler, if necessary, before the late dinner.

GLAZED HAM LOAF AND SWEET POTATOES

Zucchini*
Waldorf Salad*
Ice Cream and Cookies

GLAZED HAM LOAF AND SWEET POTATOES

3 cups or 1 pound ground ham	¾ cup milk
1 small onion, chopped	½ cup soft bread crumbs
1 egg, slightly beaten	Canned or cooked sweet potatoes

Mix all of the ingredients except potatoes and shape into 2 loaves. Place in shallow baking dishes, allowing room for the sweet potatoes. The loaves may be made any time during the day and refrigerated. Bake the loaves together in a 350° F. oven for 15 minutes. In the meantime, make a glaze by mixing the following ingredients:

⅓ cup brown sugar	1 teaspoon dry mustard
¼ cup cider vinegar	

Bring glaze to a boil. Remove the loaves from the oven. If you want to be fancy, decorate them with maraschino cherries. Dribble half of the glaze over the loaves and return to the oven for another 15 minutes. Remove again and place sweet potatoes around each loaf and dribble the rest of the glaze over the loaves. Return the children's loaf to the oven for the final 15 minutes of baking.

The adults' loaf and potatoes may be refrigerated, to be baked 20 minutes before serving.

COLD HAM LOAF

Macaroni and Cheese*
Cole Slaw with Green Pepper*
Melon with Orange Ice

The ham loaf on the preceding page is especially good cold. It is a good idea to double all of the ingredients except the sweet potatoes and make and bake 1 large loaf in addition to the 2 small ones. The large loaf may be refrigerated and served cold a day or two later.

[71]

SAUSAGE AND APPLES WITH CORNBREAD TOPPING

Baked Acorn Squash*
Cole Slaw with Water Cress*
Pudding Delights*

SAUSAGE AND APPLES WITH CORNBREAD TOPPING

1-pound package bulk pork
 sausage, cut into ½ inch slices

4 medium-size apples, pared and
 thinly sliced
12-ounce box corn muffin mix

Fry sausage slices in a medium-size skillet, pouring off fat as it accumulates. When well browned, drain on paper towels. Place in bottom of 2 1- or 1½-quart casseroles. Top with apple slices. Stir up the corn muffin mix according to package directions and spread on top of the apples. Bake both casseroles in 375° F. oven for 25–30 minutes. Serve the children. Reheat the adults' casserole 15–20 minutes in a 350° F. oven.

LAZY LIZ'S SAUSAGE 'N' RICE

Peas*
Pickled Beets on Greens*
Corn Sticks
Chocolate Ice Cream Sundae (Crème de Cacao
 for the adults)*

This is the perfect family dish. It takes about 10 minutes to prepare, it's very inexpensive, and it is good. Remember that it's the sausage that flavors the dish, so the better the sausage, the better the dish.

LAZY LIZ'S SAUSAGE 'N' RICE

1 pound sausage meat
1 medium-size onion, chopped
¼ cup chopped green pepper
1 cup raw rice

2 cups liquid—beef or chicken
 consommé, or bouillon
1 teaspoon salt

[72]

Crumble sausage in a skillet and brown well. Pour off fat. Add other ingredients and pour into 2 well-greased casseroles with tight-fitting covers, or cover tightly with foil. Bake the casseroles for 1 hour in a 400° F. oven, checking at least once and adding water if necessary. You may cook this in the skillet on top of the stove, if you prefer. Re-heat the adults' portion before serving.

SAUSAGE SUPPER WITH RICE AND GREEN BEANS

*Apple Cider Salad**
Doughnuts

SAUSAGE SUPPER WITH RICE AND GREEN BEANS

8 slices canned pineapple, drained
1 pound sausage meat
Sherry (optional)
1 cup raw rice

10-ounce package frozen cross-cut
 or whole green beans
Salt
Pepper

Lay the pineapple slices in a baking dish or dishes. Shape the sausage meat into 8 patties and put 1 patty on top of each pineapple slice. If you like, you may spoon 1 teaspoon of sherry over each of the 4 adult sausage patties. Bake 30 minutes in a 350° F. oven.

In the meantime, cook the rice and beans according to package directions. Season to taste with salt and pepper.

When the sausage has baked for ½ hour, remove it from the oven and serve the children their sausage and pineapple, rice, and beans. Spoon the rest of the rice onto an ovenproof platter or baking pan. Lay the adults' sausage and pineapple slices on top of the rice and surround them with the beans. Spoon another teaspoon of sherry on each sausage patty. Cool and cover the platter with foil and refrigerate to be re-heated, covered, for 15 minutes in a 350° F. oven.

HODGE PODGE

Carrot and Celery Sticks
*Brown Bread or Corn Muffins**
*Dessert Fruit Salad**

This is one of those dishes made of ingredients you can keep on your kitchen shelf to be assembled on days when the meat supply has dwindled and you can't get to the store. Keep a can of brown bread to go along with it.

HODGE PODGE

2 cans Vienna sausages, drained
1 tablespoon oil
1 medium onion, chopped
1-pound can limas, or 10-ounce package frozen limas, cooked
1-pound can pork and beans
8-ounce can red kidney beans

12-ounce can vacuum-packed whole kernel corn
½ cup chili sauce
¼ cup molasses
1 teaspoon dry mustard
½ teaspoon Worcestershire
Few drops hot pepper sauce

In large skillet, brown Vienna sausages in oil. Add the onions and sauté briefly, adding more oil if necessary. Remove half of the sausages. Add all of the other ingredients, mixing well. Turn into a 2-quart casserole. Lay the remaining sausages across the top. Cover and bake in a 350° F. oven for 1 hour. Serve to the children and cool and refrigerate the casserole to be reheated for 20 minutes in a 350° F. oven.

SAUERKRAUT AND SAUSAGE

*Surprise Salad**
Bread Sticks
Chocolate Cake

SAUERKRAUT AND SAUSAGE

1-pound can sauerkraut (2 cans for family of hearty eaters)
3 medium-size potatoes, sliced
1 carrot, sliced
1 small onion, sliced

1 bay leaf
8 whole black peppers
Italian link sausages
2 cups chicken broth or dry white wine

Drain the sauerkraut, squeezing out as much moisture as possible. Put ¼ of the kraut in each of 2 casseroles. Top kraut with the potatoes, carrots, and onions. Put the rest of the kraut on top of the vegetables. Tuck ½ bay leaf and 4 peppercorns in each casserole. Top with the sausages, which have been lightly browned and then drained. Pour ¾–1 cup of chicken broth (fresh, canned, or made with a bouillon cube) over the children's casserole and 1 cup of either broth or white wine or a combination of the two over the adults' casserole. Bake both casseroles at least 1 hour in a 350° F. oven. The baking time may be increased without affecting the casseroles, so, if the adults are to eat soon after the children, just turn the oven down and leave the casserole in it. You may also cool the adults' casserole and reheat it for about 20 minutes before the adults' meal.

You may substitute frankfurters for sausages. If you use frankfurters, skip the browning process and add them to the casserole the last ½ hour of baking.

This dish can be put together in the afternoon and refrigerated and then baked before eating.

HAM OR LUNCHEON MEAT WITH SWEET POTATOES AND PINEAPPLE

Cabbage in Cheese Sauce *
Pumpernickel Slices
Sherbet and Cookies

This is another "emergency" meal from cans which stand ready for action on your kitchen shelf.

HAM OR LUNCHEON MEAT WITH SWEET POTATOES AND PINEAPPLE

Canned ham or luncheon meat (or leftover ham)
Canned sweet potatoes
Pineapple rings
About ½ cup brown sugar
About ¼ cup butter

Cut ham or luncheon meat in serving-size pieces. Place in 2 lightly buttered shallow baking dishes. Surround with canned sweet potatoes and pineapple rings. Sprinkle brown sugar on top of each casserole and dot generously with butter. Refrigerate adults' casserole. Bake each casserole 20 minutes in a 350° F. oven.

CANADIAN BACON, APRICOTS, AND STUFFING BALLS

*Corn Deluxe**
Tiny French Peas in Butter Sauce
Sponge Cake

CANADIAN BACON, APRICOTS, AND STUFFING BALLS

½ pound Canadian bacon—
about 16 slices

1-pound can apricots,
whole or halves

GLAZE:

⅓ cup apricot syrup
⅓ cup brown sugar
1 tablespoon vinegar

1 teaspoon dry mustard
4 cloves

STUFFING BALLS:

¼ cup butter or margarine
¾ cup liquid—apricot syrup, with
water if necessary

3 cups seasoned stuffing mix
1 egg white

Overlap the bacon slices in the bottoms of 2 buttered shallow casseroles. Drain the apricots, saving the syrup.

To make the glaze, combine ⅓ cup apricot syrup, brown sugar, vinegar, mustard, and cloves. Simmer 2 or 3 minutes. Spoon about ⅓ of the glaze over the bacon slices.

To make the stuffing balls, melt the butter in the ¾ cup syrup. Add the stuffing mix. Beat the egg white until stiff and add to the stuffing. Using a ¼-cup measure, scoop out the stuffing and with your hands form into 8 tight balls. Place the balls and the apricots in an attractive pattern on top of the bacon slices. Pour the rest of the glaze over them.

Bake the children's casserole in a 350° F. oven for 15 minutes until the glaze begins to bubble. Refrigerate the adults' casserole, to be baked 20 minutes in a 350° F. oven just before the later dinner.

Variety and Other Meats

This is a catch-all chapter for meats that don't fall elsewhere. First come the menus and recipes for cold cuts, luncheon meat, and frankfurters. These meats may be either beef, veal, or pork or a combination. These are followed by menus and recipes for "organ" meats—liver, tongue, kidney, heart, and tripe. These may be beef, veal, pork, or lamb.

Although organ meats are considered to be great delicacies in Europe, they are frequently spurned in this country and thus are surprisingly inexpensive. Popularity determines price of these meats—as well as of many other things. Calves' liver is by far the most popular and is, therefore, the most expensive. Beef, pork, and lamb liver are all inexpensive, as are the other variety meats with the exception of tongue.

In terms of nutritive value, variety meats are great bargains. One small serving of cooked liver contains enough vitamin A to satisfy the body's needs for a week. In addition, it is an excellent source of iron and riboflavin. If not overcooked, it is also a good source of vitamin C.

CORN AND LUNCHEON MEAT BAKE

*Lettuce and Tomato Salad**
*Bran Muffins**
*Peaches with Vanilla Ice Cream and Raspberry Sauce**

CORN AND LUNCHEON MEAT BAKE

1 large onion, sliced
½ green pepper, sliced
2 tablespoons oil
12-ounce can luncheon meat,
    cubed, or 2 cups bite-size
    cubes cooked ham

1-pound can cream-style corn
½ cup shredded Cheddar cheese
2 tablespoons butter, melted
½ cup dry bread crumbs

Sauté the onion and pepper in the oil in a skillet. Stir in the meat. Divide half of the corn between 2 well-greased 4-cup casseroles (or use 4 individual casseroles). Put the onion-ham mixture on top of the corn and add the cheese. Put the rest of the corn on top of the cheese. Mix the butter with the crumbs and sprinkle on top of the casserole. Bake 30–40 minutes in a 350° F. oven. Refrigerate the adults' casserole, to be baked just before the later meal.

LUNCHEON MEAT AND APPLES

*Broccoli**
*Baked Acorn Squash**
Cheese Muffins
*Coco Mocho**

LUNCHEON MEAT AND APPLES

12-ounce can luncheon meat, or
    slices of cooked ham
1-pound 4-ounce can unsweetened
    sliced pie apples

¼ cup sugar
½ teaspoon cinnamon

Cut the luncheon meat into 8 slices and arrange in 2 flat baking pans. Pour the apples over the meat and sprinkle with sugar and cinnamon. Refrigerate the adults' portion. Bake each dish for 20 minutes in a 350° F. oven until hot and bubbly.

PENNIES FROM HEAVEN

*Scalloped Potatoes**
*Buttered Peas and Celery**
*Lettuce Wedges with Beet Dressing**
Apricot Pie

PENNIES FROM HEAVEN

These frankfurter circles are so named, I assume, because of their shape and the economy they represent. To prepare, simply slice frankfurters into thin circles and sauté. Then serve in one of the following ways:

1. Add bottled barbecue sauce and heat.
2. Serve on top of potato salad, scalloped potatoes, macaroni and cheese, Spanish rice, scrambled eggs, creamed cabbage, or broccoli.

HOT DOG TOWERS AND PEACHES

*Lettuce and Red Onion Salad**
Toasted Buns
*Chocolate Nut Sundaes**

You won't want to serve this when your rich aunt comes to dinner, but it's good, quick, and inexpensive fare for "just family."

HOT DOG TOWERS AND PEACHES

Frankfurters	Melted butter
Sauerkraut	Peach halves, well drained
Mashed potatoes (instant or regular)	

Split the frankfurters lengthwise almost in half so they will lie flat and place in 2 baking pans. Drain the sauerkraut well and spoon some on top of each frankfurter. Top with mashed potatoes and dribble butter over the top. Refrigerate the adults' portion. Place peaches around the children's "towers" and bake in a 400° F. oven for 10 minutes, until the potatoes are lightly browned. Bake the adults' "towers" and peaches the same way, allowing a little extra time if they have been refrigerated.

STUFFED FRANKFURTERS

*Baked Beans**
*Spinach Salad**
*Fruit Gelatin and Cup Cakes**

STUFFED FRANKFURTERS

Frankfurters   Sweet pickles
American cheese   Bacon

Split the frankfurters lengthwise *almost* in half. Cut the cheese and pickles into thin slices that will fit into the slit in the frankfurter. Wrap each in ½ slice bacon, securing the bacon with toothpicks. Ten minutes before serving, place the frankfurter, cut side up, on a rack (you may use your broiling pan) in a pan. Bake in a 425° F. oven until bacon is crisp.

POT-ROASTED LIVER AND VEGETABLES

*Escarole with Tomato Slices and Green Pepper Rings**
*Cherries Jubilee**

POT-ROASTED LIVER AND VEGETABLES

2-pound piece beef, pork, or lamb liver
2 cups boiling water
Flour
¼ cup bacon fat
1 tablespoon dried parsley
1 bay leaf
Pinch thyme

Few grinds pepper
2 teaspoons salt
1 onion, sliced
4 carrots, sliced
4 small parsnips or turnips, sliced
4 medium-size potatoes, cut in eighths

This recipe serves 8. See next menu and recipe.

Wash liver. Pour boiling water over it, saving the water to be used later. Remove outer membrane from the liver. Dry meat and dredge in flour. Heat fat in a Dutch oven and brown liver on all sides. Add seasonings, onion, and the water used for blanching. Cover and simmer 1 hour. Add the carrots, parsnips, and potatoes and continue to simmer, covered, until vegetables are tender. Cut the liver in 2 pieces. Refrigerate one to be served a day or two later. (See next recipe and menu.) Slice the other and serve the children. Return the adults' slices to the Dutch oven, to be reheated about 15 minutes before the later meal.

LIVER WITH TOMATO SAUCE AND RICE

Wax Beans Vinaigrette on Greens*
Raspberry Sherbet and Vanilla Ice Cream with Cookies*

LIVER WITH TOMATO SAUCE AND RICE

Liver (see preceding recipe)
2 cups canned tomato sauce with
mushrooms

1 cup brown rice cooked according
to package directions

Slice leftover liver and heat in tomato sauce. Serve over rice.

2-MINUTE LIVER SAUTÉ

Buttered Carrots with Thyme*
Creamed Whole Onions*
Sliced Tomatoes on Water Cress
Whole Wheat Toast
Fruit Cup with Grenadine and Cookies*

You really can prepare this liver in just 2 minutes, so there is no
need to cook and hold. Prepare for the children, then repeat for the
later meal. The recipe below serves 2.

2-MINUTE LIVER SAUTÉ

½ pound thinly sliced liver
1 tablespoon butter or margarine
Salt
Pepper

1 tablespoon lemon juice
1 tablespoon capers (optional)
Chopped parsley

If you have a regular meat man, ask him to cut the liver for you. It
must be *very* thin. If you buy packaged liver, you can easily slice it yourself if you will first freeze it partially. Remove the skin and cut in serving-size pieces. Then slice with a sharp knife.

Melt the butter in a large skillet. Sauté the liver for 1 minute on
each side. Season with salt and pepper. Put the liver on plates and add
lemon juice and capers to the pan. Heat and pour over the liver.
Sprinkle with parsley. Repeat for later dinner.

LIVER, BACON, AND ONIONS

*Broiled Tomatoes**
*Brussels Sprouts Vinaigrette**
Dinner Rolls
Butternut Ice Cream with Maple Sauce

LIVER, BACON, AND ONIONS

4 slices bacon
1 pound thinly sliced beef or
   calves' liver
Salt
Pepper

Flour
2 large onions, sliced
2 tablespoons butter or margarine
⅓ cup milk

Fry the bacon slices and drain on a paper towel. Remove all the membranes from the liver and cut into serving-size slices. Sprinkle with salt and pepper and dip into flour. Brown quickly on both sides in the bacon fat. Put the adults' slices on an ovenproof platter or shallow casserole. If the remaining slices are not cooked to desired doneness, cover and continue to cook for a few minutes.

In the meantime, sauté the onions in the butter. When they begin to brown, cover and continue to cook until tender. Stir in 2 teaspoons of flour, allow to bubble, and add the milk. Continue to stir until the sauce thickens. Spoon the onions over the liver and top with bacon strips. This may be done directly on the children's plates.

The adult servings may be refrigerated until 20 minutes before serving time, when they should be placed in a preheated 350° F. oven until heated through, about 15 minutes.

LIVER AND SAUSAGE LOAF

*Scalloped Potatoes**
*Broccoli Spears**
Carrot and Cucumber Sticks
*Cherry Crisp**

LIVER AND SAUSAGE LOAF

1 pound beef liver
1 pound sausage meat
1 egg, beaten
¼ cup flour

1 teaspoon minced parsley
1½ teaspoons salt
Few grinds pepper
1 clove garlic, minced

This recipe serves 8 (see menu below).

Put liver through food chopper using fine blade. Mix with the rest of the ingredients. Pack into a large loaf pan. Place pan in a shallow pan of water and bake in a 300° F. oven for 2 hours. Serve the children. To reheat slices for the adult meal, cover and place in a 300° F. oven for 20 minutes. Refrigerate the rest of the loaf for a meal later in the week.

Potatoes will cook in 2 hours at 300° F.—the same as the loaf.

Vegetable Soup

COLD LIVER AND SAUSAGE LOAF

*Macaroni Salad**
Sliced Tomatoes
Hard Rolls
Apples and Candy Bars

See preceding recipe for Liver and Sausage Loaf.

Turkey Noodle Soup

TOMATO CUPS WITH EASY LIVER PÂTÉ

Stuffed Eggs
*Spinach Salad**
Sliced Pineapple and Bananas (Crème de Menthe for Adults)

EASY LIVER PÂTÉ

¼ pound fresh mushrooms, minced
2 tablespoons butter
1 pound liverwurst, at room temperature
6 ounces cream cheese, at room temperature

1 tablespoon Worcestershire
¼ teaspoon black pepper
3 tablespoons minced green onion tops or chives
Dash cayenne
2 tablespoons mayonnaise

Brown mushrooms in butter. Blend together thoroughly with the rest of the ingredients. Refrigerate until serving time. If desired, turn into an oiled mold and unmold to serve. Or refrigerate in a covered container for up to 2 weeks. Use in any of the following ways:

1. Slices or mounds for a delicious cold dinner meat.

[83]

2. As a spread or dip (warmed to room temperature). May be made softer by adding more mayonnaise.

3. Spread generously on toast and topped with creamed eggs, vegetables, meat, or seafood.

4. Spread on toast and topped with crisp bacon slices.

5. As a stuffing for tomatoes, cucumber boats, or scooped-out rolls as a cold main course.

Tomato Soup

COLD CUTS AND CHEESE

Mixed Vegetable Salad*
Assorted Breads*
Hot Apple Pie*

COLD CUTS AND CHEESE

Preparation for this main dish involves nothing but a trip to the store.

FRIED TRIPE "OYSTERS"

Succotash*
Asparagus and Pimiento on Greens
Individual Strawberry Baked Alaskas*

FRIED TRIPE "OYSTERS"

1 pound tripe
Packaged seasoned fine bread
   crumbs

1 egg beaten with 1 tablespoon
   water
Deep fat for frying
Lemon wedges or catsup

Use tripe that is fresh, boiled until tender, or canned; do not use pickled tripe.

Cut tripe into pieces about 1–1½ inch square. Dip first in crumbs, then in egg, and again in crumbs. You may need a second egg. Refrigerate until just before serving time—at least ½ hour. Fry "oysters" a few at a time in hot fat until golden brown. Drain on paper toweling and keep in a warm place until all the "oysters" for one dinner hour are done. Serve with lemon wedges or catsup. Fry "oysters" for adults' dinner just before serving.

SPICED SMOKED BEEF TONGUE WITH CURRY SAUCE

Rice*
Mixed Vegetable Salad*
Toast Fingers*
Lemon Sherbet and Sugar Cookies

A whole smoked beef tongue will make slices for at least 8 servings, and the root end may be used in other ways. It seems to be an extremely rich meat, so the portions may be smaller than for other meats.

The part toward the center and tip of the tongue is the most attractive for slicing. The part toward the base may best be used in split pea or bean soup (use the cooking iiquid, too) with scalloped potatoes, or ground for sandwich filling.

Excellent canned small cooked tongues are also available.

The recipe below calls for cooking the tongue with pickling slices. You may, if you prefer, omit the spices.

SPICED SMOKED BEEF TONGUE

1 smoked beef tongue, about 3 pounds
Water
2 tablespoons mixed pickling spices

1 onion
1 stalk celery with leaves
1 tablespoon dried parsley

This recipe serves 8 (see next recipe menu).

Place tongue in a large kettle. Cover with cold water and add the rest of the ingredients. Cover. Simmer until tongue is tender, about 2 hours. Leave in the water until cool enough to handle. Skin the tongue. This is a surprisingly simple job, as the skin peels off like a loose-fitting glove. Also remove any gristle and small bones from the root end. Reheat the amount that will be eaten at each dinner in a little of the cooking liquid. Refrigerate the rest.

CURRY SAUCE FOR SPICED TONGUE

2 tablespoons margarine or butter
2 tablespoons chopped onion
1½ tablespoons flour
1 cup tongue broth (see preceding recipe)

1 teaspoon curry powder
¼ teaspoon salt
¼ teaspoon sugar
Few grinds pepper

Melt butter and sauté onion. Stir in the flour and add the broth, stirring constantly until the sauce thickens. Add the seasonings and serve hot over the tongue.

COLD SLICED TONGUE

*Macaroni Salad**
Tomato and Cucumber Slices, Raw Carrots
Hot Rolls
*Ice Cream with Chocolate–Peanut Butter Sauce**

See recipe for Spiced Smoked Beef Tongue*.

INDIVIDUAL STEAK AND KIDNEY PIES

*Lettuce Wedges with Tiny Canned Beets in
    Vinaigrette Sauce**
Baked Apples

INDIVIDUAL STEAK AND KIDNEY PIES

1 beef kidney
¾ pound round steak, cut ½ inch thick
Flour
2 tablespoons margarine
1 onion, chopped
1 teaspoon salt
Few grinds pepper
1½ cups water
1 bay leaf
Few sprigs parsley, or 1 tablespoon dried minced parsley
Few celery leaves
¼ pound mushrooms, sliced
2 teaspoons Worcestershire
Dash hot pepper sauce
Pastry—enough for a double-crust pie
1 egg beaten with 1 teaspoon water

Remove outer membrane of kidney. Split and remove fat and tubes. Soak in cold water for 30 minutes. Drain and cut kidney and steak in 1-inch pieces. Dredge in flour and brown in margarine with onion. Add the rest of the ingredients except the pastry and egg, and simmer until tender, about 1 hour. Remove bay leaf and celery leaves. Thicken liquid with 2 tablespoons flour mixed with a little cold water. Bring to a boil, stirring constantly until sauce thickens. Taste for seasoning. Pour into 4 12-ounce custard cups or individual round casseroles. Roll out pastry and cut to fit the top of each casserole. Arrange on top and flute edges. Brush with egg. Bake two of the pies in a 450° F. oven for about 20 minutes until crust is lightly browned. Refrigerate the other two, to be baked in the same way just before the later dinner.

BRAISED BEEF HEART WITH VEGETABLES

Green Salad with Garlic Croutons*
Merry Berry*

BRAISED BEEF HEART WITH VEGETABLES

1 beef heart	1 tablespoon chopped parsley
Water	1 stalk celery, chopped
2 teaspoons salt	Onions
Few grinds pepper	Carrots
1 bay leaf	4 medium-size potatoes

Wash heart and cover with cold water. Add salt, pepper, bay leaf, parsley, celery, and 1 chopped onion and 1 chopped carrot. Cover and simmer until meat is tender, about 1½–2 hours. Remove the heart. Continue to simmer the liquid, uncovered, for another ½ hour or until the liquid is reduced to about 1 cup. Strain.

Slice the heart, 4 carrots, 4 onions, and the potatoes. Place half of the vegetables in the bottom of a baking dish or casserole. Top with all of the sliced heart and the remainder of the vegetables. Pour the liquid over the vegetables. Cover with lid or foil and bake 1 hour in a 375° F. oven until the vegetables are tender. Serve the children. Reheat in the oven before the later meal. There may be leftover meat slices. Use cold for sandwiches, or cut in strips and add to soups for lunch.

Cream of Asparagus Soup

MUSHROOMS AND KIDNEYS ON TOAST

Extra Slices Cracked Wheat Toast
Fruit Salad with French Dressing*

MUSHROOMS AND KIDNEYS ON TOAST

1 pound veal or lamb kidneys	1 teaspoon salt
1 small onion	Few grinds pepper
¼ cup butter	1 teaspoon bottled gravy coloring
2 tablespoons flour	(optional)
6-ounce can chopped broiled	4 slices buttered cracked wheat
mushrooms	toast
Water	2 tablespoons sherry (optional)

Remove any fat from the kidneys. Cut in half and remove core and tubes. Cut into ½-inch cubes. Sauté onions in butter in a skillet for about 3 minutes and add the kidneys. Continue cooking until lightly browned. Stir in the flour. Drain the mushrooms into a measuring cup and add enough water to make 1¼ cups. Stir liquid, salt, pepper, gravy-making liquid, and the mushrooms into the kidney mixture. Bring to a boil, stirring constantly. Cover and cook over very low heat until kidneys are tender, about 10 minutes. Serve on slices of toast to the children. Add the sherry and reheat over low heat in a double boiler just before the adults' dinner.

BACONY CHICKEN LIVERS

Brown Rice*
Buttered Carrots*
Green Salad*
Strawberry and Mandarin Orange Cup with Cookies*

BACONY CHICKEN LIVERS

2 slices bacon, cut in squares	1 cup water
1 pound chicken livers	1 chicken bouillon cube, or 1
Flour	envelope instant chicken broth
Butter or margarine	Salt
¼ cup chopped onion	Pepper

Fry the bacon and remove with a slotted spoon to a piece of paper towel. Dip the livers in flour and fry quickly in the bacon fat. If necessary, add butter. When the livers are brown and crispy, remove. Add the onion and sauté briefly. Add more butter so that there will be 1 tablespoon butter in the skillet. Stir in 1 tablespoon flour and allow to bubble briefly. Stir in the water, mixed with the bouillon cube, and stir until thickened. Add the children's portion of the livers and cook in the sauce until hot and tender. This will take only a few minutes. Taste for seasoning. Serve with some of the sauce on the rice. Top with a few pieces of bacon.

Add the rest of the chicken livers to the remaining sauce. Cool and refrigerate. When the adults are ready to eat, simply reheat their portion.

FESTIVE CHICKEN LIVERS AND MUSHROOMS

*Boiled Potatoes**
*Mixed Vegetable Salad on Greens**
Cherry Pie

FESTIVE CHICKEN LIVERS AND MUSHROOMS

4 slices bacon, quartered
1 pound chicken livers (if frozen, thaw)
1 cup sliced fresh or frozen mushrooms
1 medium-size onion, thinly sliced
1 cup sour cream
1 tablespoon catsup
1 teaspoon salt
Dried parsley

In top of double boiler, fry bacon and drain on paper towel. Cut chicken livers in half and cook, covered, in bacon fat until no longer red, about 10 minutes. Add mushrooms and onion and continue to cook until mushrooms are done. Stir in sour cream and catsup. Heat over very low heat or boiling water until sour cream is hot. Serve the children's liver on boiled potatoes. Garnish with half of the bacon quarters and parsley. Refrigerate the rest, to be reheated over boiling water just before the adults' meal.

Poultry

Chicken used to be a symbol of prosperity. Remember when "a chicken in every pot" was a great slogan pointing to a better day? That day has arrived and chicken is so inexpensive in relation to other meats that every budget-conscious housewife serves it often. Turkey is in the same category. It just doesn't make sense to serve turkey on Christmas and Thanksgiving only.

Economy is only one of the several attractive features of both chicken and turkey. Another is size. You can now buy tiny broilers and large capons, small 5-pound turkeys and the traditional holiday-size birds.

Versatility is another asset. There are so many different ways to prepare turkey and chicken. The two may be used interchangeably in many of the recipes that follow. You can also buy poultry by the part, either fresh or frozen, and you can buy boneless rolls.

But perhaps poultry's most appealing feature from our point of view is the ease with which it can be reheated.

In addition to many chicken and turkey recipes in this chapter, you will also find a recipe for Rock Cornish Game Hens and one for duck. Although I have included no recipes for geese, keep your eye on these birds. Modern agricultural science has developed small lean geese that will be increasingly useful for everyday meal planning. They are already available in some areas.

TURKEY ROLL

*Sweet Potatoes**
*Braised Celery**
*Fruit Salad Mold**
*Coconut Cream Pie**

TURKEY ROLL

Because they are boneless and come in a variety of sizes, turkey rolls are especially convenient for the small family. Look at all of the different kinds available in your supermarket freezer. You can buy rolls that are all white meat and some that have gravy with them. Select the one that seems best for your family. Cook according to package directions. Slice off the children's portion and reheat the rest of the roll, covered, for about 30 minutes before the adults' dinner.

DUCK IN ORANGE SAUCE

*Parsley Potatoes**
*Brussels Sprouts**
*Lettuce and Tomato Salad**
*Cream Puffs**

DUCK IN ORANGE SAUCE

4–5-pound duck, quartered
10-ounce can mandarin oranges
Orange juice
½ teaspoon salt
1 tablespoon cornstarch mixed with 2 tablespoons cold water
Dash hot red pepper sauce
Dash nutmeg

Pull all excess pieces of fat out of the duck and rub a little on the bottom of a Dutch oven. Brown the duck, pricking with a fork, in the Dutch oven. When well browned, drain off any excess fat. Drain the oranges, adding enough orange juice to the canned liquid to make 1½ cups. Add the liquid and the salt to the duck in the Dutch oven. Cover tightly and simmer until the meat is tender, about 45 minutes. Remove the duck and skim the fat off the sauce. Add the oranges, cornstarch, pepper sauce, and nutmeg, and simmer until the sauce thickens. Taste for seasoning. Serve the children's duck with some of the sauce. Put the adults' portion in the Dutch oven with the remaining sauce. Cool and refrigerate to be reheated by simmering, covered, for about 15 minutes.

ROASTED GAME HENS WITH APRICOT-RICE STUFFING

Brussels Sprouts*
Sliced Radishes and Chicory*
Parker House Rolls
Baked Custard or Vanilla Pudding

The recipe below calls for four game hens and will serve four adults generously. It is entirely possible that your children will be happy to share a hen. If so, prepare only three and reduce the other ingredients accordingly. If you find reducing a recipe as difficult as I do, be assured that the proportions here don't matter much.

ROASTED GAME HENS WITH APRICOT-RICE STUFFING

4 Rock Cornish Game Hens,
   1½–2 pounds each
1 teaspoon salt
1½ cups water
¾ cup brown rice
1 cup well-drained apricot halves
1 cup celery

2 tablespoons chopped onion
1 teaspoon salt
½ teaspoon sage
½ teaspoon dry mustard
½ cup butter
½ cup apricot jam
2 tablespoons vinegar

Thaw, if frozen, wash, and dry the game hens. Chop the giblets and cook in salted water with the rice, according to package directions. You may substitute liquid from the apricots for some of the water. When the rice is tender, cut each apricot half into about 4 pieces and add to the rice and giblets along with the celery, onion, salt, sage, and mustard. Use this mixture to stuff the hens. Refrigerate the hens for the adult meal and place those for the children's dinner, breast side up, in an open roasting pan in a 350° F. oven.

In the meantime, make a glaze by heating together the butter, jam, and vinegar. After the hens have been in the oven for 15 minutes, spoon some of this glaze over them. Roast until tender, about 1 hour, basting several times with the jam mixture. Use your favorite method for checking doneness—pinching the thigh, moving the leg, or, if you must, piercing the breast. Serve the children. Roast the adults' hens as you did the children's, basting with the rest of the glaze. Or you may roast the adults' hens with the children's and reheat for about 20 minutes before serving.

PARTY CHICKEN

*Green Salad**
Hard Rolls or Bread Sticks
*Ice Cream Pie**

This chicken-and-rice dish, which is flavored with a variety of herbs, orange juice, and sherry, is different—and it's perfect party food because you can put it in the oven and forget it. It's especially elegant if you bone the chicken.

PARTY CHICKEN

Salt
Pepper
Chicken breasts and/or legs and
  thighs
Flour
Oil
1 cup uncooked rice
2 medium-size onions, sliced
1 clove garlic, minced

4-ounce can mushroom pieces,
  undrained
1 teaspoon salt
½ teaspoon orégano
½ teaspoon savory
½ teaspoon basil
Dash nutmeg
½ cup sherry
2 cups orange juice

Salt and pepper the chicken and dip in flour. Put ¼ cup oil in a large skillet and brown the chicken well. As it browns, remove and drain. When all of the chicken is browned, add the rice to the skillet and brown it. Divide the rice between 2 greased casseroles. Lay the chicken pieces on top of the rice. Then add another 2 tablespoons oil to the skillet and sauté the onions and garlic until the onions are limp. Add the rest of the ingredients and simmer about 5 minutes to blend the flavors. Lift out the onions and mushrooms with a slotted spoon and scatter evenly over the chicken. Pour the liquid into the casseroles and cover tightly with casserole lids or with foil. Bake in 350° F. oven for 1 hour. Feed the children their casserole. Reheat the adults' casserole for 20 minutes just before serving.

CHICKEN FRICASSEE PLUS

Lettuce Wedges with Thousand Island or
* Blue Cheese Dressing**
Cranberry Sauce
Toasted Corn Muffins
Apple Crisp*

CHICKEN FRICASSEE PLUS

2½–3-pound frying chicken,
  cut in quarters or pieces
Salt, pepper, and paprika
Margarine
2 carrots, halved
1 small onion, sliced
1½ teaspoons dried tarragon
½ teaspoon poultry seasoning
Neck and giblets
2 cups water, or a combination of
  water and liquid drained from
  canned mushrooms and onions
¼ pound mushrooms (or
  3-ounce can mushrooms,
  drained)
Mashed potatoes, freshly prepared
  or instant, enough for 1 meal
8-ounce can small white onions,
  drained
3 tablespoons flour
2 cups strained broth
½ cup cream or evaporated milk

Dry chicken pieces and rub with salt, pepper, and paprika. Brown in a large skillet in ¼ cup margarine. When golden, add carrots, sliced onion, tarragon, poultry seasoning, neck and giblets, and liquid. Simmer, covered, about 45 minutes, or until chicken is tender. In the meantime, sauté the fresh mushrooms in another ¼ cup margarine and cook and mash the potatoes. Arrange chicken pieces and carrots in 2 casseroles. Lift mushrooms from margarine with a slotted spoon and scatter over the chicken. Add onions to the casseroles.

Make a sauce in the pan in which the mushrooms were cooked by adding the flour to the margarine and cooking a minute or so. Add the strained chicken broth to the flour-butter mixture, stirring with a wire whisk. Then add the cream and adjust the seasonings. Pour over the chicken and vegetables. Place mounds of mashed potatoes at one side or either end of each of the casseroles and sprinkle liberally with paprika. Put squares of foil over the potatoes—to prevent a crust from forming —and bake each casserole about ½ hour in a 350° F. oven.

If your children are not fond of mushrooms or onions, you may substitute cooked peas in their casseroles; you might even add a few to yours for color. You'll be glad to know that this dish is practically indestructible. The last time I made it, I baked the adults' casserole once, then heated it up again when we got ready to eat—it was delicious.

ALL-IN-ONE CHICKEN CASSEROLE

*Green Salad**
*Toast Fingers**
*Cottage Pudding**

ALL-IN-ONE CHICKEN CASSEROLE

2–4 chicken breasts, halved
1 cup water
1 stalk celery
1 large onion, halved
1 teaspoon salt
1 cup raw rice
1 package frozen asparagus spears, or fresh or canned asparagus or broccoli

¼ cup butter
3 tablespoons flour
¼ cup cream
Dash nutmeg
Parmesan cheese
2 tablespoons sherry (optional)
Pimiento strips (optional)

Put chicken breasts, water, celery, ½ onion, and salt in a saucepan. Cover and simmer until the chicken is tender, about 40 minutes. Strain broth into a large measuring cup. Discard onion and celery and cool chicken until it can be handled. Remove the skin and bones, leaving the meat in large pieces.

In the meantime, cook the rice and the asparagus according to package directions, being very careful not to overcook the asparagus. Spoon the rice into 4 individual baking dishes. Six-inch pie plates are a good size. Arrange the chicken and asparagus on top of the rice.

To make the sauce, add the cooking liquid from the asparagus and water to the chicken broth to make 1⅓ cups. Chop the other ½ onion and sauté in the butter until limp. Stir in the flour, allow to bubble briefly, and remove from the heat while you add the liquid. Return to the heat and stir until the sauce is thick. Add the cream, nutmeg, and 3 tablespoons grated Parmesan cheese. Spoon the sauce over the children's chicken and asparagus. Add about 2 tablespoons sherry to the remaining sauce before you put it on the adults' casseroles. Sprinkle 1 teaspoon cheese on each casserole and top with pimiento strips. Bake in a 350° F. oven for 20 minutes, or until the sauce is bubbly, or cover lightly and refrigerate until 25 minutes before serving time. Bake uncovered.

CHICKEN PARMESAN

*Macaroni Salad on Greens**
Sliced Tomatoes
*Chocolate Pie**

CHICKEN PARMESAN

1 clove garlic
⅓ cup butter or margarine,
    melted
¾ cup soft fresh bread crumbs
¼ cup grated Parmesan cheese

2 teaspoons salt
Few grinds pepper
2½–3-pound frying chicken, cut
    in pieces

Crush garlic into butter. (If you do not have a garlic press, use ⅛ teaspoon garlic salt.) Combine crumbs, cheese, salt, and pepper. Dry chicken pieces on paper towels and dip in butter and then in crumb mixture. Place pieces side by side but not touching in 2 shallow baking dishes. Pour extra butter over chicken. Put children's portion in a 350° F. preheated oven and bake, without turning, for 1 hour. In the meantime, refrigerate adults' portion until 1 hour before you expect to serve it. Bake it, too, in a 350° F. oven for 1 hour. Or, you may bake the 2 casseroles together and reheat the adults' portion in the oven for about 15 minutes.

CHEESY CHICKEN

*Potato Salad**
*Three Bean Salad**
Toasted Buns
Gingerbread with Bananas and Whipped Cream

CHEESY CHICKEN

2½–3 pound frying chicken,
    cut up
½ cup oil

1 cup cheese cracker crumbs
Seasoned salt

Dry the chicken pieces with paper towels. Dip each piece in the oil and then in the cracker crumbs and lay in a shallow baking dish. The pieces should not touch one another. Sprinkle lightly with the seasoned salt. Drizzle any extra oil over the chicken and bake uncovered in a 375° F. oven for about 45 minutes or until tender when pierced with a fork. The adults' portion may be reheated in the oven—cover with foil if the crumbs are well browned. However, this is especially good cold—so good that you may wish to prepare the chicken early in the day and refrigerate.

CHILI CHICKEN

Lima Beans*
Warmed Peaches
Brown-and-Serve Rolls
Butterscotch Sundaes*

CHILI CHICKEN

3-pound frying chicken, cut up
Flour
Chili powder
Salt
⅓ cup oil
1 onion, sliced
2 tablespoons chopped green pepper
1 clove garlic, minced
1-pound can tomatoes
2 teaspoons sugar
12 pitted ripe olives, drained
12-ounce can vacuum-packed whole-kernel corn
½ cup crushed corn chips

Wash and dry chicken and shake in a bag with ⅓ cup flour, ¼ teaspoon chili powder, and 1 teaspoon salt. Heat oil in large skillet and brown chicken lightly on all sides. Remove chicken and drain on paper towels. Sauté onion, green pepper, and garlic in the same skillet. Stir in 2 tablespoons flour. Add ½ teaspoon salt, 1 teaspoon chili powder, tomatoes, and sugar and stir until thickened. Remove from heat and add olives. Oil 2 1-quart casseroles and put half of the corn in each. Place the chicken on top of the corn and pour the sauce on top. Cover and bake in a 350° F. oven for 45 minutes. Remove the adults' casserole, cool, and refrigerate. Sprinkle corn chips on the children's casserole and return to the oven, uncovered, for an additional 15 minutes. Twenty minutes before the adults' meal, uncover the adults' casserole, sprinkle with chips, and bake.

CRANBERRY CHICKEN

*Baked Potatoes**
*Buttered Celery and Peas**
Carrot Sticks
*Ice Cream with Maple Syrup**

CRANBERRY CHICKEN

Butter or margarine
Legs and thighs or breasts of
chicken

Salt and pepper
Juice of 1 lemon
1 cup jellied cranberry sauce

Generously butter a shallow baking dish. Dry the chicken on paper towels and lay in the pan in a single layer. Sprinkle with salt, pepper, and lemon juice. Spoon the cranberry sauce on top. Bake in a 400° F. oven for 15 minutes. Turn pieces and break up any lumps of the sauce. Continue to bake until chicken is tender, another 30–40 minutes, turning occasionally in the sauce. Serve the children their part of the chicken and sauce. Reheat the adults' portion in the oven 20 minutes before serving.

PEACH-GLAZED DRUMSTICKS AND RICE

*Broccoli Spears**
*Lettuce Wedges with Dressing**
Mocha Cake

PEACH-GLAZED DRUMSTICKS AND RICE

About 12 chicken drumsticks
1½ cups water
2 chicken bouillon cubes
1 onion
1 teaspoon salt
Few grinds pepper

8-ounce can peach slices
1 cup white rice, or mixed white
and wild rice
½ cup peach preserve
½ teaspoon dry mustard
2 tablespoons brown sugar

Wash chicken legs and put in a large saucepan with water, bouillon cubes, onion, salt, and pepper. Cover and simmer until meat is tender, about 30 minutes. Remove and drain chicken. Discard onion. Drain peach liquid into a measuring cup. Add chicken broth and water to peach liquid to make 2 cups. Return to saucepan and use to cook rice according to package directions.

In the meantime, make the peach glaze by combining preserves, mustard, and brown sugar in a small saucepan. Bring to the boiling point, stirring constantly. Lay the chicken legs in 2 9-inch metal pie pans or shallow baking dishes. Brush well with the glaze. Top with peach halves. Refrigerate the adults' portion. Put the children's portion in a preheated broiler, about 2 inches from the heat. Broil until bubbly and well browned. Total broiling time will be about 10–12 minutes. Serve the chicken with the rice and peaches. When the adults are ready to eat, reheat their rice and broil their chicken and peaches, using the rest of the glaze.

CHICKEN AND PRUNE CASSEROLE

*Baked Potatoes**
*Buttered Beets**
*Slaw**
*Crunchies**

This dish reheats so beautifully that you may wish to double the recipe and plan to serve it twice. If you use unpitted prunes, be sure to either warn all eaters, especially children, to look out for the pits, or remove them yourself before serving.

CHICKEN AND PRUNE CASSEROLE

2 tablespoons oil	Salt
3 medium-size onions, sliced	Few grinds pepper
1 tablespoon flour	½ pound pitted prunes, or ¾
1 frying chicken, cut up, or pieces	pound unpitted prunes
of chicken	8-ounce can tomato sauce

Put oil in the bottom of a casserole or Dutch oven. Lay all of the onion slices in the casserole and sprinkle with flour. Add half of the chicken and sprinkle with salt and pepper. Add half of the prunes, then the rest of the chicken, more salt and pepper, and the rest of the prunes. Pour tomato sauce on top. Cover and bake in 350° F. oven for 2 hours. Serve the children. Reheat in 350° F. oven for about 20 minutes before the later dinner.

CHICKEN-RICE SALAD

Cold Tomatoes, Asparagus, and Cucumber Slices*
Assorted Crisp Breads or Hot Rolls
Pineapple Cubes and Crème de Menthe or Mint Sauce

I concocted this recipe on the hottest day of the year in honor of visiting relatives from Seattle. In Seattle the natives start talking about a heat wave when the temperature hits 80 for 2 consecutive days. The day they came to visit me was hot by anyone's standards. Since we don't have air conditioning, I wanted to use the stove as little as possible. On the other hand, I wanted to serve something that would be hearty enough for sight-seers. Incidentally, this is just as good the second day as the first and still good on the third day.

CHICKEN-RICE SALAD

2–3-pound frying chicken
1 onion
1 carrot
1 stalk celery with leaves
3 cups water
1 teaspoon salt
Few grinds pepper
Dash nutmeg
½ cup uncooked rice

1 hard-boiled egg, sliced
¼ cup chopped green pepper
¼ cup chopped green onions
¼ cup chopped pimiento
¼ cup sour cream
1 tablespoon chili sauce
1 tablespoon bottled French
    dressing

In a large kettle, put the chicken, either whole or cut up, and giblets with the onion, carrot, celery, water, salt, pepper, and nutmeg. Bring to a boil, reduce heat, cover, and simmer until the chicken is tender, about 45 minutes. (You could use your pressure cooker.) Drain the chicken, saving the broth and discarding the vegetables. Set the chicken aside until it is cool enough to handle. Cook the rice according to package directions in 1 cup strained broth. Remove the chicken from the bones and cut into bite-size pieces. Combine the chicken, rice, and all of the other ingredients. Taste for seasoning. Add more sour cream for a moister salad. If you want to be fancy, you can press it into a mold or in bowls large enough to hold individual servings—I use 12-ounce custard cups for the adults and 8-ounce custard cups for the children. Refrigerate. When ready to serve, you can unmold the large salad on a serving plate and surround with lettuce leaves, or you can unmold the individual salads on the dinner plates. Otherwise, just put the salad mixture in a bowl. Spoon the children's servings out when they are ready to eat, and spoon more out for the adults later.

There will be broth left over. You could turn it into soup for another meal by returning the extra broth, all of the denuded bones, and the cooked vegetables to the kettle. Add 2 cups of water and a chicken bouillon cube and simmer for another hour. Strain and refrigerate this broth. If you have more chicken than you need for your salad, add some chicken pieces to the broth. When you get ready to make the soup, add noodles, vegetables, or what have you, and, if necessary, a can of chicken, to the broth. That's almost 2 meals for the price of one.

CHICKEN TETRAZZINI

Cold Zucchini Vinaigrette*
Hot Garlic French Bread*
Fresh Fruit and Cookies

CHICKEN TETRAZZINI

1½ cups spaghetti, broken into 2-inch pieces
Cooked chicken or turkey—large slices are best
4-ounce can mushrooms, drained
¼ cup butter or margarine
1 small onion, chopped
2 tablespoons flour

1½ cups chicken broth, canned or homemade
1 teaspoon salt
Dash pepper
Dash nutmeg
⅓ cup sherry (optional)
3 tablespoons cream
Grated Parmesan cheese

Cook spaghetti according to package directions and drain. Divide between 2 shallow casseroles. Lay chicken and then mushrooms on top of spaghetti. In the meantime, make sauce. Melt butter in small pan and sauté onions until limp. Stir in flour and allow to bubble for a few seconds. Stir in broth, salt, pepper, and nutmeg. Stir until smooth and add sherry and cream. Pour over chicken and sprinkle with grated cheese. Bake children's casserole in 400° F. oven until bubbly and lightly browned. Set other casserole aside until 20 minutes before ready to serve and bake as children's casserole was baked.

PRETTY SHELLS

Pickled Watermelon Rind
Celery and Cucumber Sticks
Strawberry-Blueberry Compote

PRETTY SHELLS

⅓ cup chopped onion
¼ cup chopped green pepper
¼ cup butter or margarine
3 tablespoons flour
1 teaspoon salt
1½ cups chicken broth
1 package frozen mixed vegetables, cooked and drained

2 pimientos, chopped
2–3 cups bite-size pieces of cooked chicken or turkey, or 1 cup each chicken and cooked ham
2 egg yolks
½ cup light cream
Patty shells, biscuits, or toast points

In the top of a double boiler, over direct heat, sauté the onion and pepper lightly in the butter. Stir in the flour and salt. Bubble briefly and add the broth, stirring until thickened. Add the pimiento, chicken, and vegetables. Beat the egg yolks with the cream. Stir some of the hot chicken mixture into the yolks to heat them and then stir the egg mixture into the chicken mixture. Now put the top of the double boiler over boiling water and heat for just a few minutes. Serve with frozen patty shells, prepared according to the package directions. Or, serve with split biscuits, toast points, rice, or noodles.

When the adults are ready to eat, you can carefully reheat the mixture in the top of the double boiler, stirring often, and crisp up the patty shells as directed on the package. Do not overheat.

FANCY DANCY LEFTOVERS

*Peas**
*Cranberry Crunch Salad**
Pumpkin Pie

FANCY DANCY LEFTOVERS

6 brown-and-serve link sausages, quartered crosswise
6-ounce package seasoned rice and wild rice mix, prepared according to package directions
5-ounce can mushrooms

Approximately 3 cups leftover turkey or chicken, cut in bite-size pieces
1½ cups gravy, or 1 can of cream of chicken soup, thinned with mushroom liquid

Brown the sausage. Divide half of the cooked rice between 2 greased casseroles. Put the sausages, mushrooms, and turkey pieces on top of rice. Top with the rest of the rice and the gravy. Cover. Refrigerate the adults' casserole and bake the children's casserole in a 350° F. oven until bubbly, about 30 minutes. Bake the other casserole in the same way ½ hour before the adults' meal.

BAKED CHICKEN CROQUETTES

*Spinach with Sliced Egg**
*Molded Fruit Salad**
*Biscuits**
*Grandma's Cracker Pudding**

Although croquettes are usually fried in deep fat, these are baked in a hot oven until they become crispy and brown. Almost any other leftover meat could be substituted for the cooked chicken.

BAKED CHICKEN CROQUETTES

½ cup mayonnaise or salad
  dressing
1 tablespoon chopped onion
1 tablespoon chopped green
  pepper
1 tablespoon chopped pimiento
½ teaspoon salt

Few grinds pepper
1½ cups cooked rice
2 cups minced or ground cooked
  chicken or turkey
Corn meal
Gravy or mushroom soup sauce
  (optional)

Combine all of the ingredients, except the corn meal and gravy and chill for several hours. Half an hour before the children's dinner, remove from the refrigerator and shape with your hands into smooth ball- or log-shaped croquettes, using ½ cup of the mixture for each croquette. Roll in corn meal and place in 2 heavily greased shallow baking dishes. Return the adults' portions to the refrigerator. Bake the children's portion in a preheated 450° F. oven for 20–25 minutes or until well browned. Serve plain or with hot leftover or canned chicken gravy, or a hot mushroom sauce made by thinning canned mushroom soup with milk. Twenty-five minutes before the adults expect to eat, remove their portion from the refrigerator, and bake and serve in the same way.

CHICKEN AND BISCUIT PUFF BAKE

*Lettuce Wedges**
Spiced Crab Apples
Coffee Ice Cream Pie

CHICKEN AND BISCUIT PUFF BAKE

¼ cup butter or margarine
¼ cup chopped onion
2 tablespoons chopped green
  pepper
3 tablespoons flour
2 cups chicken broth

2–3 cups cooked chicken, turkey,
  or chunk tuna, cut into bite-size
  pieces
2 cups mixed vegetables (carrots,
  peas, limas, green beans, corn),
  fresh-cooked, canned, or leftover

BISCUIT PUFF DOUGH:

1 cup all-purpose flour
1 teaspoon double-action baking
  powder
½ teaspoon salt
2 tablespoons shortening

1 egg
Milk
¼ teaspoon poultry seasoning
½ teaspoon dried parsley

Melt butter in a saucepan and sauté onion and green pepper until limp. Add flour and allow to bubble briefly. Add broth and stir until sauce is thick and smooth. Stir in chicken and vegetables and taste for seasoning, adding salt and pepper if necessary. Spoon the chicken mixture into 2 greased casseroles. In the meantime, make the biscuit dough.

Sift together the flour, baking powder, and salt. Add the shortening, working it in with a pastry blender or your fingers. Crack the egg into a measuring cup and add enough milk to make ⅔ cup. Mix well and add to the flour mixture with the poultry seasoning and parsley. Stir with a fork. Using a teaspoon, drop marble-size balls of dough onto the chicken mixture in the children's casserole. Remember that the dough will puff, so leave room for expansion. Use about half of the dough. Refrigerate the rest of the dough and bake the children's casserole in a 450° F. oven for about 15 minutes, until the dough is lightly browned and firm. Serve immediately. Twenty minutes before the adults' dinner, drop the rest of the dough onto the chicken in their casserole and bake as the children's casserole was baked.

Seafood

Fish is said to be brain food; this may or may not be true. That it is health food we know for sure. The incidence of heart disease is very low in regions of the world where fish is a staple.

Fish and shellfish are also excellent forms of protein. Boneless sirloin and boneless flounder or sole have about the same amount of protein per pound. A 1-pound can of salmon has even more protein than 1 pound of boneless sirloin.

Seafood at least once a week, therefore, will provide your diet with important nutrients. It can also keep your food costs and calorie intake down and provide variety in your menus.

Fresh fish, when it is really fresh, is magnificent. When it is not available there is a large selection of excellent canned and frozen fish from which to choose.

FISH AND POTATO BAKE

Tartar Sauce or Cucumber Sauce
(see Salmon Loaf recipe)*
Brussels Sprouts*
Sunshine Salad*
Lazy Daisy Cake*

FISH AND POTATO BAKE

1½ pounds fillet of haddock, sole, or flounder
1 package flavored fish coating mixture

Medium-size potatoes, boiled, peeled, and quartered, or small canned potatoes left whole
Salt
Pepper
Butter

Cut fish in serving-size pieces. Shake in coating mixture as indicated on package. Place children's fish in one buttered shallow baking dish and adults' in another. Lay potatoes beside the fish and sprinkle with salt and pepper and dot with butter. Bake children's portion in a 400° F. oven until fish flakes easily with a fork—about 20 minutes. Cover and refrigerate adults' portion to be uncovered and baked later.

Instead of using the commercial coating mixture, you may dip the fish pieces in milk and then in cornflake crumbs seasoned with onion salt. Put fish in the baking dishes and dribble butter on top.

OVEN-POACHED FILLETS OF SOLE

Frozen Potato Puffs
Baked Tomatoes
*Lima Beans Vinaigrette**
Crunchies and Fruit*

OVEN-POACHED FILLETS OF SOLE

1½ pounds fillet of sole or
  flounder
Salt
Butter or margarine
¼ cup finely chopped onion

¼ cup finely chopped carrot
8-ounce bottle clam juice
3 tablespoons flour
Dry white wine or bouillon
½ cup grated Swiss cheese

If you use frozen fish, thaw completely.

Butter two shallow baking dishes or 4 individual baking dishes. Lightly score the fillets. Sprinkle with a little salt. Fold each fillet in half, skin side in, and arrange in the bottoms of the baking dishes. They should be arranged in a single layer, overlapping only slightly.

In a saucepan, melt ¼ cup butter and lightly sauté the onions and carrots. With a slotted spoon, remove the vegetables from the butter and scatter them over the fish. Set saucepan aside for later use. Pour enough clam juice over the fillets to almost cover them. Cover with pieces of buttered brown paper, cut to fit the dishes. Do not tuck in. (The paper will keep the fish from browning but will allow steam to escape.) Put in a preheated 350° F. oven for 8–10 minutes until the fish flakes easily with a fork. Do not overcook.

Drain the liquid from the fish into a 2-cup measure. Set adults' casserole aside. Put the children's baking dish over boiling water to keep warm.

Melt butter in the saucepan. Add flour and bubble briefly. Stir in the liquid drained from the fish, any clam juice that remains in the bottle, and enough white wine to make a total of 1½ cups liquid. When the sauce is thick and smooth, stir in ¼ cup cheese and taste for seasoning. (You may want to add a little lemon juice and white pepper.) Pour the sauce over each of the fish dishes and top with the remaining ¼ cup cheese. Dot with 1 tablespoon butter. Refrigerate the adults' casserole. Run the children's casserole under the broiler until lightly browned.

Twenty minutes before the adults are ready to eat, put their baking dish in a preheated 350° F. oven and bake until bubbly and lightly browned.

FOIL FILLETS

*Parsley Potatoes**
*Sliced Tomato and Green Pepper Salad**
*Peaches, Ice Cream and Raspberry Sauce**

FOIL FILLETS

4-ounce can mushroom caps
Milk
3 tablespoons butter or margarine
3 tablespoons flour
¼ cup chopped green onion,
  including part of the green

¼ teaspoon dried tarragon
¼ teaspoon salt
1¼ pounds fillet of sole, halibut,
  or flounder

Drain the mushroom liquid into a measuring cup. Add enough milk to make 1 cup liquid. Melt the butter and stir in the flour, allowing to bubble briefly. Add the liquid, stirring until the sauce is thick and smooth. Stir in the green onions, tarragon, and salt. Chill.

Cut 4 12-inch squares of double-thickness foil. Butter lightly in the center. Lay a piece of fish on each square. Top with the chilled sauce and mushroom caps. Fold the sides of foil up loosely over the fish and secure with double folds. Crimp the ends so that no steam can escape. Place on a pie plate and bake 20 minutes in a 425° F. oven or refrigerate and bake for 25 minutes.

LEMON FLOUNDER BAKE

Crunch Broccoli II*
Vegetable Salad Mold*
Merry Berry*

LEMON FLOUNDER BAKE

¼ cup chopped onion
2 tablespoons butter or margarine
2 tablespoons flour
1 cup milk or light cream
¼ cup lemon juice
Grated peel of ½ lemon

1 cup raw rice, cooked according
  to package directions
1½ pounds flounder fillets
  (thawed, if frozen)
Seasoned salt
Lemon twists

Sauté onion in butter, add flour, and allow to bubble briefly. Stir in milk and continue stirring over low heat until sauce is thick and smooth. Then add lemon juice and grated lemon peel.

In the meantime, spoon the hot rice into 2 greased baking dishes. Sprinkle the fish with seasoned salt and roll each one tightly. Place rolls, seam side down, on rice. Pour sauce over the rolls and bake the children's portion in a 400° F. oven for 20 minutes or until the fish flakes easily. Garnish with lemon twists and serve immediately. The adults' casserole should be refrigerated until 25 minutes before the later meal, when it will be baked and served in the same manner.

Unfortunately, a 1-pound package of frozen fish fillets serves only 3, which may be enough if you have very young children. If you are catering to heartier appetites and want to use frozen fish, buy 2 packages. Poach a few pieces of the fish from one package according to package directions. Serve in cream sauce, or in sandwiches, or add to canned clam chowder for lunch the next day.

FISH STICKS AND EGG SAUCE

Brown Rice*
Bright Beauty Mold on Shredded Cabbage*
Apple Pie and Cheese*

FISH STICKS AND EGG SAUCE

Frozen fish sticks
2 tablespoons butter or margarine
1 tablespoon chopped onion
1 tablespoon chopped green
  pepper
2 tablespoons flour

1 cup milk
1/4 teaspoon dry mustard
1/2 teaspoon salt
1 pimiento, chopped (optional)
2 hard-boiled eggs, chopped

Bake the children's portion of fish sticks, or heat in a skillet according to package directions. In the meantime, make the sauce by melting the butter and sautéing the onion and pepper. Add the flour and allow to bubble for a moment before adding the milk. Stir until sauce thickens. Add the rest of the ingredients.

Serve the children their fish sticks with part of the sauce spooned over them. Refrigerate the rest of the sauce, to be reheated while you are heating the fish sticks for the adults' meal. You may wish to add a little milk to the sauce when you reheat it.

GARLIC SCALLOPS

Brown Rice*
Okra*
Tomato Aspic on Greens*
Melon Rings with Sherbet*

GARLIC SCALLOPS

1½ pounds scallops
½ cup oil
2 cloves garlic, split
2 tablespoons minced onion

½ teaspoon dried tarragon
½ teaspoon seasoned salt
Few grinds pepper

About 1 hour before the children are to eat, mix all of the above ingredients together in 2 shallow flame-proof baking dishes large enough to hold the scallops in a single layer. Be sure to put 1 garlic clove in each dish. Cover and refrigerate. Ten minutes before the dinner hour, place a baking dish 3 inches below the heat in a preheated broiler. Broil 5–10 minutes, until the scallops are just tender. Remove the garlic and serve.

SCALLOP-LOBSTER CASSEROLE

Rice*
Green Salad with Cucumbers and Tomato*
Hot Rolls
Blueberry Shortcake*

SCALLOP-LOBSTER CASSEROLE

1 onion, sliced
Butter
7½-ounce can lobster meat
1 pound scallops

1 can cream of mushroom soup
Sherry, milk, or water
Dry bread crumbs

Sauté onion in butter. Divide between 2 casseroles. Put lobster and raw scallops in each casserole. Mix mushroom soup with as much sherry as possible without making the soup too runny (or substitute milk or water for the children's portion). Pour over fish and top with crumbs. Bake in a 350° F. oven for 20 minutes before serving time. This is excellent company fare.

CLAM BUNNY

Toast Points
Buttered Carrots*
Slaw with Peanuts*
Cherry Cobbler*

CLAM BUNNY

¼ cup chopped onion
3 tablespoons chopped green
   pepper
¼ cup butter or margarine
¼ cup milk
⅓ cup chili sauce

2 teaspoons Worcestershire
Dash hot red pepper sauce
1 cup diced American process
   cheese
2 7-ounce cans minced clams,
   drained

Sauté onion and pepper in butter (in top part of double boiler but over direct heat) until limp but not browned. Put pan over boiling water and add the rest of the ingredients, stirring occasionally, until the cheese is melted and the sauce is thick. Serve to the children over toast points or rice, or in patty shells. Refrigerate the adults' portion, to be heated over hot water just before they are ready to eat.

This is also a delicious hot dip, served with crackers or toast rounds at a party.

Refrigerate or freeze the clam liquid for clam–tomato juice cocktail or future fish cookery, or to add to canned soup.

QUICK SHRIMP JAMBALAYA

Spinach Salad
Hard Rolls
Apples and Candy Bars

QUICK SHRIMP JAMBALAYA

6-ounce package "instant" Spanish
   rice mix
Canned tomatoes
Water
Butter, margarine, or bacon fat

1 or 2 7-ounce cans shrimp
Cooked peas, about ½ cup
   (optional)
Crisply fried and crumbled bacon,
   about 4 slices (optional)

Prepare the rice in the top of a double boiler according to package directions using the tomatoes, water, and butter called for. Add the shrimp and peas. Serve topped with crumbled bacon. Reheat over boiling water.

CRABBY SHRIMP

Rice or Biscuits*
Slaw with Dill*
Sliced Tomatoes
Fruit and Cookies*

This is a recipe I like to crow about. It's like "basic black"—you can dress it up or down. One word of warning, however. This will serve a family of 4 only if the children are small. You may want to double the recipe.

CRABBY SHRIMP

2 tablespoons butter or margarine
1/4 cup chopped onion
1/4 cup chopped green pepper
7½-ounce can crab meat
1 pimiento, chopped

10½-ounce can frozen cream of shrimp soup, partially thawed
Salt
Pepper
About 2 tablespoons sherry (optional)

Melt the butter in a saucepan and sauté the onion and pepper lightly. Pick over the crab meat, removing any cartilage. Add crab meat with the pimiento, soup, salt, and pepper to the saucepan. Heat. You may also add the sherry, or you may serve the children first and then add the sherry to the adults' portion. Taste to get the right amount.

That's the basic recipe. What you do with it next is up to you. You can serve it as is, over toast points, split biscuits, toasted corn bread, rice, or in pastry shells. You can put it in flat casseroles and top with buttered crumbs to be heated in the oven until the crumbs are brown and the crab mixture is bubbly. This is a nice company touch.

Be sure that you refrigerate the adults' portion, unless you plan to eat less than an hour after the children eat. It may be reheated in the oven, in a double boiler, or in a saucepan directly over low heat.

CRAB CREPES

*Buttered Corn***
*Spinach and Tomato Salad***
Hard Rolls
Apple Crisp or Fresh Apples*

Fear not, these festive crepes are not complicated—thanks to 2 mixes. Furthermore, you may make them during the afternoon and refrigerate them until baking time.

CRAB CREPES

1 cup pancake mix
Melted butter
Milk
2 eggs
7¾-ounce can crab meat
⅓ cup chopped celery
1 tablespoon chopped pimiento

1 tablespoon chopped green pepper
1 envelope tuna casserole sauce mix
⅓ cup mayonnaise
½ cup dry bread crumbs

Prepare pancake mix according to package directions, using 3 tablespoons butter, 1¼ cups milk, and 2 eggs. Oil the griddle, if necessary, and heat. Use a scant ¼ cup batter for each crepe, making a total of 12. (You may, of course, use a crepe pan or small frying pan, which will make neater crepes but will take longer.)

While the crepes are cooking, pick over the crab meat, discarding any cartilage, and breaking the meat into small pieces. Add the celery, green pepper, and pimiento.

In a small saucepan, combine the sauce mix with 1½ cups milk, stirring according to package directions until thick. Stir in the mayonnaise. Add ⅓ cup of this mixture to the crab mixture, mixing lightly but well. Then add another ½ cup milk to the sauce.

Combine 3 tablespoons melted butter and crumbs.

You are now ready to assemble the crepes. Butter 2 small flat baking pans—au gratin dishes, if you have them. Put a rounded tablespoon of the crab mixture on one end of a crepe and roll up. Lay, fold side down, in a baking dish. Continue until you have used up all of the crab mixture. (You may have an extra crepe. If so, it is the cook's bonus. Enjoy it.) Pour the sauce over the crepes. Top with buttered crumbs. Cover and refrigerate.

Twenty minutes before each dinner, remove the cover from a pan of crepes and bake in a 350° F. oven until the crumbs are brown and the sauce bubbles.

SALMON LOAF

Baked Acorn Squash*
Wilted Cucumbers*
Biscuits
Lemon Pie

SALMON LOAF

2 eggs
1-pound can salmon
1 cup fine cracker crumbs

1 can condensed vegetarian
vegetable soup

Beat eggs. Add the rest of the ingredients and mix well. Spoon into well-greased individual baking dishes—12-ounce custard cups are a good size. Bake 25 minutes in a 350° F. oven, or refrigerate and bake 30 minutes before serving.

JELLIED SALMON SALAD

Assorted Cold Vegetables*
Hot Rolls
Apricot Upside Down Cake*

JELLIED SALMON SALAD

1 package lemon-flavored gelatin
1 cup boiling water
2 tablespoons lemon juice
Dash hot pepper sauce
2 tablespoons chili sauce
½ cup mayonnaise
1-pound can red salmon, flaked

¼ cup sliced celery
2 tablespoons sliced green onions
2 tablespoons chopped green
  pepper
¼ cup minced or shredded carrots
2 teaspoons capers (optional)
Pimiento strips

Dissolve gelatin in boiling water. Add lemon juice and pepper sauce. Refrigerate until slightly thickened. Stir in chili sauce, mayonnaise, salmon, celery, onion, green pepper, carrots, and capers. Oil 4 individual molds and arrange pimiento strips in the bottoms of the molds. Spoon salmon mixture into molds and refrigerate until firm.

Serve on greens surrounded by an assortment of vegetables—tomatoes, cooked or canned asparagus, cucumber slices, etc.

Tomato Juice

SALMON CUPS WITH CREAMED PEAS AND CELERY

Hard Rolls
Strawberry Shortcake*

The following recipe will serve 4 small to average eaters well. However, if you have a family of big eaters, you may want to double the recipe and have leftovers to serve cold at lunch the following day.

SALMON CUPS WITH CREAMED PEAS AND CELERY

SALMON CUPS:

1-pound can salmon
Water
⅓ cup raw rice
⅓ cup chopped onion

⅓ cup chopped green pepper
½ teaspoon dry mustard
1 tablespoon lemon juice
2 eggs, lightly beaten

CREAMED PEAS AND CELERY:

1 cup sliced celery
Water
1 cup frozen peas
2 tablespoons butter or margarine

2 tablespoons flour
Salt
1 cup milk or a combination of
milk and cooking liquid

Drain the liquid from the salmon into a measuring cup. Add water to make ¾ cup liquid. Combine the liquid with the rice in a small saucepan and cook, covered, for 15 minutes, or until rice is tender.

Combine the cooked rice with the salmon, onion, green pepper, mustard, and lemon juice. Add the eggs and spoon into 2 small loaf pans or 4 custard cups. Refrigerate the adults' servings and place the children's loaf or custard cups in a baking pan with about 1 inch of water. Bake in a 350° F. oven until firm, 25–35 minutes.

In the meantime, cook the celery in a very small amount of water for 10 minutes or until crunchy-tender. Add the peas and continue to cook for 3 more minutes. Drain, saving any cooking liquid. Make a sauce by melting the butter, stirring in the flour and salt, bubbling briefly, and adding the milk or a combination of milk and cooking liquid. Cook the sauce until it thickens and add to the vegetables. If you use instant-type flour, follow the directions on the package, using these proportions and ingredients.

To serve, run a knife around the edge of the cooked loaf and un-mold. Spoon the sauced vegetables over the salmon.

Bake the adults' loaf or custard cups just before the later meal and reheat the vegetables.

COLD SALMON LOAF WITH CUCUMBER SAUCE

Assorted Chilled Cooked Vegetables*
   (Asparagus, Carrots, Beans, etc.)
Tomatoes
Hot Rolls
Peach and Blueberry Pie

COLD SALMON LOAF WITH CUCUMBER SAUCE

Prepare salmon loaf (see preceding recipe), baking in 1 large loaf pan or in 4 custard cups. Refrigerate for several hours and serve with a sauce made by combining the following:

1 cucumber, pared, chopped, and
   drained
¼ teaspoon salt

Few grinds pepper
½ cup sour cream

HOT TUNA SALAD

*Cold Vegetable Platter**
Hard Rolls
*Marble Cake with Mint Frosting**

HOT TUNA SALAD

2 7-ounce cans white-meat tuna
1 cup thinly sliced celery
½ cup chopped green pepper
2 tablespoons chopped pimiento
  (optional)

¼ cup chopped onion
1 tablespoon prepared mustard
1 cup mayonnaise
1 cup Chinese noodles

Break up the tuna into large chunks. Add the celery, green pepper, onion, and pimiento. Stir the mustard into the mayonnaise and pour over the tuna mixture, stirring lightly with a fork. Spoon the mixture into 4 individual baking dishes. Sprinkle noodles on top. Bake, or refrigerate and bake, for 25 minutes in a 350° F. oven.

TUNA-EGG BURGERS

*Butternut Squash Rings**
*Green Bean Salad**
*Ginger-Lemon Treat**

TUNA-EGG BURGERS

4 English muffins
2 7-ounce cans tuna
¼ cup mayonnaise
4 hard-boiled eggs
2 tablespoons butter or margarine

2 tablespoons flour
1 cup milk
½ teaspoon seasoned salt
Grated Cheddar or American
  cheese

Split the muffins and toast lightly on cut side. Mix the tuna with the mayonnaise and mound on the 8 muffin halves, spreading to the edges. Peel and slice the eggs. Put the attractive middle slices of the eggs on top of the tuna. Chop up the remaining eggs. Make a sauce by melting the butter and stirring in the flour. Allow to bubble for a moment and add the milk, stirring until the sauce is thick and smooth. Stir in the chopped eggs and seasoned salt. Top the muffin halves with the sauce and sprinkle with the cheese. Put the children's muffins on a baking sheet and bake in a 350° F. oven for 15 minutes until heated through. Refrigerate the adults' muffins, to be baked in a 350° F. oven 20 minutes before the adults' meal.

TUNA SHEPHERD'S PIE

Lettuce Wedges with Russian Dressing*
Fruit and Cereal Crunch Cookies*

TUNA SHEPHERD'S PIE

¼ cup chopped onion
2 tablespoons chopped green
  pepper
Butter or margarine
3 tablespoons flour
½ teaspoon salt
2 cups milk

Few grinds pepper
10-ounce package frozen mixed
  vegetables, cooked
2 7-ounce cans tuna
1 pimiento, chopped
4 servings well-seasoned mashed
  potatoes

Sauté onion and green pepper in ¼ cup butter. Add flour and salt and allow to bubble briefly. Stir in milk and continue stirring until sauce is thick and smooth. Add pepper, vegetables, tuna, and pimiento. Divide the mixture between 2 casseroles. Top with mashed potatoes. Dot the potatoes with butter. Refrigerate 1 casserole. Bake the children's in a 375° F. oven for 20–25 minutes until heated through and browned on top. Thirty minutes before the adults' dinner hour, remove their casserole from the refrigerator and bake as the children's casserole was baked.

TUNA CASSEROLE

Green Beans with Almonds*
Raw Carrots, Celery, and Cherry Tomatoes
Fresh Fruit and Sugar Cookies

TUNA CASSEROLE

1 cup uncooked elbow macaroni
2 eggs
½ cup condensed cream of
  mushroom soup
1 cup milk
7-ounce can tuna

¾ cup dry bread crumbs
¾ cup shredded American cheese
¼ cup chopped green pepper
2 tablespoons chopped pimiento
1 teaspoon salt

Cook macaroni according to package directions. Drain. Beat the eggs in a large mixing bowl and beat in ½ cup of the soup and the milk. Stir in the macaroni and the rest of the ingredients and pour into 2 flat casseroles or into 4 12-ounce custard cups. Bake, or refrigerate and bake, for 40 minutes in a 350° F. oven, until the custard is barely firm.

Serve with a sauce made by heating the mushroom soup that remains in the can with 2 tablespoons of milk.

Golden Mushroom Soup

SEA AND GARDEN SALAD

Hot Rolls
Berry Cobbler*

SEA AND GARDEN SALAD

1 pound scallops
1 package frozen mixed vegetables
½ teaspoon salt
1 cup boiling water
1 tablespoon lemon juice
Italian dressing
Salad greens
¼ cup chopped green onions

½ cup chopped celery
1 cup cooked shrimp
4 hard-boiled eggs, halved
Tomato slices
Cucumber slices
¼ cup mayonnaise
¼ cup chili sauce

Unless you are able to buy small scallops, cut the scallops in small pieces of uniform size. Cook the vegetables in 1 cup boiling salted water. When just barely tender, drain the vegetables, saving the liquid. Return the liquid to the saucepan and add the lemon juice. Cook the scallops in this liquid for 5 minutes. Drain. Drizzle dressing over the vegetables and the scallops and refrigerate in 2 separate bowls.

To serve, line plates or soup plates with greens. Add the green onions and celery to the vegetables and spoon into the center of the plates. Surround with the scallops, shrimp, eggs, tomato and cucumber slices. Pass a dressing made by combining the mayonnaise and chili sauce.

Eggs and Cheese

Eggs and cheese are two rich sources of protein and can, therefore, be substituted for meat in your dinner menus. They are also inexpensive and versatile.

Very fresh eggs are best for eating. Those more than 3 days old are best for baking. You can test the freshness of your eggs by breaking one in a saucer. If the yolk stands up considerably above the white, the egg is fresh. If the yolk settles down to the level of the white, or just slightly above it, the egg is not fresh and had better be used in a dish where it will lose its identity—in a cake instead of an omelet—as soon as possible.

Keep eggs in the refrigerator. Do not wash, for this can destroy nature's seal. Don't stock up on eggs. Buy just what you will need—plus a few extras—until your next shopping day. Remember, too, that eggs cannot stand severe heat in cooking. Fry or scramble them over low heat; boil them at a point just below the simmer.

As for cheeses, the variety is staggering. In some large cities there are specialty stores devoted to domestic and imported cheeses. Most supermarkets carry American, Cheddar, Swiss, Edam, Gouda, and Parmesan cheeses. All of these are good sources of protein. Cottage cheese also has quite a bit of protein. Cream cheese has very little.

Omelets

OMELET AUX FINES HERBES

Salad Plate with Assorted Cooked and Raw Vegetables*
Bran Muffins*
Peach Crisp*

CHEESE OMELET

Bean and Onion Casserole*
Pickled Beets*
Toast Fingers*
Sliced Oranges and Toasted Coconut

CREAMED CRABMEAT OMELET

Cabbage Slaw with Grated Carrot*
Sliced Tomatoes
Biscuits*
Raspberries and Sherbet

The omelet is so cloaked in epicurean mystery that many of us are timid about even attempting so royal a dish. That's silly. If you produce a poor omelet, what do you have? Good scrambled eggs.

Omelets—or scrambled eggs—make fine dinner fare, particularly if you fill or top them with sautéed mushrooms, cheese, or bits of cooked meat, chicken, or fish. No omelet should cook more than 1 minute, so you can get dinner on the table in a hurry. Remember to call the children to the table *before* you put the eggs in the skillet. Nothing is less appealing than a cold omelet.

For 2 servings use 3 or 4 very fresh eggs. Remove them from the refrigerator an hour or so before you want to serve them so that they can warm up to room temperature. If you forget to take them out, put them in tepid—not warm—water for a few minutes.

Select a *heavy* skillet that measures about 7 inches across the bottom. It should have rounded sides. Some gourmets insist that the pan should never be used for anything else, but few of us have the storage space to keep a pan for only one purpose. Do be sure that the pan is smooth inside. Teflon-coated pans are nice for egg cookery. Use just enough butter to coat the inside of a Teflon pan.

Break the eggs into a bowl and add 3 tablespoons tepid water. Beat slightly with a fork. Most people prefer to salt the eggs after they are cooked.

Melt a rounded tablespoon of butter, preferably sweet butter, in the skillet over medium low heat. Swirl it around to coat the sides of the pan. When the butter is bubbly but has not yet begun to brown, pour in the eggs. The proper way to cook an omelet is to slide the pan back and forth over the heat with your left hand while you stir the eggs in a circular motion with a fork. This is a bit like the children's trick of patting the head while rubbing the stomach—very difficult, but possible with practice. You may also want to lift the edges of the cooked egg mixture so that the uncooked part can run underneath. The omelet is done when the eggs are no longer runny but are still soft. To fold, grasp the skillet by the handle and tilt it away from you, guiding the omelet with a fork so that part of the mixture falls over the other part. Hold a heated plate in one hand and raise the skillet to a sharp angle so that you can flip the omelet out of the pan onto the plate making another fold. Sprinkle with salt, cut in half, and serve. You may, if you like, brush the finished omelet with melted butter.

That's all there is to it. If you wish to make a more elegant omelet, try one of the suggestions below.

Omelette aux Fines Herbes sounds French and fancy. Add 1 tablespoon fresh or dried herbs to the egg and water mixture before you beat them together. Appropriate herbs are parsley, chives, chervil, and tarragon. You can also use minced water cress.

Cheese Omelet. Sprinkle about 3 tablespoons grated Swiss or Cheddar cheese over the eggs before folding. You may then sprinkle more cheese on top of the omelet and run it under the broiler for an instant until the cheese melts.

Vegetable Omelet. Spread well-drained vegetables over the eggs before folding. You may, if you like, spread 2 tablespoons heavy cream or sour cream over the eggs before you add the vegetables. Be sure that the vegetables are warm before you add them to the eggs. Try sautéed mushrooms, cooked-potato cubes, cooked mixed vegetables, sautéed onions or green pepper, chopped cooked spinach, or finely diced and drained raw tomato.

Chicken, Seafood, and Meat Omelet. Spread diced cooked chicken, diced or flaked fish or shellfish, or diced ham, pork, beef, veal, or crisp bacon over the eggs before folding. The fish or meat may be creamed before adding to the omelet, in which case you will probably want to serve more of the cream sauce over the omelet after it has been folded.

For two servings, mix up to 1 cup cooked seafood, chicken, or meat with 1 cup white sauce, leftover or canned gravy, or slightly thinned canned cream soup. Canned cheese soup is a good choice.

Italian Omelet. Spoon spaghetti sauce, with or without meat, over the omelet after it has finished cooking.

Western Omelet. First fry bacon squares in the skillet. When the bacon is brown, remove it and drain on paper towels while you sauté 1 tablespoon chopped onion and 1 tablespoon chopped green pepper in the skillet. Swish the bacon fat around the edges of the skillet and pour off any excess. Return the bacon with the egg mixture and cook like any other omelet. You may use cubes of ham or canned luncheon meat and butter instead of the bacon.

Any of the above additions are also suitable for scrambled eggs.

Packaged Omelets are now available and are usually quite good and relatively inexpensive. You may find them useful to keep on hand for emergency meals.

Quiches and Gratins

Both quiches and gratins are basically egg and cheese dishes, with only one difference: quiches are baked in pastry shells; gratins are baked in flat casseroles. If you are going to make quiches, you will need individual pie plates. Although they are delicious cold, they should not be reheated. Quiches prepared in tiny pastry shells or cut in small pieces also make magnificent appetizers.

BACON AND CHEESE QUICHE

Mixed Vegetable Salad*
Melon or Berries with Lemon Ice

BACON AND CHEESE QUICHE

2 pie crust sticks, or pastry for a
    double-crust 9-inch pie
6 slices bacon, cut in squares, or
    sausage, cut in circles
1 tablespoon flour
6 ounces Swiss cheese, cut in small
    pieces

4 eggs
1 teaspoon salt
Dash nutmeg
2 cups milk
2 tablespoons butter

Roll out pastry and line 4 individual pie plates. Fry the bacon until crisp and drain on paper towels. Mix the bacon with the flour and cheese and arrange in the bottoms of the 4 pie shells. Beat the eggs well and then beat in the salt, nutmeg, and milk. Fill 2 of the pastry shells, using about half of the egg mixture. Put small dots of butter on top of the milk mixture and bake in the 375° F. oven for 25–30 minutes until the quiches are puffed and brown. Refrigerate the adults' pastry shells and the bowl with the milk mixture. Thirty minutes before the adults' dinner, pour the egg mixture into their pie shells, dot with butter, and bake.

CLAM QUICHE

Yellow Squash*
Spinach Salad*
Fruit Gelatin and Cookies*

CLAM QUICHE

Pastry for double-crust 9-inch pie
2 7½-ounce cans minced clams
4 slices bacon cut in quarters
1 small onion, thinly sliced
4 eggs

2 tablespoons chili sauce
½ teaspoon salt
1¾ cups liquid—clam juice and milk

Roll out pie crust dough and line 4 individual pie pans. Drain the clams into a measuring cup. Fry the bacon and drain well on paper towels. Add the onion to the bacon fat and sauté until slices separate into rings and are limp. Remove from fat with a slotted spoon and combine with clams and bacon. Spread in the pie shells. Then beat the eggs. Add the chili sauce, salt, and liquid. Pour half of the egg mixture over the clam mixture into 2 pie shells. Dot with butter. Bake in a 375° F. oven for 25–30 minutes until puffed and brown. Refrigerate the adults' pie shells and egg mixture separately. Thirty minutes before the later meal, pour the egg mixture over the clams, dot with butter, and bake.

GRATIN OF CREAMED FISH OR POULTRY

*Zucchini Vinaigrette**
Carrot Sticks
Assorted Crisp Breads
*Peach Shortcake**

GRATIN OF CREAMED FISH OR POULTRY

3 tablespoons butter
1 small onion, chopped
3 tablespoons flour
5-ounce can mushrooms
1-pound can salmon, or 2 7-ounce
   cans crab or tuna, or 2 cups
   diced cooked chicken or turkey

1½ cups liquid
¼ cup whipping cream
Salt
Pepper
Thin slices Swiss or Cheddar
   cheese

Heat the butter in a saucepan and add the onions. Sauté over low heat just until the onions are limp. Stir in the flour and allow to bubble for a few seconds. Remove from the heat.

In the meantime, drain the mushrooms and fish into a large measuring cup. If necessary, add milk to make 1½ cups.

Stir liquid into the flour and return to heat. Bring to a boil, stirring constantly. When the sauce begins to thicken, add the whipping cream. Stir in the fish (or poultry) and mushrooms. Add salt and pepper to taste.

Put the fish mixture in individual casseroles, arrange the cheese on top of it, dot with butter, and bake, or refrigerate and bake, in a 400° F. oven until browned, about 15 minutes. If you wish, you may use pie shells which have been baked 15 minutes in a 400° F. oven. Add the fish mixture. Top with cheese and butter and bake 15 minutes in a 400° F. oven.

EGG AND POTATO GRATIN

Broccoli*
Fruit Salad Mold on Greens*
Brown-and-Serve Rolls
Chocolate Sundaes*

This mixture is so hearty that you will probably want to bake it in a casserole rather than in a pie shell. However, if you prefer a pie shell, follow the instructions in the recipe for Bacon and Cheese Quiche*.

EGG AND POTATO GRATIN

4 eggs
¼ cup milk
6 slices Swiss cheese, cut in small pieces
½ cup finely diced cooked ham, fried bacon, or fried sausage (optional)

½ cup finely chopped onion
⅛ teaspoon garlic powder (optional)
½ teaspoon salt
3 medium-size potatoes
Butter

Beat eggs and add milk. Stir in the cheese, onion, meat, garlic powder, and salt. Peel the potatoes and grate them, using the largest holes on the grater. Pick up a handful of potatoes, squeeze out as much liquid as possible and add to the egg mixture. Continue until all of the potatoes have been squeezed and added. Stir again. Refrigerate covered.

About 40 minutes before each meal, heat 1 tablespoon butter in a flameproof casserole or skillet. Roll around to coat the casserole. Add half of the egg mixture. Dot with butter and bake 25–30 minutes in a preheated 375° F. oven until puffy and brown. Serve at once.

BACON AND EGG SPAGHETTI

Tossed Vegetable Salad*
French Bread or Toast
Apples and Candy Bars

Although this dish cannot be reheated, it can be prepared in a very short time. I "found" it in a tiny little restaurant in Rome and am very proud of it. It's wonderful for those occasions when you get home late and find your cupboards in a state that would embarrass Mother Hubbard.

BACON AND EGG SPAGHETTI

Spaghetti
Bacon—2 slices per person, cut in
  squares
Eggs—1 per person

Milk—1 teaspoon per person
Salt
Pepper
Grated Parmesan cheese

While the spaghetti is cooking according to package directions, fry the bacon and also beat up the eggs with the milk, salt, and pepper. When the spaghetti is tender, drain it quickly and return it to the pot in which it was cooked. Pour the bacon and eggs over the spaghetti and stir quickly with a fork. If the spaghetti is hot enough it will cook the eggs. If not, turn the heat on under the pot and toss the spaghetti very quickly until the eggs are just barely creamy. Spoon a generous amount of cheese over the mixture and serve immediately. Repeat the process for the later meal.

EGGS ALMANDINE

Baked or Broiled Tomato*
Asparagus Salad with Vinaigrette Dressing*
Whole Wheat Toast
Berry Cobbler*

EGGS ALMANDINE

3 tablespoons butter or margarine
1/3 cup sliced or slivered almonds
2 tablespoons flour
1 1/2 cups milk
1/4 cup mayonnaise

1 teaspoon salt
1 canned pimiento, diced
8–10 hard-boiled eggs, shelled and
  quartered

[*128*]

Melt butter in heavy saucepan. Add almonds and brown lightly. Remove almonds with a slotted spoon and drain on paper towel. There should be approximately 2 tablespoons butter left in the pan. Add more if necessary. Make a sauce by stirring flour into butter and cooking for a moment or two. Remove from heat, add milk, and return to heat stirring until sauce is boiling and thick. Remove from heat and stir in mayonnaise, salt, and pimiento. Divide eggs in 2 well-buttered shallow casseroles. Cover with sauce and sprinkle with almonds. Place children's casserole in a 350° F. oven for 15 minutes or until bubbly. Refrigerate adults' casserole to be heated in a 350° F. oven for 20 minutes before serving.

CHEESE PUFF

*Cooked Radishes**
*Lima Beans Vinaigrette in Lettuce Cups**
*Ginger Bread with Lemon Sauce**

CHEESE PUFF

6 slices firm white bread
½ pound Cheddar cheese
¼ cup mayonnaise
2 tablespoons chopped onion
2 tablespoons chopped green
   pepper

2 eggs
½ teaspoon salt
1½ cups milk
Paprika

Early in the afternoon, cut 3 slices of bread into small squares. Put the squares in a single layer in the bottoms of two well-greased casseroles. Each casserole must be at least 2 inches deep and may be deeper. Cut the cheese into small cubes and mix with the mayonnaise, onion, and green pepper. Spoon over the bread. Cut each of the remaining 3 slices of bread into triangular-shaped quarters and arrange over the cheese mixture. Beat the eggs with a rotary beater or whisk and beat in the salt and milk. Pour over the bread and cheese and sprinkle paprika liberally on top of each casserole. Refrigerate. Bake the casseroles in a 350° F. oven about 40 minutes until they have puffed up and started to brown. Serve immediately.

MACARONI AND CHEESE

*Carrots Diable**
*Green Salad**
*Blueberry Cobbler**

MACARONI AND CHEESE

8-ounce package elbow macaroni
8 ounces sharp Cheddar cheese,
  grated
1 tablespoon minced onion
Butter

1⅔ cups milk
½ teaspoon salt
1 egg
⅓ cups dry bread crumbs

Cook macaroni according to package directions. Drain well and put half of the macaroni in a well-greased 1½–2-quart casserole. Top with about ⅔ of the cheese and the onion. Add the rest of the macaroni and then the rest of the cheese. Melt 2 tablespoons butter and add the milk. Beat in the salt and egg. Pour into the casserole. Cover the top layer of cheese with bread crumbs and dot with 1 tablespoon butter. Bake about 40 minutes in a 400° F. oven until the top is browned and most of the milk has been absorbed. Serve the children and reheat in the oven for the later dinner, adding more milk if necessary.

EGG, CHEESE, AND CORN CUSTARD

*Zucchini Vinaigrette**
Frozen Potato Puffs
Toasted English Muffins
Rhubarb and Strawberry Compote

EGG, CHEESE, AND CORN CUSTARD

6 eggs
¾ cup milk
1 teaspoon salt
Few grinds pepper
¼ teaspoon dried basil

1 teaspoon chopped dried parsley
1 tablespoon dried onion flakes
1 cup canned whole-kernel corn,
  drained
1 cup cubed Swiss cheese

Beat the eggs and add the milk, salt, pepper, basil, parsley, and onion flakes. Beat again and stir in the corn and cheese. Pour into 4 buttered 12-ounce custard cups or casseroles.

Put the children's casseroles in a 350° F. oven and bake about 30 minutes until puffy and lightly browned. They will still be not quite set in the center. Unmold on dinner plates.

Refrigerate the adults' casseroles. Forty minutes before the later dinner, remove from the refrigerator, stir gently with a fork, and bake.

MANICOTTI

Tossed Salad*
French Bread
Fruit and Cookies

MANICOTTI

5 eggs
¾ cup milk
1 cup all-purpose flour, sifted
½ teaspoon salt
1 pound ricotta cheese (or cottage
  cheese)

½ pound mozzarella cheese at
  room temperature
2 tablespoons dried parsley
3 cups meatless spaghetti sauce
  with mushrooms
¼ cup Parmesan cheese

Make crepes by beating 4 of the eggs and stirring in the milk, flour, and salt to make a very thin batter. Heat slightly greased or Teflon griddle. Pour the batter onto the griddle, using about 3 tablespoons of batter for each crepe. When the crepes have bubbled just a bit and turned a brighter yellow all the way to the center, turn them over and cook on the other side for just a few minutes. They will not brown. Remove to a plate and continue until all of the batter has been used up. The traditional way to make crepes is to use a small frying pan—about 6 inches in diameter—and make 1 crepe at a time. However, you can make them much faster on a griddle.

While you are making the crepes, mix together the ricotta, the mozzarella (which has been brought to room temperature), the fifth egg, and the parsley. If you use an electric mixer, the mozzarella will break up into the ricotta.

Put a little spaghetti sauce in the bottom of each of 2 baking dishes.

Place about 2 tablespoons of the cheese mixture on each crepe, making a strip of filling that goes along the diameter of the crepe. Fold one side of the crepe over the filling and the other side of the crepe over the first side to make a filled tube. Put the crepe, fold side down, in one of the baking dishes. Continue filling crepes until all of the cheese mixture is used up. Put the rest of the spaghetti sauce over the crepes and sprinkle with Parmesan cheese.

Refrigerate the adults' manicotti. Bake the children's serving for 20 minutes in a 350° F. oven, until bubbly and browned. Bake the adults' portion in the same way.

Vegetables

Let's face it, vegetables don't need to be a bore. However, many of us who give a lot of thought to the main dish on our menu too frequently just go to the freezer and take out a box of vegetables. We cook and serve them with a sort of "eat it, it's good for you" attitude. No wonder children, who are good eaters otherwise, scorn vegetables. Wise Dr. Spock says that it is the mother's attitude that makes children dislike vegetables. According to him, if we served spinach as a special treat and ice cream as a duty—"eat up all your ice cream and then I'll give you some yummy spinach"—children would love spinach and hate ice cream.

Vegetables provide more than vitamins; they provide variety and eye appeal to a dinner. Select your main dish first and then choose vegetables that will complement it. Crisp or raw vegetables to add "crunch" to the texture, "strong" or sharp vegetables or sauces to complement a bland main dish, bright vegetables to add color to a drab plate.

Fresh Vegetables

There is nothing better than carefully selected and cooked fresh vegetables. How long has it been since you served "real" green beans? If you are like many American mothers, it has been such a long time that you have forgotten how good they are.

Remember to cook fresh vegetables in as small a pan as is practical in as little water as possible. Most vegetables should be tightly covered. The exceptions are those vegetables that cause the liquid to "creep" up the side of the pan and boil over if the pan is tightly covered. Covered skillets are good utensils for cooking broccoli and asparagus spears, okra, corn on the cob, and any of the greens that "shrink" during the cooking process. Don't overcook vegetables.

Canned Vegetables

Canned vegetables are particularly handy for the cook-now-serve-later mother. Cans come in such a wide variety of sizes. You may open a can and take out the vegetables the children will eat, cover, and refrigerate the rest of the contents in the can, and heat just before the adults' meal. But canned vegetables are often dreary, so shop carefully. If you find a brand you like for a particular vegetable, stick to it.

To preserve the nutritive values, drain canned vegetable liquid into a small skillet or saucepan. Boil it down to about 2 tablespoons, add vegetables and seasonings, and *heat*. Canned vegetables do *not* need boiling.

Frozen Vegetables

Frozen vegetables are a great convenience and they have become increasingly interesting in the past few years. Combinations of vegetables with seasonings or sauces are now available, and new ones are added frequently. Take time to study the products in the frozen-food department at your supermarket and experiment with them. Read the "serving suggestions" on the package. Just a pinch of an herb will often perk up a monotonous flavor.

Unfortunately, the regular 10-ounce package of frozen vegetables is not big enough for a family of 4 good eaters—and 2 packages are too much. The big family-size bags or cartons of vegetables are, therefore, a good choice. You just pour out the quantity you need and return the remainder to the freezer. They also make it possible for you to cook vegetables separately for children and adults. Although it is possible to cook the adults' vegetables while you are cooking for the children, you are apt to lose flavor and vitamins in the reheating process. Furthermore, it is just as easy to cook some vegetables (for example, frozen peas) as it is to reheat them.

If you are using the 10-ounce-size package for your family, pour out the children's portion, close the box, and return it to the freezer, to be cooked just before the adults' meal.

Elsewhere in this chapter you will find a number of suggestions for combining vegetables, so if 1 10-ounce package is not enough, cook 2 and refrigerate the leftovers to be served later in the week with other vegetables or tossed into a mixed salad.

All cooking and canning liquids should be saved *and used* to conserve vitamins and minerals and add interesting flavors to soups, stews, sauces, aspics, gravies or vegetable juice cocktails. (Beet and sauerkraut juices combine to make a delicious ruby red cocktail.) Tightly covered, they may be held for a few days in a good refrigerator—several months in a freezer. Why not keep a pint jar for juices in your refrigerator? When it is full, if you have no immediate plans for it, move it to the freezer. Incidentally, if you are freezing in a regular glass jar, remember that freezing foods expand, so fill only to within 1 inch of the top of the jar.

Let me repeat: Freshly cooked vegetables are best, so, whenever possible, cook the vegetables fresh for each sitting. If you're cooking a last-minute steak, you might just as well cook a vegetable at the same time. However, we're trying to make it easy to get that second meal on the table with as few minutes in the kitchen as possible—that's the point of this book after all—so here are some suggestions for reheating.

You can reheat without overcooking if you will remove the vegetables for the adults' meal about 2 minutes before they are done. If, for example, the package says return to a boil and cook 10 minutes, you could lift the adults' portions out of the boiling water with a slotted spoon after they have cooked 7–8 minutes. Continue to cook the children's vegetables until tender, then serve. Reheat the adults' vegetables in butter—no water—and they will be perfectly tender and brightly colored.

Frozen vegetables may also be cooked in the oven. Put the children's vegetables in one small casserole and the adults' in another. Sprinkle with salt and pepper and dot with butter. You may want to add a little liquid, but never add more than 2 tablespoons per casserole. Cover tightly and place in the oven. Remove the adults' casserole when the vegetables are just beginning to be tender. Return them to the oven about 10 minutes before their meal. If the children's vegetables are tender before the main dish is finished, remove them, to be reheated in the oven just before serving time. Don't overcook. I can't give you any definite times for this procedure, because it varies from vegetable to vegetable and depends on the temperature of the oven. Generally, count on 30–40 minutes at 350° F. and 50–60 minutes at 325° F.

SAUCED VEGETABLES

Sauces make reheating vegetables a cinch. Furthermore, they are one way of taking vegetables out of the "duty" class. But don't overdo it. One sauce or gravy per meal is a good rule. More than that means a messy plate and too little variety in texture.

The French or wire whisk is a great aid to the sauce maker. If you have any trouble with lumpy gravies or sauces, buy a whisk. Formerly available only in gourmet shops, they are now being manufactured in the United States and are becoming available in large housewares departments throughout the country. If you have the storage space, you may want to own 3. The tiny one is useful for mixing flour and water or vinegar and oil—anything that can be mixed in a cup. The medium-size one goes to work on sauces and puddings—anything that is cooked in a small saucepan. The largest one is handy for stirring up the holiday gravy.

PREPARED SAUCES

We've all been using canned or packaged cream of mushroom and cream of celery soup as a sauce for ages. And who could cook without tomato sauce? Now, however, there is such an abundance of sauces and sauce mixes available on the grocery shelves that there is no excuse for not having interestingly sauced vegetables anytime you want them.

To be honest, I seldom used canned and packaged sauce mixes and gravies because I prefer to make my own. Besides, I'm something of a miser and prepared sauces are more expensive than the ones you make yourself. However, prepared sauces and gravies are wonderful for two reasons. They offer variety and save you time. Both of these can be very important. So keep your eyes open for new sauces and new ideas and keep a few prepared sauces and gravies handy for those "hurry-up days."

CREAMED VEGETABLES

Although you can buy prepared white sauce, it is one of the easiest and most basic sauces there is. Now with the advent of instant-type flour, it is even easier. Following are recipes for vegetables in old-fashioned white sauce and one for vegetables in white sauce made with instant-type flour:

CREAMED VEGETABLES OLD STYLE

2 tablespoons butter or margarine
2 tablespoons flour
1 cup liquid (milk, cream, cooking liquid, broth or a combination)

2–3 cups cooked vegetables
Salt
Pepper

Melt butter in a heavy saucepan and stir in the flour. Allow to bubble for a few seconds. Remove from the heat and stir in the liquid with a wire whisk. Return to the heat until the sauce comes to a boil and thickens. Add the vegetables and seasoning.

"INSTANT" CREAMED VEGETABLES

2–3 cups vegetables cooked in ¾ cup water, or 2–3 cups canned vegetables, heated in liquid
½ cup milk

2 tablespoons instant-type flour
Salt
Pepper

When the vegetables are tender, check to see that there is about ½ cup liquid left in the saucepan with the vegetables. Stir the flour into the milk and then stir into the vegetables and liquid. Allow to bubble for a minute or two and taste for seasoning. If the sauce is too thick, add a little more milk.

To vary: Add 2–3 tablespoons chopped onion, green pepper, or a combination of the 2 to the butter and sauté for 2–3 minutes before adding the flour. If you are using instant-type flour, add the onion or green pepper to the vegetables during the last 3 minutes of cooking. Add butter if desired.

Add 1 chopped pimiento to the sauce.

Add ¼ to ¾ cup cubed or shredded American or Cheddar cheese or grated Swiss or Parmesan cheese to the sauce.

Enrich old-fashioned white sauce with a beaten egg yolk. Be careful to beat the egg well with a little milk or water. Add a little of the hot sauce to the egg to warm it before adding the egg to the rest of the sauce.

Add a teaspoon of curry powder to the flour.

Add ¼ cup chopped blanched almonds to the butter in old-fashioned sauce and stir until lightly browned before adding the flour.

Substitute onion or celery salt for regular salt.

To serve and hold: Actually, making white sauce with instant-type flour is so easy that you may prefer to cook the children's and adults'

[*136*]

vegetables separately. However, if you want to cook all 4 portions at once you may cool and refrigerate the adults' portion to be reheated gently on top of the stove or in a double boiler just before the later meal. Or, you can put the adults' portion in a casserole, sprinkle with buttered crumbs or cheese and refrigerate to be baked 15 to 20 minutes until the sauce bubbles and the topping is browned.

COLD VEGETABLES

Cold vegetables are served frequently in Europe—such a pleasant addition to most menus and a great convenience to the woman who is planning meals for two sittings.

VEGETABLES VINAIGRETTE

¼ cup vegetable or olive oil
2 tablespoons wine, tarragon, or cider vinegar
½ teaspoon sugar

½ teaspoon dry mustard
½ teaspoon salt
Few drops red hot pepper sauce
About 2 cups cooked vegetables

Mix all of the ingredients except the vegetables together, shaking or stirring vigorously. Pour the dressing over the vegetables and refrigerate for 1 or more hours. Serve the children and continue to refrigerate the adults' portions until just before their dinner.

Do not use leafy vegetables. Do use any, or any combination, of the following: celery, summer squash, all types of beans, broccoli, Brussels sprouts, peas, carrots, asparagus, beets, okra, artichokes, onions.

ARTICHOKES

Fresh Artichokes. Allow 1, average size, per person. Wash thoroughly, running water right down among the petals to remove any grit. Cut stem off even with the bottom, snip off the prickly points of the petals with scissors, and remove any discolored petals. Put in a saucepan with about 2 inches boiling water. Add 2 tablespoons lemon juice or vinegar. Cover and simmer until an outer leaf pulls off easily—about ½ hour. Drain upside down. Remove the choke, if you like. Serve hot with individual dishes of melted butter, or refrigerate and serve cold with vinaigrette sauce or mayonnaise thinned with lemon juice.

Eating artichokes is an art. You tear off a leaf, dip the bottom in butter or sauce, hold on to the tip and put the dipped end in your mouth, scraping it against your teeth as you pull it out. The succulent pulp that sticks to your teeth is all that you eat. When you have eaten the pulp from all of the petals, you come to the choke, a fibrous, prickly center substance which must be removed with a knife. Below this is the artichoke heart, which is delicious and well worth working to get.

Canned Artichoke Hearts may be drained and sautéed in butter until delicately brown and sprinkled with salt and pepper, or they may be tossed in vinaigrette sauce and chilled to serve alone or as part of a salad.

Frozen Artichokes and Artichoke Hearts should be prepared according to package directions.

To vary: Combine artichoke hearts with cooked peas or sautéed mushrooms for a bit of elegance.

ASPARAGUS

Fresh Asparagus. Buy 2 pounds for 4 generous servings. Select fresh-looking spears with very tight green tips. Try to have all the spears approximately the same size. Wash each one carefully and cut off the lower scales to dislodge any grit. Snap off the "woody" white lower part of the stalk. The important thing about cooking asparagus is to get the stalks done without overcooking the tips. To do this I tear off a piece of foil about 8 inches wide and crumple it to make a long narrow "pillow" to fit one side of my large covered skillet. Then I lay the asparagus spears in the pan with the tips resting on the "pillow." I pour boiling water into the skillet to cover the stalks but not the tips, add 1 teaspoon salt, cover, and simmer until tender, about 15 minutes. Then I lift the spears out, drain, and place them on a plate or in a shallow bowl. A pancake turner or kitchen tongs makes this easier. If you use tongs, be sure to grasp the ends of the asparagus rather than the tips.

If you are going to serve immediately, just spread butter over the asparagus and add a little freshly ground pepper.

Cold asparagus, which is also delicious, is practical for serving at a later meal. Refrigerate and serve plain or with vinaigrette sauce, hollandaise sauce, or with mayonnaise mixed with lemon juice.

If, however, you insist on hot asparagus and do not wish to cook it separately at the later meal, remove it before it is quite tender—cook about 12 minutes—and lay it in an ovenproof pan or dish. Spread with butter, cool, and cover, to be baked about 10 minutes in a 350° F. oven.

For creamed asparagus, break the spears into 2-inch pieces. Put the stalks in a saucepan with water to cover. Simmer 10 minutes and add the tips. Continue to simmer until tender. Drain. Serve in a cream sauce or a cheese sauce, or put creamed asparagus in baking dishes. Sprinkle with buttered crumbs or grated cheese and bake 15 minutes in a 350° F. oven.

Canned Asparagus is a poor substitute for the appearance and flavor of fresh, but it is a good nutritive buy. If well chilled, canned asparagus in a nice addition to a salad plate. It can also be doctored up with a cream sauce. It comes bleached white or green. While Europeans insist on the white, Americans find the green more like the fresh.

Frozen Asparagus should be cooked according to package directions and served as you would serve fresh asparagus.

Fresh Beans. One pound serves 4. Select small, young beans with bright color and smooth skins and an audible "snap" when you break them. Wash well. Thanks to science, the strings in string beans seem to have disappeared. However, just to be sure, break off the ends and pull down toward the spine of the bean. If there is a string, it should come off with the end. If you do 3 or 4 beans this way and find no strings, break or cut off the rest of the ends. If the beans are small, leave them whole. If they are larger, cut or break them in pieces of the same size. You can use your knife to vary beans. Dice them, cut them French style, sliver them or split them lengthwise for a change.

Put beans in a saucepan that will hold them snugly, and pour about 1/2 inch boiling water and 1/2 teaspoon salt on them. Cook, covered, for about 12 minutes, until they are tender but not limp. Drain, if necessary. Season and serve.

Or, you can cook them in a pressure cooker for 2 minutes at full pressure. Reduce the pressure by putting the cooker under cold water.

If you have the patience to cut your beans French style reduce the cooking time.

Beans are best served as soon as they are cooked, but you may, if necessary, reheat them in butter over low heat.

Canned Beans. Reduce the liquid before heating.

Frozen Beans. Cook according to package directions. For a special treat, try the small whole beans.

To serve: Add butter, salt, and freshly ground pepper.
To vary: Cut 4 slices of bacon into small pieces and fry in a small skillet until the bacon is crisp. Pour the bacon and some fat over the cooked beans and toss with a fork.

Add a little sweet or sour cream and a dash of sugar.

Serve in a cream, celery, onion, or cheese sauce.

Sauté slivered almonds in butter and toss with the beans.

Sprinkle thyme or dill on the beans with the butter.

Combine several different kinds of beans—green beans with wax, lima, and/or kidney beans.

Combine with small white onions, corn, or mushrooms.

Chill in a vinaigrette sauce.

BEAN CASSEROLE

2 packages frozen cross-cut green
   beans
1 can condensed cream of
   mushroom soup

3-ounce can French-fried onion
   rings

Cook beans according to package directions. Drain well. Stir in soup and pour into 2 buttered casseroles. Put half of the onion rings on one casserole and bake 10–15 minutes in a 350° F. oven. Refrigerate the other casserole. Bake 10 minutes in a 350° F. oven, then add the onion rings and bake another 10 minutes.

3-BEAN SALAD

1 package frozen green beans,
   cooked, or 1-pound can, drained
1 package frozen wax beans,
   cooked, or 8-ounce can, drained
8-ounce can kidney beans, drained
2 tablespoons minced green onion

2 tablespoons minced green
   pepper
Vinaigrette sauce with 1
   tablespoon of sugar and lots
   of freshly ground pepper

Combine the above ingredients and chill for several hours or overnight, stirring occasionally. Drain and serve plain or on lettuce. Chick peas and lima beans may also be added.

LIMA BEANS

Fresh Limas. Buy 1 pound limas without shells, or 1½–2 pounds with shells, for 4 servings. Wash and cook 15–20 minutes in a tightly covered pan with boiling salted water 1 inch deep.

Canned Limas. Reduce the liquid before heating.

Frozen Limas. Cook according to package directions.

Dried Limas. See section on Dried Beans.

To serve: Add butter, salt, and pepper.
To vary: Stir in a little heavy cream or sour cream or serve in cream, onion, celery, or cheese sauce.

Sprinkle with chopped parsley or chives.

Add a can of tomato or tomato-mushroom sauce.

Combine with corn to make succotash.

Combine cooked limas with sliced cucumbers and scallions. Add ¼ cup vinegar, salt, and pepper. Cover and chill.

Serve cold with vinaigrette sauce.

FROZEN LIMAS AND TOMATOES

1 package frozen lima beans
8-ounce can stewed tomatoes
½ cup water

1 teaspoon sugar
1 teaspoon onion salt

Combine all of the above ingredients and cook according to package directions. If there is liquid left in the pan when the beans are tender, remove the cover and boil down quickly.

DRIED BEANS

Dried beans are so inexpensive that we sometimes forget how good they are. There are several recipes in this book in which dried beans are combined with meats to make main dishes. See pages 5, 6, and 53.

Since the beans more than double in bulk during the cooking process, 1 cup will serve 4 people as a side dish. You may, however, wish to cook more while you are at it, for a second meal later in the week.

Wash the beans, discarding any discolored ones. Put in a saucepan and cover with water. Boil 2 minutes and remove from the heat. Let stand an hour or more. This eliminates the soaking-overnight process.

Then add 1 teaspoon salt and bring to a boil again and simmer for 1–3 hours, depending on the type of bean. Add more water from time to time. Season with salt, pepper, and butter—or include in one of the following dishes:

WESTERN BEANS

4 slices bacon, cut in small pieces
1 clove garlic, chopped
1 onion, chopped
8-ounce can tomatoes
½ teaspoon dried marjoram

1 teaspoon chili powder
1 teaspoon salt
2 cups cooked dried white beans, drained

Fry bacon in a large skillet. Remove the bacon and drain. Add the garlic and onion and sauté briefly until the onion is limp. Pour off about half of the fat. Stir in the rest of the ingredients and the bacon and simmer 10 minutes. The liquid should have disappeared but the beans should be moist. To reheat, add more liquid and simmer over a low heat.

BAKED BEANS

Carrot and Celery Sticks and Assorted Pickles
Canned Boston Brown Bread
*Apple Crisp with Ice Cream**

Since baked beans are rich in protein they may be used as a substitute for meat.

OLD-FASHIONED BAKED BEANS

1 pound dried white beans
Water
Small piece salt pork, cubed
1 large onion, thinly sliced

½ cup dark molasses
2 tablespoons catsup
½ teaspoon dry mustard

Put beans in a large saucepan and cover with water. Boil 2 minutes and remove from the heat. Let stand 1 hour, then simmer for 1½ hours, adding more water if necessary. Put beans and remaining ingredients in a beanpot, Dutch oven, or heavy casserole. Cover tightly and bake 4 hours at 300° F., uncover, and bake another 2 hours. Add water as needed. Reheat in the oven or in the top of a double boiler.

1-pound can pork and beans
1 small onion, minced
1 tablespoon dark molasses

2 tablespoons brown sugar
½ teaspoon dry mustard

Combine the above ingredients in a beanpot or casserole. Bake, covered, in 350° F. oven 30 minutes or longer. Serve the children and reheat for the adults.

BEETS

Beets are beautiful! Furthermore, children like them and they are one of the few really delicious *canned* vegetables.

Fresh Beets. One–1½ pounds serves 4. Buy only fresh-looking, small- to medium-size beets. Wash thoroughly. If the beets are tiny—marble-size —cook them with their greens in just enough salted water to keep the pan from burning. When tender, drain, if necessary. Cut the greens with scissors. Add salt, pepper, and butter to taste. If the beets are larger, cut off all but 1 inch of the tops and discard. Leave the roots on. Cover with boiling water and simmer 30–60 minutes or cook in a pressure cooker with 1 cup water for 15–25 minutes. When tender, drain and drop in cold water for just a minute. The skins will slip off in your fingers. Leave whole or cut in quarters or slices. Reheat in butter.

Canned Beets come in a variety of conditions—whole, sliced, diced, or julienne. Boil down the liquid and heat in the liquid.

To serve: Add butter, salt, and pepper.
To vary: Add sour cream.
   Add orange, lemon, or grapefruit juice.
   Serve in cream sauce with 1–3 tablespoons prepared horseradish added.
   Serve cold with a dressing made of ½ teaspoon dry mustard, ½ teaspoon salt, 2 tablespoons vinegar, and ⅓ cup oil.
   Serve in an orange sauce made by combining butter and orange marmalade.

1-pound can sliced beets or cooked
  fresh beets
½ cup beet liquid
½ cup cider vinegar

1 stick cinnamon
6 cloves
1 tablespoon sugar
¼ teaspoon salt

Drain the beets and add the ½ cup liquid to the other ingredients. Bring to the boiling point and pour over the beets. Cover and refrigerate at least 5 hours, stirring from time to time. Drain well before serving.

My husband's mother, who is Pennsylvania Dutch, saves the pickle juice and pours it over peeled hard-boiled eggs in a jar. After the eggs have soaked long enough to pick up the red color, they may be served as part of a salad, a snack, or with spinach. They're pretty.

BROCCOLI

Fresh Broccoli is a very good source of both vitamins A and C. Buy 2 pounds for 4 or 5 servings. Select crisp, short, bright green stalks with tightly closed buds. If the buds are beginning to turn yellow, the broccoli is past its peak. Soak in cold, salted water for about 15 minutes. The soaking draws out any little bugs that may be hiding among the leaves. Cut off the tough part of the stalks and any leaves that are withering. Split the stalks lengthwise for several inches so that they will cook more quickly. If especially large, cut into individual portions. Lay in a saucepan. Pour in 1 inch of boiling water. Cover tightly and simmer until the stalks are tender, about 12 minutes. Do not overcook.

Frozen Broccoli should be cooked according to package directions; be careful not to overcook.

To serve: Add butter, salt, and pepper.
To vary: Serve in cream or cheese sauce.
  Chop broccoli and add to a cream or cheese sauce, top with crumbs and bake until crumbs brown.
  Dress with hollandaise sauce.
  Season with marjoram or basil.
  Serve cold with favorite salad dressing.

CRUNCHY BROCCOLI I

1 package frozen chopped broccoli
¾ cup chicken broth
1 onion, chopped

4 tablespoons butter
1 cup prepared stuffing mix or
    seasoned croutons

Boil broccoli in broth for 3 minutes. Pour into 2 baking pans or individual casseroles. Sauté the onion in the butter. Add the stuffing mix and toss together. Put the stuffing mixture on top of the broccoli mixture and bake in a 350° F. oven for 20 minutes, or refrigerate and then bake 25 minutes. This will make 4 *small* servings.

CRUNCHY BROCCOLI II

1 package frozen broccoli spears
Water
2 tablespoons butter

3 tablespoons dry bread crumbs
3 tablespoons Parmesan cheese

Cook frozen broccoli spears in a small amount of boiling water for 5 minutes. Drain and place in buttered baking dishes. Melt butter and stir in crumbs and cheese. Sprinkle over the broccoli. Bake 15 minutes in a 350° F. oven, or refrigerate and bake.

BRUSSELS SPROUTS

Fresh Brussels Sprouts are rich in vitamin C; they supply some vitamin A, but not as much as broccoli. One pound serves 4. Buy tight little sprouts that have no brown spots on them. Remove the wilted leaves and cut off any protruding stems. Cut crosswise slits in the stem ends of large sprouts so that they will cook more quickly. Large sprouts may also be cut in half. Soak 15 minutes in cold salted water. Drain and simmer, covered, in boiling salted water until the sprouts are tender, about 10 minutes.

Frozen Brussels Sprouts should be cooked according to package directions.

To serve: Add butter, salt, and pepper.
To vary:
    Add sautéed mushrooms.
    Add green onions, chopped and sautéed in butter.
    Add 4 slices fried bacon, crumbled, with bacon fat.

[*146*]

Serve in a cream sauce.

Add cream sauce to the sprouts, top with crumbs, and bake.

Sprinkle with buttered crumbs and bake until crumbs are brown.

Add vinaigrette sauce and chill.

Cook with sliced celery. Add a white sauce.

Top with grated cheese and bake.

CABBAGE

Cabbage is rich in vitamin C, inexpensive, available the year round, versatile, and delicious. Years ago, people cooked cabbage for hours until the house was filled with an unpleasant odor and the vegetable was a soggy mass. Cook it only until it is crisp-tender, and it will be entirely different; the air will be pleasant, too.

There are several types of cabbage. They come in assorted sizes, sold by the pound. Try new green heads, solid white heads, the crinkly savoy type, Chinese cabbage, and red cabbage. Buy heads that are relatively heavy for their size. For cooked cabbage, allow about 2 pounds, or 1 small head or ½ larger head, for 4 servings. If you are serving the cabbage raw, you will need slightly less.

Remove the coarse or spotted outside leaves and wash the head. Then it may be cut in wedges or shredded. To shred, cut the cabbage in half and lay the cut side flat on a cutting board. With a long, thin, very sharp knife, cut in fine slices. You may also grind it in the food chopper or blender.

Cabbage Salad or Cole Slaw is particularly popular and is a wonderful dish for the cook-now-serve-later meal. Every cook has her own method of preparing slaw—which is probably the same one her mother used. Some used boiled dressing; others use mayonnaise; I prefer sour cream. This is the way I make slaw: I shred the cabbage. Then I add salt, pepper, vinegar, and sugar to taste. I add sour cream to lightly moisten the cabbage. I like to refrigerate slaw for at least 1 hour to mellow it.

To vary slaw, add any of the following:

Chopped onion, cucumber, and/or green pepper

Grated carrot or turnip

Sophia's Dressing*

Finely sliced olives

Chopped apple—leave the skin on to add color

Pineapple chunks

A combination of chopped apple, pineapple chunks, chopped dates, and a few walnuts

Fresh salted peanuts

Canned kidney beans, drained; diced celery, green pepper, and onion; chopped salted peanuts; and mayonnaise

Chopped pimiento and parsley

Chopped water cress

Crisp crumbled bacon

Capers and dried basil

Pickled beets

Chopped raw cranberries

Pickle relish

Curry powder, powdered ginger, and mayonnaise

Lemon juice and diced banana

Fresh or dried dill

Caraway or poppy seed

Cooked Fresh Cabbage is best if it is served immediately, unless it is sauced. However, the cooking time is short. Put the cabbage in a small amount of boiling water, cover tightly, and cook 7 minutes if shredded —about 15 minutes if quartered.

To serve: Add butter, salt, and pepper and serve immediately.

To vary: Add a cream or cheese sauce.

Add a cheese sauce, top with shredded or sliced cheese and bake about 15 minutes in a 350° F. oven or refrigerate and bake. This is a favorite in my family.

Add a sauce made by frying 4 slices of bacon diced. Remove the bacon and sauté 1 small minced onion in the bacon fat. Add 8-ounce can tomato sauce and 2 tablespoons brown sugar. Pour over the cooked cabbage. Add the reserved bacon and toss lightly. This may be reheated in the top of a double boiler or in a baking dish in the oven.

Cook cabbage and celery together. Serve in a cream sauce with 1 tablespoon minced pimiento and ⅓ cup chopped peanuts.

Cook cabbage in ½ cup white wine, ½ cup chicken broth, and 1 tablespoon vinegar. Add butter, minced onion, and dill.

Sauerkraut is generally marketed cooked or uncooked in plastic bags and cans. To make it milder, cook it with a potato. I am particularly fond of the recipe below:

1-pound can sauerkraut   1 tablespoon oil
⅓ cup chopped carrot   1 chicken bouillon cube
⅓ cup chopped onion   ½ cup water

Drain sauerkraut, squeezing out as much liquid as possible. Brown carrots and onions lightly in oil. Add bouillon cube dissolved in water and sauerkraut. Divide into 2 casseroles, cover and bake both in 350° F. oven for 30 minutes. Serve the children. The adults' casserole may be left in the oven turned to its lowest temperature, or may be taken out of the oven to be reheated 15 minutes before serving time.

If you are not using your oven for other parts of the meal, you may cook the sauerkraut—just at the simmering point—on top of the stove. *To vary:* Add sliced potatoes to the sauerkraut dish. Or add a grated red apple and caraway seed.

CARROTS

Carrots are certainly among the most maligned vegetables God made. Why, I don't know. They are pretty, can be served in such a variety of ways, are packed with vitamins, and are inexpensive. Furthermore, they can be reheated with ease. In fact, you really can't ruin a carrot unless you burn it.

Fresh Carrots should have a permanent home in your vegetable crisper. One pound serves 4. Scrub. Don't peel unless they are very old or you want to be very fancy. There are vitamins in those peels. Serve them whole, sliced crosswise, or lengthwise, cubed, or slivered. Serve raw for crunch and color with any dinner. Raw, they are also a wonderful appetite appeaser when you have a starving child underfoot as you are preparing dinner.

Cook in a little boiling salted water until tender, 10–20 minutes, depending on their age and how you have cut them.

Frozen and Canned Carrots are available in a wide assortment of cuts. I seldom use them because fresh carrots are less expensive. However, the little fat baby carrots are wonderfully attractive party fare, and you can't buy them fresh.

To serve: Add butter, salt, and pepper.

To vary: Add a sprinkling of minced parsley or dried orégano. Orégano is one of my favorites. Try it.

Add a cream sauce.

Combine with celery or peas.

Add either cooked or raw carrots to vegetable salads.

Cool in a vinaigrette sauce.

Sprinkle with brown sugar or add maple syrup or honey.

Cook with 1 cup golden raisins. Drain and sprinkle with brown sugar, butter, and lemon juice.

Roll cooked whole carrots in butter and dry cereal crumbs. Bake until lightly browned.

Drain tiny canned or cooked carrots and chill in garlic dressing with chopped onion.

Grate raw carrots. Add seedless raisins and mayonnaise for a relish salad that delights children. You can even use it as a sandwich spread.

CARROTS DIABLE

About 6 carrots, cut in halves
   lengthwise and then in quarters
   or sixths
½ cup water
4 tablespoons butter
4 tablespoons brown sugar
2 teaspoons dry mustard
Few drops hot pepper sauce
½ teaspoon salt
Few grinds pepper

Put the carrots in a saucepan and pour boiling water over them. Cover and cook 10 minutes. Drain immediately. (Save the cooking water in a jar in the refrigerator to be added to soup or gravy). Add the rest of the ingredients to the saucepan, cover tightly, and cook over very low heat for another 10 minutes until the carrots are tender. Shake the pan frequently. The carrots may be reheated in the same sauce.

You may want to use just a little mustard and a hint of pepper sauce in the children's dish. If so, add more of each when you reheat the adults' portion.

If you are planning to use the oven for something else, cook the carrots for 10 minutes, drain immediately, and divide between 2 small well-greased covered casseroles. (Use the 3-cup size or use au gratin dishes, which you will cover tightly with foil.) Divide the rest of the ingredients among the 2 casseroles. Cover and shake. Refrigerate the adults' casserole and bake the children's, adjusting the time and temperature to fit whatever else is in the oven.

CARROT MÉLANGE

4 slices bacon, cut in 1-inch pieces	1-pound can tomatoes
¼ cup chopped onion	1 teaspoon salt
¼ cup chopped green pepper	3 turns of pepper mill
½ cup sliced celery	¼ teaspoon orégano
1½ cups sliced carrots	1 teaspoon brown sugar

Fry the bacon until crisp in a saucepan. Drain on a piece of paper towel. Sauté the onion and the pepper in the bacon fat. Pour off the fat and add all of the other ingredients, with the exception of the bacon pieces. Simmer, covered, over a low heat for 15–20 minutes until the carrots are tender. If the mixture is too runny, boil the liquid down quickly with the lid off. If it is too dry, add water, tomato juice, or broth. Add the bacon pieces. The mélange is now ready to serve. It may be reheated on the top of the stove or in an ovenproof serving dish in the oven.

CAULIFLOWER

Cauliflower, which is one of my favorite vegetables, is also one of the least attractive from the point of view of this cookbook. It simply does not reheat well. So, if you don't have time to cook it at the last moment before the later dinner hour, save it for a time when the whole family will be eating together or serve it raw.

Fresh Cauliflower comes in all sizes. For a family of 4, select one that weighs about 2 pounds. It should be white with no dark spots. Cut off the leaves and the stalk. Wash well and leave whole or separate into flowerettes. If you are leaving it whole, pierce the stem end with a knife so that it will cook more evenly. Cook covered in a small amount of boiling salted water. Flowerettes will be tender in 10–15 minutes—a whole head in 20–25 minutes.

Raw Flowerettes are delicious in a mixed salad. Slice, if large.

Frozen Cauliflower is a poor substitute for fresh. However, freezing methods may improve, so it's worth trying the frozen vegetable from time to time.

To serve: Add butter, salt, and pepper.
To vary: Surround the whole cauliflower with creamed peas or combine flowerettes and peas in cream sauce.

Combine with mushrooms in cream sauce.

Serve in a cheese sauce.

Sprinkle the cooked cauliflower with browned buttered bread crumbs or sesame seeds.

Combine flowerettes with Brussels sprouts.

Serve cold in vinaigrette sauce.

CELERY

Raw celery is almost always good. Cooked celery can be either awful or elegant, depending on how it is prepared. If you don't believe that it can be elegant, try the recipe for braised celery.

Raw Celery is so popular that it hardly needs mentioning. However, it may be glamorized by stuffing with sour cream, crunchy peanut butter, cottage cheese, or a cheese spread. Blue cheese is particularly tasty.

Fresh Celery. Two cups thinly sliced celery will serve 4. Wash and remove the strings. Slice any way you like, thinly or in 1 to 3 inch pieces. Cook covered in a small amount of boiling water for 8 minutes or until tender.
To serve: Add butter, salt, and pepper.
To vary: Add a cream, cheese, or tomato sauce.

Combine with peas, mushrooms, green beans, or carrots—with or without a cream sauce.

Season with curry powder, dill, or nutmeg.

Chill in vinaigrette sauce.

BRAISED CELERY

Celery
2 tablespoons butter
½ cup chicken or beef broth
½ teaspoon salt
1 teaspoon sugar

Cut celery stalks in 3- or 4-inch lengths or remove the leaves and quarter celery hearts. Brown lightly in butter in a skillet or flameproof baking dish. Add the other ingredients and bring to a boil. Cover and simmer until the celery is tender—about 15 minutes. Or bake, covered, in a slow or moderate oven until tender.

[*152*]

4 cups 1-inch pieces celery
1 cup water
5-ounce can water chestnuts,
  drained and sliced
¼ cup chopped pimiento

1 can condensed cream of chicken
  soup
¼ cup dry bread crumbs
2 tablespoons melted butter

Put celery and water in a saucepan. Cover and simmer 10 minutes or until cooked but still crisp. Drain off any liquid. Stir water chestnuts, pimiento, and soup into the celery. Pour into 2 casseroles. Combine bread crumbs and butter and sprinkle over the vegetables. Refrigerate one casserole and bake the other in a 350° F. oven for 35 minutes. Forty minutes before the adults' meal, remove their casserole from the refrigerator and bake as the children's casserole was baked.

CORN

Thank the Indians for introducing corn! It is an especially convenient vegetable for the cook-now-serve-later mother, since fresh corn cooks very quickly and frozen and canned corn are both delicious.

Fresh Corn is best just after it is picked. Unfortunately, unless you live near a farm where corn is grown and sold, it is difficult to buy really fresh. Nevertheless, look for corn that looks moist and juicy with kernels that are soft—pierce with your fingernail to be sure. Keep refrigerated with the husks on until cooking time.

To cook shucked corn on the cob, put enough water in a kettle to cover the corn, bring to a boil, and add the ears, one at a time, so that the water never stops boiling. Cook 5 minutes. Lift out with tongs and serve with salt, pepper, and butter.

To cook fresh corn kernels, cut the corn from the cob with a sharp knife. Scrape the cob with the back of the knife to get out any "milk." Put in a pan with butter, salt, and pepper and a small amount of milk or cream. Cover tightly and simmer until the corn is tender—about 5 minutes.

Canned Corn comes in a wide variety. I particularly like the vacuum-packed whole-kernel corn. And do try the white shoe peg corn.

Frozen Corn is also most satisfactory.

To serve: Add butter, salt, and pepper.
To vary: Bake cooked or canned corn kernels in a cream sauce with crumbs on top.

Combine with lima beans (succotash), green beans, peas, okra, tomatoes, or mushrooms.

Combine corn and green beans and top with sautéed onion and green pepper rings or chopped pimiento.

Add cold to salads.

Cream and use to stuff green peppers.

Season with chopped green pepper, tomato, onion, and/or pimiento.

Season with leaf sage or marjoram.

CORN DANDY

4 slices bacon, halved	1-pound can cream-style corn
¾ cup chopped onions	½ teaspoon salt
1 egg	Few grinds pepper
½ cup undiluted evaporated milk	1 pimiento, chopped

Fry bacon until crisp and drain on a paper towel. Fry onion in bacon fat until golden. In the meantime, beat the egg with a wire whisk and beat in the evaporated milk. Add the corn, salt, pepper, and pimiento. Crumble and add 4 of the bacon halves. Remove the onions with a slotted spoon and add to the corn mixture. Mix well and pour into 2 well-greased shallow casseroles. Bake each casserole in a 350° F. oven for 30 minutes before serving. During the last 5 minutes of baking, arrange 2 bacon halves on the top of each casserole.

EGGPLANT

One and a half pounds of eggplant serves 4. Buy small ones with perfectly smooth skins. Eggplant is usually fried, baked, or broiled. It need not be peeled.

Frying is a last minute sort of thing and is therefore not useful for this book.

To bake or broil, marinate in French dressing for at least 15 minutes. Drain and place on a baking pan. Bake in a 400° F. oven for about 15 minutes, turning once. Or, place under the broiler. Turn when brown and continue to broil until tender—about 10 minutes.

Or, you may dip the eggplant in seasoned flour or fine dry bread crumbs. Dot liberally with butter and place under the broiler. Broil slowly. When browned on one side, turn, dot with more butter and return to the broiler until tender. Baked or broiled slices may be topped with cheese, grilled tomato slices, creamed vegetables, or chopped parsley.

SCALLOPED EGGPLANT

1 medium-size eggplant
1 small onion, sliced
½ cup boiling water

¼ cup butter
¼ cup dry bread crumbs

Peel eggplant and cut in ½–1-inch cubes. Put the eggplant, onion, and water in a saucepan. Cover and simmer until tender, about 15 minutes. Drain well and place in 2 baking dishes. Melt butter and add crumbs. Sprinkle over the eggplant. Bake, or refrigerate and then bake, in a 350° F. oven for about 15 minutes.

RATATOUILLE

¼ cup oil
1 medium-size onion, chopped
1 clove garlic, minced
1¼ pound eggplant, peeled and
    cut in cubes
2 medium-size zucchini, sliced but
    not peeled

1 large or 2 small green peppers,
    cut in strips
½ teaspoon dried basil
1 teaspoon salt
1-pound can solid pack tomatoes

In a large saucepan, heat the oil and sauté the onion and garlic until limp. Add the rest of the ingredients and simmer until tender. Watch carefully to prevent burning. If you have too much liquid when the vegetables are tender, remove the cover and boil down rapidly. Serve the children and reheat for the adults. Or refrigerate and serve cold.

This is the perfect cook-now-serve-later dish. It can easily be reheated and it is delicious cold.

ENDIVE

Endive is very elegant—and, unfortunately, very expensive, since it is usually imported from Belgium. Use as a salad green either alone or in combination with other greens, or braised.

To braise, buy 4–8 heads endive. Wash well under running water. Leave heads whole unless they are very large, in which case they may be sliced in half, lengthwise. Brown lightly in a little butter in a skillet. Add about ½ cup bouillon or broth. Season with salt and white pepper. Simmer, covered, until tender, about 10 minutes. Reheat in additional broth if needed.

CUCUMBERS

One seldom thinks of cucumbers as a cooked vegetable. However, cooking vegetables we usually serve raw is one way of adding variety to our dinners. Select small, firm, glossy dark cucumbers. If they feel soft or have yellow spots on them, they are too old to be good.

Cooked Cucumbers. Cut in thick rounds or short fat sticks and put in a saucepan with just enough water or chicken broth to keep from burning. Cover and simmer until tender, 5–15 minutes. Serve in a cream sauce. Or add a cream sauce, put in a baking pan with buttered crumbs on top, and bake until the crumbs are browned.

Raw Cucumbers are, of course, delicious in salads, as part of a cold vegetable platter or wilted. Don't peel unless the peel is waxed or especially thick or tough. To "fancy," run the tines of a fork lengthwise down the cucumbers before you slice them.

WILTED CUCUMBERS

About 2 cups sliced cucumbers
Salt, preferably the coarse kosher
    type
2 tablespoons vinegar
¼ cup oil (optional)

1 tablespoon sugar
Freshly ground black pepper
1 small onion, thinly sliced and
    divided into rings (optional)

Peel the cucumbers if necessary and slice very thinly. Put in a bowl that will not quite hold them. Sprinkle each layer with a little salt. Press down and put a saucer or plate on top. Weight the saucer with something heavy—an unopened can of soup is a good weight. Refrigerate for several hours or overnight. To serve, put the cucumbers in a sieve to drain well and return to the bowl. Add the rest of the ingredients. Refrigerate until serving time.

[*156*]

2 cucumbers
½ cup dry bread crumbs
1 tablespoon minced green onion
2 tablespoons grated Parmesan
  cheese

¼ cup melted butter
½ teaspoon salt
Few grinds pepper
½ cup chicken or beef broth

Cut cucumbers in half lengthwise and then in half crosswise—making a total of 8 pieces. Remove the seeds with the tip of a spoon. Mix together the crumbs, onion, cheese, butter, salt, and pepper. Use to fill the cucumbers and place in 2 baking dishes. Put half of the broth in each pan and bake each one 30 minutes in a 350° F. oven.

GREENS

Greens are delicious and may be used to add variety and vitamins to your menus. Try tender young beet tops, Swiss chard, dandelion greens, collard, chickory, kale, escarole, lettuce, mustard greens, spinach, and young turnip tops. All of these are delicious raw in salad. They may be used in combination for variety.

One to 1½ pounds serves 4. Wash well and then wash again to be sure that the leaves are completely free of all sand and grit. Throw away any discolored leaves and cut off the roots and tough stems. The water that clings to the leaves after washing may be enough to prevent scorching. If not, add a very little bit more. Salt and simmer, covered, until barely tender. Drain, if necessary, and chop fine or just cut through a few times. Or, greens may be shredded first then cooked in a matter of minutes.

Spinach is the green most readily available frozen or in cans. Be sure not to overcook. By the time frozen chopped spinach is completely thawed and the water returns to a boil, it is done. It may also be cooked in butter only—no water added.

To serve greens: Use raw in salads—see section on green salads.
Add butter, salt, and pepper to cooked greens.
To vary: Add a cream sauce. Nutmeg—just a dash—is a nice addition to the sauce.
Stir in a little sour cream.
Add cream sauce to chopped greens and put in baking dishes. Top with crumbs and bake until crumbs are browned.
Season buttered greens with vinegar or lemon juice.
Add some pickle relish.

Serve buttered greens with sliced hard-boiled egg or sautéed chopped onion or onion salt.

Serve with hot pepper sauce and sliced raw onion.

Cooked chopped lettuce is delicious with peas, particularly the tiny young ones.

Season with crisply fried bacon and bacon fat.

SPINACH CUSTARD

1 package frozen chopped spinach	Pinch sugar
1 small onion, finely chopped	Dash nutmeg
2 tablespoons butter	1/2 teaspoon salt
1 egg, slightly beaten	Few grinds pepper
1/2 cup milk	2 teaspoons vinegar

Cook the spinach and onion in the butter in a tightly covered saucepan. Add the rest of the ingredients and pour into 2 small baking dishes. Bake in a 350° F. oven until firm, about 20 minutes, or refrigerate and bake. This recipe really makes about 3 good portions. Double for a family of 4 good eaters.

Frozen chopped broccoli is equally good.

KOHLRABI

Eight small pale bulbs will serve 4. Wash well, cut off the tops, peel, and slice. Cook, uncovered, in boiling salted water until tender, about 30 minutes. If the tops are young and tender, chop and add during last 10 minutes of boiling. Drain. Season with butter, salt, and pepper or serve in a cream sauce.

LEEKS

Leeks, which look like huge green onions, are delicious. Buy 2 large ones for each person. Cut off most of the green part, wash very well, split in half lengthwise and braise. See the instructions for Endive*.

LENTILS

*Wilted Cucumbers, Carrot, Celery, and Green Pepper Strips
and Beet Pickles
Pumpernickle
Cream Puffs with Ice Cream and Chocolate Sauce*

Dried lentils are homely which may be why they are not popular. Poor things! Once you get past their muddy complexions, however, you'll find that they are good and especially rich in protein—so rich that you do not need to serve meat when you serve them. They are also inexpensive. Cook according to instructions in the Dried Bean section or use the following recipe which will remind you of Boston Baked Beans. If you want to serve meat with it, serve cold sliced lamb or grilled frankfurters.

LENTILS

¾ cup dried lentils	⅓ cup rice
Water	3 slices bacon
1 teaspoon salt	2 medium onions, chopped
Pepper	2 tablespoons brown sugar
1 can condensed tomato soup	½ teaspoon dry mustard

Pick over lentils and discard any bad-looking ones. Rinse thoroughly. Put in a saucepan with 2 cups water, salt, and pepper. Cover and cook until tender, about 30 minutes. Do not drain. Add the soup and rice, cover, and cook another 15 minutes, until the rice is tender. This has a tendency to stick so watch it, adding water if necessary. When the rice is done, the lentil-rice mixture should be the consistency of baked beans. If too thin, boil down quickly with the cover off, while stirring with a fork.

In the meantime, cut the bacon in squares and brown in a skillet. Remove the bacon with a slotted spoon and drain. Add the onions and sauté lightly. I like it better if the onions are a little crunchy. Then stir the onions, bacon, brown sugar, and mustard into the lentils.

You may reheat over low heat or in a casserole in the oven.

If you are serving no other meat with this dish, you might like to serve strips of bacon. Fry them when you fry the 3 slices called for, but be sure to pour off some of the fat before you brown the onions.

MUSHROOMS

There is something rather elegant about mushrooms. Combined with other vegetables or served alone, they are a nice addition to most menus. Furthermore, they are rich in vitamin C and low in calories.

Fresh Mushrooms. One pound serves 4. Select white, unblemished mushrooms of uniform size. On truly fresh mushrooms—which may be impossible to find—the underside of the cap will fit tightly around the top of the stem so that the black gills are completely hidden. As the mushrooms age, they expand, revealing more and more of the gills.

Unless they are very old and very dark, they do not need peeling. Just wipe them with a damp cloth. If peeling is necessary, lift the skin at the outside edge of the cap and pull off toward the crown. The mushrooms may be served whole, halved, quartered, or sliced lengthwise through the stem. If you wish to serve mushroom caps, cut the stems even with the bottom of the cap—do not pull out the whole stem. Save the rest of the stems, to be sliced or minced and served in another dish another day. Fresh mushrooms may be boiled, steamed, sautéed, or broiled.

To boil, put 1 pound of prepared mushrooms in a saucepan with 1 cup water, 1/2 teaspoon salt, 1 tablespoon lemon juice, and 3 tablespoons butter. Cover and boil over moderate heat for 5 minutes. They may be reheated in their own juice. Cooked this way, they will remain white.

To steam, put 1 pound mushrooms, 2 tablespoons of butter, 1/2 teaspoon salt, and 1/2 cup milk or water in the top of a double boiler. Cover. Cook over hot water for about 20 minutes. Reheat over hot water.

To sauté, heat 1 tablespoon oil and 2 tablespoons butter in a skillet. Add 1 pound mushrooms and shake the pan over moderate heat to coat the mushrooms with the butter. Continue to cook, shaking frequently for about 5 minutes, until the mushrooms are tender. Sautéed mushrooms may be reheated in their own juices.

To broil, select large mushroom caps. Brush well with butter and place cup side down in a baking pan. Broil about 2 minutes and turn over. Put a small lump of butter in each cap and broil another 2 minutes. These, of course, must be done at the last minute.

Canned Mushrooms are a great convenience and are one of those foods that you should always have on hand. However, canned mushrooms are better added to other vegetables than served alone.

Frozen Mushrooms are very expensive but good. Cook according to package directions.

To vary: Cook with garlic, shallots, or onions.

Fill large steamed mushroom caps with puréed peas, creamed spinach, or a combination of seasoned bread crumbs, cheese, and butter.

Serve in a cream or cheese sauce.

Combine mushrooms with almost any other vegetable or with rice or pasta.

Season with tarragon.

Slice raw mushrooms very thin. Pour oil and vinegar dressing over them and refrigerate an hour or more. Serve on greens for a special salad. These are especially good with water cress.

I particularly like to combine cooked small new potatoes (or quartered larger potatoes), small white onions, peas, and mushrooms in a white sauce. I put the mixture in casseroles, top with buttered crumbs or grated cheese and bake until hot and bubbly. This is one of my favorite company vegetables, because it can be prepared early in the afternoon, refrigerated, and baked without attention during the cocktail hour.

OKRA

Fresh Okra. One pound will serve 4. Select small crisp pods. Wash well. If small, leave whole, or cut in 1-inch slices. Put in a saucepan with a little boiling salted water. Simmer covered for 10 to 15 minutes or until tender. Drain. Or, you may fry sliced okra slowly in a little bacon or salt pork fat.

Frozen and Canned Okra are available. Cook according to package directions.

To serve: Add butter, salt, and pepper.
To vary: Cook okra with tomatoes—½ pound okra to a 1-pound can stewed tomatoes—or heat in tomato sauce.

Serve hot with vinaigrette sauce.

Cook whole kernel corn with fried okra.

Use cooked chilled whole okra pods as a salad either plain or marinated in garlic-flavored oil and vinegar dressing.

ONIONS

Onions, an important part of the diet of early Egyptians, are still a universally used vegetable and seasoning. Variety may be obtained by using different types of onions and preparing them in interesting ways.

Fresh Onions. One pound serves 4 or more. Buy onions without sprouts or blemishes and store in a cool, dry place. Tears are the sidekick of onions. You may try holding a piece of bread in your mouth while you peel and slice onions or you may try holding them under running water. I don't think anything eliminates tears. Therefore I just weep as I do the job as quickly as possible.

If you plan to cook the onions whole, be sure to pierce crossed slits in the stem ends with the point of a paring knife. This helps the onions cook quickly and evenly. If you are going to slice them, cut a flat surface so you can steady the onion on your cutting board as you slice. If you are going to chop them, cut the onions in half and put the cut surface flat on the board. A sharp knife is the most important utensil for chopping or slicing. In fact, it is about the most important utensil in your kitchen.

To boil, put peeled whole small white onions or thickly sliced yellow onions in a saucepan. Pour about 1 inch boiling water and ½ teaspoon salt on them. Cover and simmer until tender. The time will vary from about 15 minutes for sliced onions to 40 minutes for largish white onions. Drain. Reheat in sauce or butter.

To braise, put peeled whole white onions or whole green onions with part of the green and all of the roots cut off in a skillet. Brown lightly in 2 tablespoons butter and add ½ cup broth or bouillon, and ½ teaspoon salt. Cover and simmer until tender, about 40 minutes for white onions, 10 minutes for scallions. Add more broth if necessary. These may be reheated in their own liquid.

To sauté, melt 2 tablespoons butter and 1 tablespoon oil in a skillet. Add sliced or chopped onions and shake to coat well with the butter. Cook over low heat until lightly browned and tender. If they brown too quickly, cover and steam for a few minutes. Reheat in butter.

Raw Onions are delicious in salad. Use scallions, red onions, or Bermuda onions. To crisp for salad, put in a bowl with ice water, ice cubes, and salt. Soak for at least 30 minutes. Drain and add an oil and vinegar dressing.

Canned Whole Onions solve the problem of tears. They are also frequently less expensive than fresh white onions. And they are uniform in size. Try draining them—saving the liquid, of course—and browning them lightly in butter and oil. Canned onions may be substituted for boiled or braised onions in all recipes. French-fried onions in 3-ounce cans are also delicious and a great favorite of many children.

Frozen Onions. You can now buy frozen chopped onions, which also solves the tear problem. And you can buy frozen creamed onions and French-fried onion rings.

Onions for Seasoning. Dried onions, onion salt, and instant onions are all useful for adding onion flavor to other dishes.

To vary: Serve boiled onions with butter, salt, and pepper, or in a cream or tomato sauce.

Combine cooked onions with almost any other cooked vegetables —peas, potatoes, beans, mushrooms, limas, etc. Sautéed, chopped, or sliced onions are particularly useful in masking the "canned" taste of vegetables.

Serve raw sliced onions or "crisped" onions on greens with cooked beets, oranges, apples, raw cucumbers, tomatoes, or green pepper. Or, put circles of raw onion on top of a mixed vegetable salad.

Bake boiled onions in a cream or cheese sauce with crumb topping.

Serve braised green onions on toast with a cheese sauce.

Combine braised green onions with asparagus.

Glaze onions by baking cooked or canned whole onions in a mixture of 2 tablespoons butter, 2 tablespoons brown sugar, 1 tablespoon honey, and ½ teaspoon salt.

Use canned or heated frozen French-fried onions as a topping for casseroles or sprinkle on top of other buttered or creamed vegetables.

BAKED ONION

4 large yellow onions
2 bouillon cubes
1½ cups boiling water

2 tablespoons melted butter or
  margarine
¼ cup dry bread crumbs
Paprika

Peel and cut the onions in halves—through the "equator," not through the stem ends. Place cut side down in a single layer in a skillet with a cover. Dissolve the bouillon cubes in the water and pour over the onions. Cover and simmer until the onions are just tender when pierced with a fork, about 20 minutes. If necessary, add more water. Place the onions cut side up in 2 greased shallow casseroles. In the meantime, stir the butter into the crumbs. Spoon the crumb mixture on top of the onions. Sprinkle with paprika. Put one casserole in 350° F. oven and bake 10–15 minutes. Refrigerate the other casserole to be baked 20 minutes in a 350° F. oven just before the adults' dinner.

HONEY ONIONS

2 or 3 large yellow onions
½ cup hot water
1 chicken bouillon cube
1 tablespoon butter or margarine

1 tablespoon honey
½ teaspoon salt
¼ teaspoon grated lemon peel
Few grinds pepper

Cut onions in half and arrange in small skillet or baking dish. Combine the rest of the ingredients and pour over the onions. Cover tightly and simmer on top of the stove or bake in a 325° F. oven until the onions are tender, about 1 hour. To brown the tops, uncover and bake about 10 minutes, or run under the broiler.

PARSNIPS

Parsnips have a very mild but distinctive flavor. Big ones are apt to be woody, so buy small ones whenever you can. One pound serves 4. Wash, and scrape or peel. Leave whole, cut in halves or quarters lengthwise, or cut in eighths crosswise. Cook covered in a small amount of boiling salted water until tender, about half an hour for halves. Drain.

To serve: Season with salt, pepper, nutmeg, and butter.
To vary: Add a cream sauce.

Sauté boiled parsnips in a combination of butter and oil until browned.

Place boiled parsnips in flat casseroles and top with butter and brown sugar. Bake about 15 minutes in a 400° F. oven, or longer in a lower oven, just before serving time.

French-fry boiled parsnips.

PEAS

Fresh Peas have been neglected in recent years in favor of frozen peas—a pity, since young fresh well-cooked peas are superb. One pound of peas in their shells will yield about 1 cup of peas or 2 servings. Buy only small peas with smooth, bright green pods. Store in the refrigerator to be shelled just before they are to be cooked.

Put the shelled peas in a saucepan with a small amount of boiling salted water. Cover and cook just until the peas are tender, about 10 minutes. Drain.

Alternatively, very young peas may be cooked in butter and the water that clings to lettuce leaves. Melt 2 tablespoons butter in a saucepan. Add 2 cups shelled peas. Rinse 2 or 3 outer leaves of lettuce in water and lay over the peas. Cover and cook over very low heat until the peas are tender. The lettuce can be snipped and served with the peas.

Snow peas—or sugar peas, as they are sometimes called—are a treat you shouldn't miss. They may be purchased at Chinese grocery stores. Buy only very young snow peas. Wash the pods. Do not shell. Remove any stems and tips and put in a saucepan with a small amount of boiling salted water. Cook covered for about 8 minutes or until barely tender. Drain and serve hot with melted butter or cold with French dressing.

Canned Peas vary tremendously from one brand and grade to the next. If you find a brand that pleases you, stick to it. I personally prefer the petit pois, the tiny young peas, though no canned peas can compare to fresh or frozen ones.

Frozen Peas are such a staple of most family diets that they hardly need to be mentioned. For variety try the tiny peas or petit pois. Overcooking is the enemy of frozen peas. Frozen snow peas are becoming more readily available and are better than no snow peas at all.

To serve: Season cooked fresh, frozen, or canned peas with butter, salt, pepper, and a pinch of sugar.
To vary: Add a little dried mint, sage, parsley, marjoram, or curry powder.

Combine peas with celery, onions, mushrooms, carrots, or water chestnuts.

Add a cream sauce or condensed cream of mushroom soup.

Serve with creamed new potatoes.

Add cooked or raw to vegetable or green salads.

Chill in vinaigrette sauce with onion rings. Serve on greens.

Stir-fry snow peas. Put snow peas in a skillet with a little oil. Cook over high heat, stirring constantly for several minutes. They should be crisp, not tender. Season with soy sauce.

PEPPERS AND PIMIENTOS

Red and Green Sweet Peppers—not the small chili peppers— are rich in vitamin C and are delectable served raw in a salad or as a relish or cooked as a vegetable. Buy only smooth, glossy peppers. Always remove the seeds and white membrane before cooking.

To sauté, cut peppers in small squares or strips. Put in a skillet with 2 tablespoons oil. Cover and simmer in the oil until crisp-tender, 5–10 minutes. Sprinkle with salt and pepper. Sauté only at the last minute before serving.

To boil, cut peppers in large squares or strips. Put in a saucepan with a small amount of boiling water. Cook, covered, until crisp-tender, about 10 minutes. Drain and serve in a cream or cheese sauce, alone or combined with another vegetable—peas, onions, celery, or corn.

Stuffed Sweet Peppers. Cut 2 peppers in half, crosswise. Remove the seeds and membrane and cook in boiling salted water for 5 minutes. Lift out of the water and drain upside down. Fill and bake, or refrigerate and bake, until heated through and lightly browned—about 20 minutes at 350° F. For filling, use one of the following combinations:

A small onion, sautéed in butter and combined with a 1-pound can creamed corn. Top with buttered crumbs.

Cooked rice, seasoned with grated cheese and bound with cream of mushroom, chicken, or tomato soup.

Creamed fish.

Creamed lima beans, celery, carrots, or spinach topped with crumbs or cheese.

Frozen Chopped Peppers are available and very convenient to use as a seasoning.

Pimientos are a special variety of sweet red pepper sold in cans and jars. They make an excellent flavoring. If you wish to use 1 or 2 out of a can or jar, you may keep the rest in the refrigerator in their original container for several days. Just cover with a thin film of salad oil. Or, you may wrap the remaining pimientos individually in plastic wrap and freeze. When you remove one from the freezer, run in under cold water for a minute and unwrap. It is easy to chop or slice while still slightly frozen.

POTATOES

See next chapter.

RADISHES

Cooked Radishes? They're flavorful and unusual. The red and the less common white are equally good. Allow about 2 cups sliced radishes for 4 people. Wash well. Slice. Put in a saucepan with a small amount of boiling water. Cover and simmer until crisp-tender, about 25 minutes. Drain and serve with butter or in a cream sauce. Alternatively you may cut off the tails and stems and cook whole. Use about 3 cups for 4 servings.

Raw Radishes are, of course, good in a salad and attractive as a garnish. They may be varied by quartering, shredding, slivering, or chopping.

SAUERKRAUT

See section on Cabbage.

SPINACH

See section on Greens.

SQUASH

Say the word "squash" and many people turn up their noses. Serve it and most people smile as they eat the first bite and ask for a second helping. Admittedly, squash is an ugly word. We might, therefore, substitute the names of individual squashes—zucchini, butternut, cocozelle —such pleasant words.

Squash falls into 2 categories: summer squash, which has a thin tender skin, and winter squash, which has a thick, pumpkinlike skin.

Summer Squash. Zucchini is a popular summer squash. Other types include straight-neck and crooked-neck squash, which have very bumpy yellow skins; cymling or patty pan, which is a flat, white round squash with a scalloped edge—it looks like something you would expect to find at the seashore—and cocozelle, which looks like zucchini but has a yellow skin. Buy small heavy squash with unblemished skin. Store in the refrigerator and eat within a day or two. Allow a pound or a little more for 4 people. Scrub well with a brush and peel only if the skins seem very tough. Do not peel zucchini, if for no other reason than that the peel is attractive.

To boil summer squash, slice or cut into squares or rings and put in a saucepan with a very small amount of boiling salted water. Cover and simmer until tender, about 10 minutes. Drain well.

To bake summer squash, dice or cut into strips and place in greased shallow casseroles. Dot with butter and sprinkle with salt or onion salt and/or a dash of nutmeg or thyme. Pour a few tablespoons of milk over each casserole. Cover tightly and bake until tender, about 40 minutes in a 350° F. oven.

To sauté summer squash, dice or cut in thin slices. Sauté in a skillet with 2 tablespoons butter and 1 tablespoon oil and 1 cup chopped onion. Sprinkle with salt and pepper. Cover and cook about 10 minutes, shaking the pan frequently to prevent sticking.

To vary: Chill boiled squash well and toss with oil and vinegar or Italian dressing and chopped scallions. Serve from the bowl or spoon onto greens. Add tomato slices, sliced pimiento, cherry tomatoes, or sweet red pepper rings for a most attractive and unusual salad.

Toss boiled or sautéed squash with crisply fried bacon squares.

Season with grated Parmesan or Cheddar cheese.

Serve boiled squash in a cream or tomato sauce.

Sauté with a minced clove of garlic.

Cook equal parts of zucchini and yellow summer squash together.

Serve raw summer squash as you would cucumbers.

[*168*]

ZUCCHINI CASSEROLE

1 pound zucchini, scrubbed and
    thinly sliced
1 cup water
4 slices bacon
½ cup sliced onions

1 tablespoon cornstarch
¼ cup sherry
¼ cup dry bread crumbs
2 tablespoons melted butter

Boil zucchini, covered, in water for 5 minutes. Drain, reserving the liquid, and put in 2 shallow casseroles.

In the meantime, fry the bacon, drain well, and crumble. Fry the onions in the bacon fat. Dissolve the cornstarch in the sherry and add to the onions with the cooking liquid and bacon. Cook until thick. Pour sauce over the zucchini. Combine the crumbs and butter and sprinkle over the sauce. Bake, or refrigerate and bake, for about 30 minutes in a 350° F. oven.

ZUCCHINI AND SOUR CREAM

1 pound zucchini, cut in slices 1
    inch thick (or young yellow
    summer squash)
1 clove garlic
Pinch fresh or dried dill
½ pound fresh mushrooms

2 tablespoons butter
1 tablespoon oil
3 tablespoons flour
Salt
1 cup sour cream
Shredded Cheddar cheese

Put zucchini, garlic, and dill in a small saucepan. Pour on a small amount of boiling water. Cover and simmer for 10 minutes, until just barely tender. Drain well reserving the liquid. Discard garlic.

In the meantime, sauté the mushrooms in the butter and oil for 5 minutes. Stir in the flour and salt and 2 tablespoons cooking liquid. Stir in the sour cream and zucchini. Heat but *do not boil*. Put in 2 buttered casseroles. Sprinkle cheese on one of them and run under the broiler to brown. Refrigerate the other to be reheated in a low oven or over hot water. Sprinkle with cheese and broil. Remember: Do not boil.

Winter Squash. Acorn, hubbard, buttercup, butternut, golden delicious, and pumpkin are all winter squashes. Butternut, hubbard, and pumpkin are especially rich in vitamin A. Buy squash with blemish-free skin. They should be relatively heavy for their size. Allow about ½ pound per person.

Scrub well with a brush. Then bake or boil.

[*169*]

To bake Acorn or Butternut Squash, select 2 squashes weighing about 1 pound each. Cut in half and remove the seeds and fibers. Slice a little of the skin off of the bottom of each half so that they will stand steadily. Turn cut side down in a pan or pans with about ½ inch of water and bake 20 minutes. Turn right side up and put 1 tablespoon butter, 1 tablespoon brown sugar, ¼ teaspoon salt, a few grinds of pepper, and a dash of nutmeg in each half. Return to the oven and continue to bake until tender, another 20 minutes. For a later dinner, remove the adults' squash halves after the first 20 minutes of baking. Fill the cavities and refrigerate until 30 minutes before serving.

Acorn and butternut squash may also be cut into 1-inch-thick round slices, which can be baked in pans with a little water and brushed with butter before serving.

To vary: Put bacon in the hollows instead of butter.

Put cooked onions or spiced crab apples in the hollows and dot with butter, brown sugar, and seasoning before the final 20 minutes of cooking.

Fill hollows with equal parts of cream and maple or maple-flavored syrup.

To mash, place a large winter squash in the 350° F. oven and bake whole until the skin can be pierced easily with a toothpick. A large hubbard squash will take at least 2 hours. When tender, cut the squash in half and scoop out the seeds and fibers. Peel and mash the pulp, adding butter, brown sugar, salt, and milk or orange juice.

You may also cut a raw squash into large pieces and boil in a little water until tender. Drain, peel, and mash.

Frozen Squash or Canned Pumpkin. Season with butter, brown sugar, grated orange peel or orange juice, sautéed onions, allspice, nutmeg, or cinnamon. Heat in the top of a double boiler or in a casserole in the oven.

TOMATOES

Technically a fruit, tomatoes are rich in Vitamin C, colorful, and available the year round.

Fresh Tomatoes. In the summer, big, juicy tomatoes, fresh from the vine, are magnificent. So are the small cherry or plum tomatoes. In the winter, when tomatoes are expensive and disappointingly bland, I use fresh tomatoes only in salads or broiled or baked. To skin tomatoes, pierce with a fork and hold over a gas flame for just a moment. This loosens the skin which will then slip off quickly. If you do not have a gas stove, plunge the tomatoes in boiling water for no longer than a minute. Drain and plunge into cold water and slip off the skins. It is never necessary to skin tomatoes, merely a matter of choice.

Baked or Broiled Large Tomatoes. Cut the tomatoes in half. Do not skin. Place cut side up in a buttered baking dish. Sprinkle the tops with salt and pepper and dot with butter. Bake 20 minutes in a 350° F. oven. The time may be adjusted to higher or lower oven temperatures. You may also broil the tomatoes until the tops are lightly browned, about 5 minutes.

To vary: Top with 2 tablespoons melted butter mixed with ¼ cup bread crumbs.

Add 2 tablespoons grated Parmesan cheese to the above mixture.

Sprinkle with dried or fresh dill, thyme, basil, or mixed herbs.

Substitute onion salt or seasoned salt for regular salt.

Sprinkle with grated onion or chopped green onions.

Baked or Broiled Cherry Tomatoes. Put the small unskinned tomatoes in a buttered baking dish and dot with butter, or put on small skewers and dot with butter. Bake about 10 minutes in a 350° F. oven, shaking the pan once or twice, or broil about 5 minutes. Do not overcook or they will fall apart.

To vary: Add tomatoes to any green or vegetable salad.

Serve raw, baked, or broiled as a garnish for meat.

Alternate sautéed mushroom caps or parboiled green pepper squares, or cooked white onions on the skewers with cherry tomatoes.

Pour heated sweet or sour cream over baked or broiled tomatoes.

Heat cherry or plum tomatoes in a skillet with butter and sugar for a few minutes. *Heat*—do not really cook them. Season to taste.

Canned Tomatoes, Tomato Sauce, and Tomato Soup are indispensable. Most of us keep a supply of these on our shelves at all times. Select your brands carefully.

Canned tomatoes may be served chilled in individual sauce dishes. Sprinkle with chopped scallions, green pepper, or cucumber. Whole tomatoes are more expensive than the "unwhole" type. Use the cheaper type for soups, casseroles, and sauces. Besides being less expensive, they are just as nutritious and less work.

To serve hot, combine a 1-pound can of tomatoes with ¼ cup chopped onion and celery, ½ teaspoon salt, and 1 tablespoon brown sugar. Simmer about 10 minutes. Stir in 2 tablespoons instant-type flour mixed with ½ cup milk or cream. Add to the tomatoes and cook just until the mixture begins to thicken.

TOMATO-OLIVE CASSEROLE

1 tablespoon butter
¼ cup chopped onion
1 clove garlic, minced (optional)
1-pound can whole tomatoes
¼ cup quick-cooking tapioca
1 teaspoon salt

2 tablespoons brown sugar
18 ripe olives, sliced
½ cup grated cheese
2 tablespoons butter
¼ cup bread crumbs

Melt the butter in a small skillet and sauté the onion and garlic until golden. Divide half of the tomatoes between 2 small casseroles. Pour the onion-garlic-butter mixture over the tomatoes. Combine the tapioca, salt, and brown sugar and add to the casseroles. Top with the olives and grated cheese and the remaining half of the tomatoes. Combine bread crumbs and butter and sprinkle over the tomatoes. Bake or refrigerate and bake 30 minutes in a 350° F. oven.

TOMATO, CORN, AND ONION CASSEROLE

2 tablespoons butter or margarine
⅓ cup chopped green pepper
2 tablespoons flour
¼ cup milk
8-ounce can tomatoes
½ teaspoon salt
½ teaspoon sugar

Pinch orégano and basil
Shredded American or Cheddar cheese
12-ounce can vacuum-packed corn
8-ounce can small white onions, drained

Melt butter and add green pepper. Sauté lightly and stir in flour. Allow to bubble briefly and add milk, tomatoes, salt, sugar, orégano, and basil. Stir until sauce begins to thicken. Add ¼ cup cheese, corn and onions. Pour mixture into 2 small casseroles. Sprinkle another ¼ cup cheese on top. Bake or refrigerate and bake 30 minutes in 350° F. oven.

TURNIPS

Small white turnips and large yellow rutabagas have a very distinctive flavor which goes especially well in stews and with game or pork.

Children frequently enjoy eating raw turnips. Cut into thin strips or sticks.

If you like a little of the turnip flavor—but not much—combine turnips with potatoes. Rutabagas and potatoes mashed together are especially attractive and delicious. Creamed white turnips also have a more milky flavor. One to 1½ pounds turnips serve 4. Use ½–¾ pound if you are going to combine them with potatoes.

Mashed Turnips. Wash, pare, and cut the turnips in large pieces. Put in a saucepan with a small amount of boiling, salted water and cook, covered, until tender, 15–30 minutes. Drain well and mash with butter, salt, pepper, and cream or milk. Reheat in the top of a double boiler or covered in the oven.

Creamed Turnips. Wash, pare, and dice or slice. Cook in a covered saucepan with a small amount of salted water. Drain well and add a cream sauce. Reheat in the sauce on top of the stove or in a buttered casserole in the oven.

Glazed Turnips. Cut rutabaga in slices and cook until tender. Combine with 1 apple, sliced, in 2 casseroles. Dot with butter, brown sugar, salt, and pepper. Bake about 30 minutes in 350° F. oven.

Potatoes, Pilaf, and Pasta

Unless you worry about overweight at your house, you will want to include something starchy—potatoes, rice, noodles, or the like—in most dinner menus. Potatoes might have been included in the vegetable chapter, but I put them here to make meal planning easier. You will have noticed many of the meat and fish recipes include a starchy food. This is to make reheating easier and to combine flavors.

POTATOES

Potatoes have been so maligned because of their high calorie count that we may have lost sight of the fact that they are also filled with necessary minerals. Consider the Irish, who before the famine prospered on a diet devoted almost exclusively to potatoes. Furthermore, an unadorned potato is not a bad "buy" for weight watchers. It is the butter and cream added to potatoes which are the real calorie culprits.

There are 3 main types: new potatoes, which may be either red or brown and have very thin skins; baking or Idaho potatoes; and plain "boiling" potatoes. Do not buy greenish, sprouted, or spotted potatoes. Buy only enough to last for a week or two.

Reheating potatoes is ticklish but not impossible.

Baked Potatoes. Select large, firm potatoes of uniform size. They need not be those sold as baking potatoes. Scrub well with a stiff brush and cut out any blemishes. Prick a few holes in the skins with a fork. Rub the skins with butter or oil and place directly on the oven rack, in a shallow pan, or on a special potato rack with spikes that go up into the potatoes. The spikes make the potatoes cook more quickly. I have some potato "nails" that I bought in a dime store. I thrust one lengthwise into each potato and the metal carries the heat and greatly reduces the cooking time. The nails are also useful for potatoes that are not the same size. You can nail the large potatoes and they will cook as quickly as the smaller ones.

Bake potatoes until soft at any convenient temperature from 325° F.–450° F. Allow about an hour for medium-size potatoes at 375° F. To test, pick up a potato in a towel or hot pad. Squeeze it gently. If it feels soft, it is done.

To serve immediately, cut a cross in the top of the potato and push the ends toward the center to release the steam. Serve with butter or with sour cream, which may be mixed with chopped onions or chives. A small pitcher of hot skimmed milk will provide flavor and moisture for the weight watcher.

To serve later, you may cut the potatoes in half, brush the cut surfaces with butter and put the halves back together. Reheat in the oven just before serving. These are not as good as those served immediately, but they are good.

If you want to *improve* the flavor of baked potatoes and add a nice fillip to the dinner plate, you can stuff them. Cut the baked potatoes in half lengthwise and scoop out the pulp. Mash thoroughly, adding milk until the mixture is fluffy and quite soft but not runny. Season with salt and pepper. Add grated cheese, minced onion, green pepper or pimiento, crumbled bacon, chopped cooked ham, or chopped olives. Refill the shells and brush with butter or sprinkle with cheese. Set on a baking sheet. Reheat in a 450° F. oven for about 10 minutes just before serving time.

Boiled Potatoes. Wash well, remove any spots or sprouts, and pare or not. There is good nutrition just beneath the skins. Leave whole or cut into pieces of the same size. Cook covered in a small amount of boiling salted water until tender—15–40 minutes depending on size. Drain well. *To serve boiled potatoes:* After the potatoes have been drained, put a folded towel over the top of the pan to absorb the steam. Leave it there for about 5 minutes, shaking the pan occasionally. Remove the towel and add butter, salt, pepper, and chopped chives or parsley, and shake again. These are best served immediately, but they may be reheated for a few minutes in the oven or in the top of a double boiler. Be sure the potatoes are well coated with butter. *To vary:* Add a cream sauce in which the potatoes may be reheated.

Combine potatoes in a cream sauce with cooked peas, mushrooms, or small white onions or with all three. These may be baked with a cheese topping. Creamed potatoes are delicious reheated on top of the stove or in the oven.

Cut the potatoes in large cubes. Cook and drain. Add cream or milk and butter and stir lightly with a fork. Reheat in a double boiler. Grated cheese may also be added.

Mashed Potatoes. Boil the potatoes as indicated above. Drain well and shake over heat for just a moment to be sure that all of the moisture is gone. Break the potatoes into pieces and mash with a potato masher or whip with a portable electric mixer, adding milk, butter, salt, and pepper until they are fluffy—not mushy. Most cookbooks call for hot milk, a procedure which dirties an extra pan. I keep the potatoes over very low heat while I beat them with cold milk. You must work fast to prevent scorching, but you save a pan which is worth a great deal if you are your own dishwasher.

If the potatoes are well brushed with butter, they may be reheated in the oven or in the top of a double boiler.

To vary mashed potatoes: Mound the potatoes in a baking pan. Combine whipping cream and grated cheese, about ⅓ cup of each, and pour over the potatoes. Bake until the cheese melts and the potatoes are lightly browned. This is called Potatoes Chantilly, if you want to be fancy.

Combine with sautéed onions or mushrooms.

Mash potatoes with an equal quantity of boiled carrots or turnips.

Mash with sour cream rather than milk or add cream-style cottage cheese or mash with cream of celery or mushroom soup.

Scalloped Potatoes. Wash, pare, and thinly slice potatoes until you have about 3 cups. Put a layer of potatoes in a well-greased casserole, dot with butter, and sprinkle with flour. Repeat the layers until you have used up all of the potatoes, 2 tablespoons of flour, about ¼ cup of butter. Pour 1¼ cups milk, mixed with 1 teaspoon salt and a little mustard and freshly ground black pepper, over the top. Bake covered for 30 minutes in a 350° F. oven. Remove the cover and bake another hour. The temperature may be increased or decreased, depending on what else is in the oven with the potatoes.

Alternatively, you may prepare the potatoes as above but substitute 1 can condensed cream of mushroom, celery, or cheese soup for the flour and milk. Scalloped potatoes may be reheated in the oven or in the top of a double boiler.

Thinly sliced onion, chopped green onions, or chives, shredded or cubed cheese, or crisply fried and crumbled bacon or cubed cooked ham may be added to the potatoes before they are baked.

Butter Baked Potatoes. Grease a shallow baking dish well and put in no more than 3 layers of sliced potatoes. Add a sliced onion, if you like. Dot each layer with butter and sprinkle with salt and pepper. Cover tightly and bake until the potatoes are tender, about 40 minutes. Remove the cover and brown for about 10 minutes. These are delicious, but don't try to prepare them in advance. I recently prepared the casserole, brushing each layer with melted butter to coat the potatoes well. I covered it tightly and refrigerated it for several hours before baking. You know what happened. Some of the potatoes turned black. They tasted fine but were unbelievably ugly.

Raw-Fried Potatoes. Peel and cut the potatoes into small cubes. Heat 1 tablespoon oil and 1 tablespoon butter in a large Teflon-lined skillet. If you do not have a Teflon skillet, double the quantities of oil and butter. Add the potato cubes and cook over low to medium heat, shaking the pan and turning the potatoes until they are lightly browned and tender. This takes about 15 minutes. If the potatoes should brown before they are soft, cover the skillet and continue cooking. Serve the children. Drain the adults' potatoes and place in a single layer on a large plate. If they are heaped, they will become mushy. Reheat in the oven or drop back in the skillet and fry them again for just a few minutes. Remember that they will brown more in the reheating, so be sure that you do not brown them too much in the first cooking. Salt just before serving.

Precooked Fried Potatoes. Boil potatoes with their skins on until tender. Cool, remove the skins, and cut in small cubes or thin slices. Just before serving, drop into a skillet with about 2 tablespoons hot butter and oil and brown quickly. Salt and serve immediately.

Baked Potato Sticks. Peel the potatoes and cut in long strips. Melt 2 tablespoons butter and 2 tablespoons oil in a shallow casserole and roll the potato sticks in the butter mixture, coating each one well. Place, uncovered, in a 400° F. oven and bake for 50 minutes. If you lower the temperature, increase the time. Serve the children, sprinkling their potatoes with salt. Set the rest of the potatoes aside to return to the oven for about 5 minutes just before dinner time. Sprinkle with salt and serve.

Potato Packets. For each serving, peel and slice one small- to medium-size potato. Lay the slices on a square of foil and top with 1 tablespoon butter, a thin slice of cheese, and salt and pepper. You may also add 1 onion slice, divided into rings. Bring the foil up over the potatoes and seal tightly, allowing space for the steam. Bake 40 minutes in a 400° F. oven, longer in a slower oven. Remove the packets and serve the children. Do not open the adults' packets, but return to the oven and bake 10 minutes before serving.

New Potatoes. Scrub them with a stiff brush and cook in boiling salted water until tender. They may be served with their jackets on or off.
To vary new potatoes: Remove the skins and sauté lightly in butter. This is a delicious way to reheat new potatoes and takes only a few minutes just before serving.

Add a cream sauce, which makes reheating easy.

Combine in a cream sauce with cooked peas, mushrooms, and small white onions.

Add butter, salt, pepper, and parsley or chives.

Potato Salad. Usually docile women can become very obstinate on the subject of potato salad. I, for one, am quite sure that I make the very best potato salad to be had, so I will tell you how I do it. You can read my instructions and then go right back to your method, which is probably the same as your mother's.

Early in the day I boil 2 or 3 medium-size potatoes with their jackets on. When tender, I drain them and wait until they are cool enough to handle. I peel them and cut them into rather large cubes, which I put in a large bowl. I drizzle a little French dressing, about 1 tablespoon, over the potatoes, give them a good shake, cover them and put them in the refrigerator. Several times during the day I shake them up a bit. Late in the afternoon I add chopped pickles, onion, green pepper, cucumber, and celery to the potatoes. I also add 2 sliced hard-boiled eggs. I mix together 2 tablespoons mayonnaise, 2 tablespoons sour cream, 1 teaspoon dry mustard, 1 teaspoon salt, and plenty of freshly ground black pepper. I pour this mixture into the bowl and toss everything together. Then I start tasting and adding. I may need more mayonnaise, sour cream, or French dressing, or a little vinegar from the pickle jar, plain vinegar, more mustard, or onion, or salt and pepper. When it tastes good to me, I put it back in the refrigerator to "meld" for at least an hour. The children eat their portions at six and my husband and I eat ours whenever we get around to it.

That's the way I do it. My husband likes it, too. The children (poor innocents!) don't know that there is any other kind of potato salad.

Another way to make good potato salad is simply to cook 3 or 4 medium-size potatoes. Drain, cool, and dice. Add 3 tablespoons French dressing, cover, and refrigerate, shaking the bowl several times. An hour before serving, add chopped onion, if you like, and salt, pepper, and enough mayonnaise to hold the potatoes together. Serve alone on a bed of greens or with hard-boiled egg halves, sliced cucumbers, and tomato wedges.

Or, you may refrigerate the diced potatoes in Sophia's Dressing*. No other dressing or seasoning will be necessary.

Canned, Frozen, Instant, and Potato Dish Mixes are all useful for the cook in a hurry. I seldom use any of these because to me they are not quite as good as fresh potatoes. They can also be more expensive. But, do keep your eyes open for new potato products and ideas. It is also a good idea to keep "prepared" potatoes in some form on hand for emergency meals. If you have a baby in your family, you will definitely want to keep instant mashed potatoes on hand.

SWEET POTATOES OR YAMS

A yam by any name is sweeter, brighter, and moister than a sweet potato. Both sweets and yams are easier to reheat than white potatoes. They are also a rich source of vitamin A. They spoil rather quickly, so buy for one meal at a time—unless, of course, you plan to eat sweet potatoes for three consecutive days.

Baked Sweet Potatoes. Prepare and bake just as you do white potatoes. Yams will take less time to bake.

[179]

Boiled Sweet Potatoes. Scrub well but do not skin. Drop in boiling salted water, cover, and cook until tender, about 20 minutes. Drain and skin. Reheat in the top of a double boiler over very low heat, or in the oven.

To vary: Mash with butter and a little milk or orange juice and season with nutmeg, rum, sherry, crushed pineapple, nuts, honey, or molasses.

Boil only 10 minutes. Peel and put in a pan with roasting meat 1 hour before the meat is to be done. Baste frequently with the pan juices.

Slice and serve with butter and any of the seasonings mentioned for mashed sweet potatoes.

Cut in halves or quarters and toss with butter and brown sugar or butter and maple syrup.

Canned Sweet Potatoes and Yams are almost as good as fresh ones and are a convenient food to keep on hand at all times. There is great variety among brands, so find one that you like and stick to it. Canned sweet potatoes may be prepared in any of the ways suggested for boiled sweet potatoes.

Instant Mashed Sweet Potatoes or Yams may also be prepared with any of the seasonings suggested above.

Frozen and Canned Candied Sweet Potatoes and Yams are also good, but expensive.

RICE

Rice is one of the foods that reheat easily and is frequently better for being warmed over.

There are many different kinds of rice and many different ways of cooking it. You can choose from brown, white, and wild. Some have been processed or precooked to cut preparation time. Wild rice—which is not really rice at all—is delicious but sky high in price. It also requires a special cooking method. Brown rice, which is crunchy, is my favorite.

Cook rice according to package directions. One cup raw rice is usually cooked with 2 cups liquid and will serve 4. Rice may be boiled in a covered saucepan or baked in the oven. It may be browned in a little butter before the liquid is added. To reheat, put over very low heat and stir until it is hot, or put in the oven or in the top of a double boiler.

Many flavored packaged rice products are on the market. While more expensive than fixing up plain rice, they are convenient and interesting. One product combines wild and white rice and is a good way to pretend you are having costly wild rice.

To vary: Sauté chopped onion or green pepper in butter. Add the rice and stir until it browns lightly. Add water, broth, or tomato juice and cook according to package directions.

Combine with almost any cooked vegetable.

Season with curry powder, chili powder, nutmeg, seasoned salt, onion salt, garlic salt, seasoned pepper, etc.

Add lots of minced parsley.

Add grated or shredded cheese.

Add chopped cooked ham, poultry, fish, or crumbled crisp bacon.

Cook rice in poultry or meat broth or bouillon. When tender, season with lemon juice and grated lemon or orange peel.

Add turmeric or saffron to color rice a pretty yellow.

Cook rice in carrot, pineapple, orange, or tomato juice rather than water, or use vegetable cooking liquids.

Add dried or fresh herbs suitable for the meat or fish being served.

GREEN RICE

½ cup rice
1 cup boiling water
⅓ cup chopped onion
10-ounce package frozen chopped spinach, cooked and drained
¼ pound shredded American cheese
½ teaspoon salt
Few grinds pepper
Dash nutmeg
1 tablespoon vinegar (optional)
2 eggs, lightly beaten
2 cups milk

Cook rice in water for 10 minutes. Drain and add the remaining ingredients. Pour into 2 buttered casseroles and bake, or refrigerate and bake, in a 350° F. oven until just firm—about 25 minutes.

RICE SALAD

2 tablespoons chili sauce
1/3 cup mayonnaise
1 tablespoon prepared mustard
1 teaspoon salt
Few grinds pepper
2 cups cooked white rice

4 hard-boiled eggs, chopped
1/4 cup chopped onion
1 pimiento, chopped
1/4 cup chopped green pepper
1/2 cup chopped celery

Combine chili sauce, mayonnaise, mustard, salt, and pepper, and pour over all of the other ingredients in a large bowl. Toss well and chill. This salad may be spooned onto greens and garnished with cherry tomatoes and cucumber slices.

PASTA

Noodles, spaghetti, and macaroni can be used interchangeably. Again, read the instructions on the package and cook accordingly. There are lovely green noodles worth seeking. Instant pasta products are now a reality. Some of the endless varieties of macaroni shapes are wonderful appetite inducers for children who need a little prodding at mealtime. I have yet to meet a child who didn't like seashells and cheese.

Do you know how to get long spaghetti into a pot that is narrower than the length of the spaghetti? When the water is boiling, put the spaghetti into the water with what won't fit sticking out. As the part in the water begins to soften, push the part that is sticking out down in. When you have worked all of the spaghetti into the water, stir it with a fork so that the individual pieces will separate.

Cook according to package directions and drain well. Do not over-cook. Properly cooked, well buttered or sauced pasta may be reheated in the top of a double boiler, in a saucepan over very low heat, or in the oven.

To vary: Toss with butter, a few tablespoons of milk and grated, shredded, or cubed cheese.

Add a cream or cheese sauce and bake to reheat.

Top with butter and chopped chives, parsley, chopped pimiento, poppy seeds, or buttered croutons.

Add sautéed onions or mushrooms.

NOODLES DELUXE

1 clove garlic, crushed
1 medium onion, chopped
2 tablespoons butter or margarine
2 tablespoons flour
1½ cups milk
8-ounce carton cottage cheese

4 ounces broad noodles, cooked
  and drained
3 hard-boiled eggs
10-ounce package frozen chopped
  spinach, cooked and drained
¼ cup grated Parmesan cheese

Sauté garlic and onion in butter. Add flour and allow to bubble briefly. Stir in milk and continue stirring until sauce is thick and smooth. Add cottage cheese, noodles, eggs, and spinach. Pour into buttered casseroles and sprinkle with cheese. Bake, or refrigerate and bake, 30 minutes in 350° F. oven.

MACARONI SALAD

1 cup uncooked macaroni—elbows
  or shells
2 hard-boiled eggs
1 cup chopped celery
¼ cup chopped onion
¼ cup chopped green pepper
1 pimiento, chopped

1 tablespoon pickle juice
½ teaspoon salt
Few grinds pepper
¼ teaspoon dry mustard
⅓ cup mayonnaise or salad
  dressing
Lettuce

Early in the day, or at least 3 hours before dinner, cook the macaroni according to package directions, and hard-boil the eggs. Drain the macaroni, slice the eggs, and mix with the other ingredients. Pack into serving-size custard cups. Chill until serving time and unmold on greens.

Salads

Salad suggestions have been scattered all through this book—in the main-dish chapters, in the vegetable chapter, in the potato and pasta chapter—even in the dessert chapter. (Check the index under "Salads" for recipes in other chapters.)

First, let's talk about dressings. There are so many delicious bottled dressings and dressing mixes that few of us make many dressings from scratch. I regularly make only three. But prepared dressings can be dressed up into new delights, and I have included many suggestions for these in the main salad sections.

The quality of the ingredients is the most important single feature of the dressings you make yourself. Most salad oils today are very good. The only one you need to be particularly careful about choosing is olive oil. If you cannot buy very good olive oil, stick to vegetable oil.

As for vinegars, those basic ones available in all supermarkets are good but frequently undistinguished. On the other hand, some of the vinegars sold in specialty and gourmet shops are magnificent. I am now using a bottle of wine vinegar that I bought in a very fancy fruit and vegetable store in my neighborhood. It was expensive, compared to supermarket vinegar, but so what? A little vinegar goes a long way. If you are serious about making good salads, you will keep a variety of vinegars on hand. Cider, malt, and wine vinegars are the basics. Wine vinegar, which may be either red or white, seems less acid. White vinegar is best for making pickles and relishes. And then there are almost endless flavored and dressed-up vinegars. Try some of these.

Salt is an item you may want to buy specially for salads. Plain old table or cooking salt is good, but coarse kosher salt is even better, and sea salt is better still. And fresh herbs are better than dried ones. So, if you want to make really superior salads, shop around for superior ingredients.

OIL AND VINEGAR DRESSING

2 tablespoons oil
1 tablespoon vinegar
1 teaspoon salt
½ teaspoon dry mustard

1 teaspoon sugar
Garlic salt (optional)
Hot red pepper sauce (optional)

Combine all of the ingredients in the bottom of your salad bowl or in a cup or small jar. I mix them in the salad bowl and lay cucumbers, onions, or green peppers over the dressing. Soaking in the oil only improves them. Then I lay the greens, which will get limp if they stay in the oil, on top of the cucumber-onion layer—well out of the dressing. I cover the bowl and refrigerate it, to be tossed at the last minute.

If you prepare the dressing in a cup or jar, you will, of course, pour it over the salad at the last minute. If you are going to prepare it this way, you will probably want to increase the ingredients and keep the dressing in the refrigerator for several future salads.

A word of warning—I like vinegar, so this is quite a tart dressing. You may want to use less vinegar and more oil—say 3 or 4 tablespoons oil to 1 tablespoon vinegar.

To vary: Add fresh or dried herbs, substitute lemon juice for vinegar, add finely chopped scallions or capers. If you want to make blue cheese dressing, mash about 1 tablespoon cheese and beat it into the dressing and then crumble another tablespoon cheese into it.

SOPHIA'S DRESSING

2 egg yolks, lightly beaten
¼ cup sugar
½ teaspoon mustard
¼ teaspoon salt

1 teaspoon flour
½ cup vinegar, or ¼ cup vinegar
  and ¼ cup water
1 tablespoon butter

Mix all the ingredients except the butter in the top of a double boiler. Cook over boiling water until thick—this takes only a few minutes. Remove from the heat and stir in the butter. Refrigerate. Serve with potato salad, tuna salad, or slaw.

PINEAPPLE DRESSING

¼ cup sugar
2 teaspoons cornstarch
¼ teaspoon salt

¼ cup lemon or orange juice
½ cup pineapple juice
1 egg

In a small saucepan combine the sugar, cornstarch, and salt. Add the juices. Place over very low heat, stirring constantly until the sauce begins to thicken. Beat the egg well, add a little of the hot mixture to the egg and then add the egg to the dressing. Cook just to the boiling point. Cool and refrigerate to be served with fruit salads.

GREEN AND VEGETABLE SALADS

Well-prepared green salads are a perfect complement for almost any dinner. They are also filled with necessary vitamins and minerals. Again, it is superior ingredients that make a superior salad. Iceberg lettuce is good but not as rich in vitamin A as many other kinds of greens. Try bibb lettuce, Boston lettuce, romaine, endive, chicory, or escarole. Try water cress, spinach, dandelion greens, or sorrel. If you don't know the names of the various greens, just pick up a head of something that looks good in the vegetable bins at your supermarket. Bring it home and be prepared for a delicious surprise. Or pick out the name of one of the greens mentioned above and ask the vegetable man for some. Be daring!

Grit is the salad bowl's mortal enemy, so be sure you wash your greens well under running water and then dry them. As you know, oil and water don't mix; neither do salad dressing and wet greens. There are several ways to dry greens. One is to drain them in a wire vegetable basket or collander. Another is to wrap them lightly in a towel. Whatever your method, be gentle. Greens wound easily.

Prepared greens can be stored in the drying towel or in a plastic bag or tightly covered bowl in the refrigerator for several hours, but don't let the dressing touch them until just before serving time. Limp lettuce is worse than a limp handshake.

Greens alone with a good dressing make a delicious salad. They also combine well with a variety of cooked and raw fruits and vegetables. Following are suggestions for salads:

1. Simplest of all are wedges of head lettuce. Try serving with a dressing made by combining mayonnaise and chili sauce in any proportions with or without a chopped-up hard-boiled egg. Or serve with bottled Russian or Thousand Island dressing.

2. Serve lettuce wedges or a mixture of greens with a blue cheese dressing. Combine equal parts of French dressing, sour cream, and mayonnaise with a little garlic salt and blue cheese.

3. Drain an 8-ounce can of diced beets. Mash with a fork and stir in ½ cup mayonnaise, seasoned with a little prepared horseradish. Refrigerate. Just before serving, spoon onto lettuce wedges.

4. Add any or a combination of the following raw vegetables to a combination of greens: carrot, celery, cauliflower, red or green pepper, onions, turnips, radishes, or tomatoes.

5. Salads may be given a new look if you don't toss them. Instead, put greens on individual plates or bowls and top with slices of cucumber, "wheels" of green pepper, whole cherry tomatoes, flowerettes of cauliflower, etc. Pass a dressing. This is a particularly good idea if your main dish is a combination of several foods. For example, if you are serving a stew with beef, potatoes, carrots, and onions, a salad with 4 or 5 more ingredients all mixed together is not as attractive as one made up of several very distinct vegetables.

6. Cooked vegetables which are suitable for salads have been discussed at some detail in the vegetable chapter. An attractive salad plate can be made by combining several of these, with or without a bed of greens. Try beet pickles, asparagus spears, artichoke hearts, green beans, zucchini—almost any of the cold vegetables mentioned in the vegetable chapter. A slice of Swiss cheese would be a nice addition to this vegetable plate.

7. You can add almost any cooked vegetables—except the leafy ones—to a tossed salad.

8. Or take a can of mixed vegetables or slightly undercook a package of frozen ones and mix with diced celery and cucumber or onions or green peppers to add crunch and zest. Serve with a dressing made by combining chili sauce and mayonnaise or make a special dressing by frying and crumbling a slice or two of bacon and adding to mayonnaise or sour cream.

9. Toss greens with croutons fried in garlic butter and an oil and vinegar dressing. Add a sprinkling of grated Parmesan cheese.

10. Combine greens with ripe or green olives and an oil and vinegar dressing.

11. Slice raw cauliflower very thin. Combine with thinly sliced radishes and green onions. Chill in a dressing made by combining 1 package garlic-cheese salad dressing mix with mayonnaise and sour cream. Serve in a lettuce cup.

12. Combine a well-drained 8-ounce can of kidney beans with 1 cup chopped celery and 1 small onion, chopped. Moisten with mayonnaise and taste for seasoning. Chill. To serve, spoon the bean mixture onto lettuce leaves and garnish with slices of hard-boiled egg.

13. Combine a variety of greens with sliced green onions, green pepper rings and pitted ripe olives. Just before serving, add a sliced avocado and well-drained canned anchovy fillets. Toss with an oil and vinegar dressing.

14. To ½ cup mayonnaise, add 2 chopped anchovy fillets, 1 tablespoon chopped onion, 2 tablespoons dried or chopped fresh parsley, ¼ teaspoon dry mustard and 1 tablespoon vinegar. Refrigerate. Just before serving, toss with a combination of greens and a sliced tomato.

15. Drain and chill 1 8-ounce can tiny whole beets, 1 8-ounce can tiny whole potatoes, 1 8-ounce can cross-cut green beans. Combine and chill ¼ cup chopped celery, ¼ cup sliced green onions, and ¼ cup radishes. Season with ½ teaspoon salt and a few grinds of pepper. Add ½ cup sour cream, 1 tablespoon of horseradish, and ¼–½ cup French dressing. Just before serving, combine all of the ingredients and serve on lettuce leaves.

16. Combine 3 tablespoons dry onion-soup mix with 3 tablespoons water, ¾ cup salad oil, and ¼ cup vinegar. Shake well and refrigerate. Just before serving, toss with mixed salad greens.

17. Thinly slice one red onion and divide into rings. Add 1 well-drained 10-ounce can mandarin oranges and about ½ cup oil and vinegar dressing. Cover and refrigerate. Just before serving, toss with salad greens and 1 sliced avocado. (The avocado is optional.)

18. Combine ¼ cup sliced radishes, ¼ cup sliced green onions, ½ cup sliced celery, and ¼ cup diced green peppers, 2 tomatoes, diced, and 1 8-ounce carton cream-style cottage cheese. Season with freshly ground black pepper. Refrigerate and serve on salad greens.

19. Cook 1 package frozen lima beans according to package directions. Add ½ cup thinly sliced celery and ¼ cup chopped scallions. Drizzle ¼ cup bottled French dressing over the vegetables and refrigerate. Skin a tomato for each person. Just before serving, place each tomato on a salad plate and cut into 6 wedges down to, but not through, the stem end. Spread the wedges and fill with the vegetable mixture. Garnish with a little sour cream.

VEGETABLE MOLDS

All of these molds are extremely pretty and very useful in transforming ordinary vegetables from a "duty" food to a "party treat" fare. Do try them.

VEGETABLE COMBO

1 package frozen mixed vegetables, or canned mixed vegetables
Water
3-ounce package lemon-flavored gelatin

1 tablespoon cider vinegar
1/4 cup chopped green onion
1/4 cup chopped green pepper
1 pimiento, diced

Cook vegetables in 1 cup boiling water. When tender, drain and dissolve the gelatin in the cooking liquid. Add 1 cup cold water and the vinegar. Refrigerate until gelatin begins to set. Add the cooked vegetables and the rest of the ingredients. Pour into individual molds and refrigerate until firm. Serve on lettuce with a mayonnaise or sour cream dressing.

If you are using canned mixed vegetables, drain into a measuring cup and add enough water to make 1 cup. Dissolve the gelatin in boiling water and add the vegetable liquid in place of the cold water.

EASY COTTAGE TOMATO ASPIC

2 cups tomato juice
3-ounce package lemon-flavored gelatin
Few drops red pepper sauce
8-ounce carton cream-style cottage cheese

1/4 cup chopped celery
1/4 cup chopped green pepper
1/4 cup chopped green onion
1/4 cup chopped cucumber

Heat 1 cup of the tomato juice to the boiling point. Stir in gelatin. Add cold tomato juice, pepper sauce, and cottage cheese, stirring well to break up any lumps. Refrigerate. When mixture begins to set, add other ingredients and pour into individual molds. Refrigerate until firm. Serve on greens with mayonnaise, creamy Italian dressing, or sour cream.

CRANBERRY CRUNCH MOLD

¾ cup boiling water
1 package pineapple-flavored
 gelatin
1 cup bottled cranberry juice
1 tablespoon vinegar

1 tablespoon sugar
½ cup finely shredded cabbage
1 small carrot, diced
½ cucumber, diced
2 green onions, sliced

Pour boiling water over gelatin. Stir until dissolved and add cranberry juice, vinegar, and sugar. Refrigerate until mixture begins to set. Add vegetables and pour into individual molds. Refrigerate until firm and serve on more shredded cabbage or greens.

BRIGHT BEAUTY

8-ounce can diced beets
Water
1 package lemon-flavored gelatin
Salt
Pepper

½ cup chopped celery
2 tablespoons chopped onions
2 tablespoons chopped green
 pepper

Drain beet liquid into a measuring cup. Add enough water to make 1 cup liquid. Pour 1 cup boiling water over the gelatin. Stir and add beet liquid. Season with salt and pepper. Refrigerate until mixture begins to set. Add beets and vegetables. Pour into individual molds and refrigerate until firm. Serve on greens—chopped raw spinach is especially good. Serve with a dressing made by combining mayonnaise with a little prepared horseradish or lemon juice.

CREAMY MOLD

1 envelope unflavored gelatin
1 cup water
1 tablespoon sugar
1 tablespoon vinegar
1 cup mayonnaise

½ cup shredded cabbage
¼ cup sliced celery
¼ cup diced carrot
¼ cup chopped green pepper

In a small saucepan, soften gelatin in 1 cup water. Stir over low heat until gelatin dissolves. Add sugar, vinegar, and mayonnaise. Refrigerate until mixture begins to set. Add vegetables and pour into individual molds. Refrigerate until firm and serve on greens.

3-ounce package lemon-lime-
flavored gelatin
Water
2 tablespoons lemon juice
1/4 teaspoon salt

1 small cucumber, peeled and
thinly sliced
Several radishes, thinly sliced
1/2 cup cubed Cheddar, American,
or Swiss cheese

Dissolve gelatin in 1 cup boiling water. Add lemon juice and salt and 3/4 cup cold water. Refrigerate until mixture begins to set. Add cucumber, radishes, and cheese. Pour into individual molds and refrigerate until firm. Serve on greens with mayonnaise or sour cream dressing.

FANCY OLD FRIEND

8-ounce can tiny green peas
Water
1 chicken bouillon cube
1/4 teaspoon dry basil
1/4 teaspoon tarragon
1/4 teaspoon salt

1/4 teaspoon sugar
1 envelope unflavored gelatin
1/4 cup lemon juice
1/4 cup thinly sliced celery
1/4 cup chopped green onions
1 pimiento, chopped

Drain pea liquid into a measuring cup. Add water to make 1 cup. Heat to the boiling point with bouillon cube, basil, tarragon, salt, and sugar. In the meantime, soften the gelatin in the lemon juice and 3/4 cup water. Add the hot mixture and stir until dissolved. Refrigerate until mixture begins to set. Add peas, celery, green onions, and pimiento. Pour into molds and refrigerate until firm. Serve on greens with mayonnaise.

JELLIED TOMATOES

1 envelope unflavored gelatin
1/2 cup cold water
1-pound 4-ounce can peeled
tomatoes
1 tablespoon brown sugar

Dash red hot pepper sauce
1 teaspoon salt
1 teaspoon instant onion
1 tablespoon lemon juice

Soften the gelatin in the cold water. In the meantime, bring all of the other ingredients, except the lemon juice, to a boil. Cut up any large pieces of tomato with a spoon or scissors. Add to the softened gelatin with the lemon juice. Stir, cool slightly, and pour into individual molds. Serve on greens with mayonnaise.

3-ounce package lemon-flavored
   gelatin
¾ cup boiling water
¼ cup mayonnaise
¼ cup prepared horseradish

¼ teaspoon salt
1 cup commercial sour cream
½ cup finely diced celery
   (optional)

Dissolve gelatin in water. Add the rest of the ingredients and stir until smooth. Pour into individual molds and refrigerate until firm.

FRUIT SALADS

Fruit salads with heavy dressing are delicious but are more suitable for desserts than to accompany meats. Therefore, you will find several salads in the dessert chapter. Here are suggestions for lighter salads.

Remember to drain canned or frozen fruits very well. I put these fruits in a sieve or collander over a bowl and refrigerate for several hours, shaking the sieve occasionally. Be sure that the bottom of the sieve stays out of the syrup. The syrup which you drain off of the fruit may be substituted for up to half of the water to make a delicious gelatin. See the next section.

1. Waldorf salad is one of the all-time favorite fruit salads. Combine cubes or slices of apples (leave the skins on to add color) with chopped celery and nut meats. Sprinkle with lemon juice and moisten with mayonnaise or sour cream. Refrigerate to be served on lettuce. Pears may be substituted for apples.

2. Add pineapple chunks, seedless or seeded grapes, raisins, or chopped dates to basic Waldorf salad. Or add all four.

3. Combine apples, celery, and seedless grapes with a dressing made by combining 2 tablespoons milk, 2 tablespoons chunky peanut butter and ½ cup mayonnaise.

4. Use the peanut butter dressing above on a combination of bananas, pineapple, and grapes.

5. Use the peanut butter dressing above on bananas sliced lengthwise on a bed of greens. Either peel the bananas at the last minute or coat them with lemon juice or fruit syrup to keep them from turning dark.

6. Drain a 10-ounce can mandarin oranges, a 13-ounce can pineapple chunks, and an 8-ounce can pear slices. Add raisins and a few coarsely chopped walnuts or pecans. Refrigerate in the sieve. Just be-

fore serving, toss with bite-size greens and an oil and vinegar or French dressing.

7. Combine torn lettuce with tangerine sections, 1 small onion, sliced and separated into rings, and walnuts. Toss with an oil and vinegar or Italian dressing.

8. Chop nuts, dates, and celery and moisten with mayonnaise. Refrigerate. Mound this mixture on spiced peach halves or spiced apple slices on a bed of greens.

9. Combine almost any canned or fresh fruits in any proportion with the pineapple dressing given at the beginning of this chapter. Serve on greens.

10. Arrange apple, peach, pineapple, and pear slices with seedless grapes and cooked prunes on lettuce-lined plates. Top with sour cream or mayonnaise.

11. Arrange any or all of the fruits mentioned in Salad 10 on a lettuce-lined plate and top with cottage cheese.

12. Combine ⅓ cup mayonnaise with 1 tablespoon vinegar and ½ teaspoon sugar. Add about 2 ounces crumbled blue cheese. Toss with lettuce, sliced banana, pared and diced avocado, and well-drained mandarin oranges.

13. Combine melon balls, strawberry halves, pineapple chunks, and banana slices. Serve on lettuce with mayonnaise, sour cream, or pineapple dressing.

14. Soften a 3-ounce package of cream cheese at room temperature and shape into 8 balls. Roll each ball in finely chopped nutmeats. Refrigerate. At serving time, place well-drained canned apricot halves on lettuce-lined plates. Put a cream cheese ball in each apricot hollow. Serve with mayonnaise.

15. Serve almost any combination of fruits with a dressing made by combining mayonnaise with grated lemon peel and a little lemon juice.

FRUIT MOLDS

Fruit gelatin can be either very dull with an aura of baby food and sickrooms, or it can be spectacularly attractive, cool, and sophisticated. It all depends on what goes into it.

One of its great virtues is that even very young children can make it themselves. My three-year-old is a whiz at making gelatin. All I have to do is pour in the boiling water and clean up after her!

The very best babysitter I know keeps large families of children occupied for most of an afternoon making striped gelatin. Here's what she says she does. She fills the teakettle and puts it on the stove. Then she arranges all of the children around the kitchen table with a bowl and spoon for each. She brings out as many packages of flavored gelatin as there are cooks, and each child chooses a package. (She's so clever that they don't all insist on red.) The children open their packages— which, if the children are young, can take a good long time right there —and empty the contents into their bowls. When the teakettle whistles, she pours a cup of boiling water in each bowl, and the stirring begins. Then she pours in the cold water, and they stir some more.

She then finds some glass bowls. A little gelatin is poured into each glass bowl and refrigerated. The children get down, wash their hands, and play. When things get a little tedious, it's time for the next layer and everyone reassembles, pours in another layer, washes hands, plays, reassembles, pours, etc., etc., all through the afternoon. The result is pure ambrosia, at least from the young cooks' point of view. I could slave all day with the rarest of ingredients and not prepare anything half so appealing to my children as this striped concoction they make themselves.

From an adults' point of view, gelatin will always taste better if fruit juice is substituted for at least part of the water. Use 1 cup boiling water and 1 cup cold fruit juice or syrup drained from canned fruits with flavored gelatin. You can use all fruit juices if you are using unflavored gelatin, in which case you may want to add a few drops of food coloring. The mixture may not congeal if you use all fruit syrup with flavored gelatin.

Almost any fruit—with the exception of fresh or frozen pineapple —goes well in gelatin. Try some of these combinations:

1. Drained frozen or fresh melon balls and canned pineapple tidbits in lemon-lime gelatin. This can also be served as a dessert in sherbet glasses.

2. Grated carrots and cabbage and drained crushed pineapple in lemon- or orange-flavored gelatin. This is called "Sunshine Salad" for obvious reasons.

3. Grapefruit sections in lemon- or lime-flavored gelatin made with grapefruit juice and ginger ale.

4. Pitted sweet cherries, sliced celery, and chopped nuts in orange or lemon-flavored gelatin.

5. Diced apples and oranges, pineapple tidbits, sliced banana, and broken walnuts in lemon- or banana-flavored gelatin. Good for dessert too.

6. Chopped avocado and celery in lemon-flavored gelatin dissolved in cranberry juice.

SURPRISE SALAD

8-ounce can crushed pineapple
1 envelope lime-flavored gelatin
Water
3-ounce package cream cheese

1 tablespoon mayonnaise
¼ cup coarsely chopped walnuts
   or pecans

Drain pineapple liquid into a measuring cup. Dissolve gelatin in 1 cup boiling water. Add cold water to pineapple syrup to make 1 cup, and pour into gelatin with crushed pineapple. Refrigerate. In the meantime, beat the cream cheese with the mayonnaise. Stir in the walnuts and shape into 4–6 balls. Pour a little of the gelatin mixture into each of 4–6 individual molds and refrigerate until set. Put the cream cheese balls in the center of the molds and pour the rest of the gelatin mixture around them. Refrigerate until firm and serve on greens with mayonnaise thinned with pineapple juice.

FRUIT AND BLUE CHEESE MOLD

1-pound can fruit cocktail
1 envelope unflavored gelatin
1 cup orange juice
¼ cup mayonnaise
6-ounce glass blue cheese spread

2 tablespoons lemon juice
1 tablespoon sugar
¼ teaspoon salt
¼ cup thinly sliced celery

Drain fruit cocktail liquid into a measuring cup. In a small saucepan, soften the gelatin in ½ cup of the fruit syrup. Dissolve over very low heat and add the orange juice, mayonnaise, cheese spread, lemon juice, sugar, and salt. Beat with an electric or rotary beater until smooth. Chill until partly set and stir in the fruit cocktail and celery. Pour into individual molds and refrigerate until firm. Serve on greens.

8-ounce can crushed pineapple
Water
1 envelope unflavored gelatin
½ cup sugar
¼ teaspoon salt

¼ cup cider vinegar
Few drops green food coloring
½ cup coarsely chopped walnuts
½ cup sliced stuffed olives
½ cup chopped sweet pickle

This tart salad is both different and attractive.

Drain pineapple liquid in a 1 quart measure. Add water to make ½ cup liquid. Soften gelatin in it. Add sugar, salt, and ¾ cup boiling water, stirring until dissolved. Add vinegar and food coloring. Refrigerate until mixture begins to set. Then add pineapple, walnuts, olives, and pickles. Pour into molds and refrigerate for several hours or more. Serve on lettuce leaves with mayonnaise and a dash of paprika.

CIDER SALAD

1 envelope unflavored gelatin
¼ cup cold water
1¾ cups cider or apple juice
½ stick cinnamon
3 cloves

1 unpeeled apple, cored and
  chopped
½ cup chopped celery
½ cup drained crushed pineapple

Early in the day soften the gelatin in the water while you bring the cider to a boil with the cinnamon and cloves. Add the gelatin and stir. Put the cover on the pan and allow the cider to steep for 1 hour off the heat. Remove the spices and add the other ingredients. Refrigerate and stir once or twice until the mixture begins to thicken. Pour into molds and refrigerate. Serve on salad greens with mayonnaise.

Breads

You may have noticed that some of the menus in this book contain suggestions for bread and some don't. Some families have bread on the table at every dinner and some never do. Other women serve bread as a substitute for potatoes or rice or pasta and some just serve it when the mood strikes. When preparing these menus, I have included a bread suggestion when I thought of some variety that would be particularly appealing or when I thought it necessary to round out the menu. Otherwise, I have left it out. After all, if your family likes bread, you don't need me to remind you to put it on the table.

If you're like me—too lazy to bake your own loaves of bread—you can fool your family by buying frozen unbaked loaves of bread. These are fun to use.

For interesting varieties of bread, check your bakery and your grocery store. Even plain old white bread can be made into a delightful treat.

FANCY BREAD FINGERS

Cut 6 slices of bread into 4 lengthwise strips each—or any other shapes that appeal to you. Or leave whole. Melt ½ cup (1 stick) butter. Dip each piece of bread into the butter and lay on baking sheets. One sheet for the adults, 1 for the children. Leave plain or sprinkle with one of the following:

Grated cheese
Sesame, poppy, dill, or caraway seeds
Poultry seasoning
Chili powder
Minced onion
Cinnamon and sugar
Seasoned salt
Garlic salt

Place in a 400° F. oven for about 10 minutes just before serving or under the broiler until lightly browned. It's simple and amazingly good.

You may also add ¼ cup frozen orange juice concentrate to the melted butter and sprinkle with cinnamon and sugar.

Remember that bread freezes well, so if you have a small family you can still buy several kinds of bread and keep them in plastic bags in the freezer. Remove as many slices as you need about ½ hour before dinner, close the package and bag tightly, and return to the freezer. Try keeping several special breads on hand this way—pumpernickel, rye, oatmeal, cheese—any good bakery will have a wide assortment of breads that can be used to add variety to your meals.

I don't think that the quality of any food varies more than the quality of French and Italian bread. I've found one brand of Italian bread in my neighborhood that is really good. The rest range from adequate to awful.

To dress up French or Italian bread: Divide the loaf into sections for each sitting. Cut the sections into thick slices cutting down to, but not through, the bottom crust. Spread softened butter between the slices and wrap in foil. Heat in the oven about 15 minutes before serving. *To vary:* Add any seasonings mentioned above under Fancy Bread Fingers, or place thin slices of cheese between the slices.

If you have a small family, you may find it convenient to substitute crusty rolls for French or Italian bread. These may be split or sliced and prepared just as you would prepare the loaves of bread.

Next to the breads on your supermarket shelves, you will find different kinds of baked and brown-and-serve rolls. These are best served warm. Bake brown-and-serve rolls just before serving. Follow package instructions for reheating baked rolls or wrap in foil and bake about 10 minutes just before serving.

Then consult the refrigerator section of your supermarket. The rolls and biscuits that come in refrigerated tubes are particularly good. I've tried baking ½ can of rolls for the children and keeping the rest of the can in the refrigerator to be baked just before the adults' meal, but it's really not very satisfactory. The best method I've found is to bake all of the rolls just before the children's dinner. Serve the children and wrap the rest of the rolls in foil to be reheated just before the later meal or put in a bun warmer if you have one.

[*198*]

Any of the seasonings mentioned previously may be used with refrigerated Parker House rolls. Just lift the top of the unbaked roll and insert the seasoning and a little extra butter. Put the top back down and bake according to package directions.

Then there are the frozen rolls and bread doughs. Some of these are better than anything you can make yourself and are convenient to keep on hand. The frozen bread dough is fun to use and the package has instructions for making several different kinds of rolls and shapes of bread from the dough.

Your grocer's "mix department" is another source of interesting breads. Yeast breads, corn breads, biscuits, muffins, and coffee cakes are all available there. Read the packages for instructions and variations. Bake before the children's meal and wrap in foil, to be reheated before the adults' meal.

BISCUITS

2 cups all-purpose flour
1 teaspoon salt
2 teaspoons baking powder

3 tablespoons butter, margarine, or vegetable shortening
⅔ cup milk

I like to make my own biscuits and find it to be almost as easy as using a mix.

Sift the flour, salt, and baking powder into a bowl. Add the shortening and work into the flour with your fingers. (If you are fastidious, use a pastry blender, but you'll find it easier with your fingers.) When the shortening is all broken up into tiny bits and mixed well with the flour, add the milk. Stir lightly and quickly with a fork, adding a little more milk if necessary to moisten all of the flour. Use your hands again to get all of the flour into the softened mixture. Pat out on a floured board and knead about 15 times until the dough is smooth. Roll or pat until about ¾ inch thick. Cut with a floured biscuit cutter or the rim of a juice glass. Place about 1 inch apart on ungreased cookie sheets. Bake the children's biscuits and refrigerate the adults' biscuits. Bake 12–15 minutes in a 450° F. oven until lightly browned.

To vary: Add ½ cup grated cheese or ½ cup crisply fried and crumbled bacon to the batter. Or, put a small dab of orange marmalade on each biscuit before baking. You may, of course, use these variations on biscuits made from a mix.

[199]

To make sweet rolls with biscuit dough, roll the mixture into an oblong, ¼ inch thick. Spread softened butter all over the dough and sprinkle with cinnamon and brown sugar. Roll jelly-roll fashion and cut into 1-inch circles. Place, cut side up, in greased muffin tins and bake about 20 minutes in a 400° F. oven.

To convert biscuit dough into shortcake, roll the dough to ⅓-inch thickness. Cut in large rounds with a big biscuit cutter or the rim of an 8-ounce glass. Spread one round with softened butter and sprinkle with sugar. Top with another round and bake.

MUFFINS

The best bran muffin recipe I know of comes on the package of bran cereal. It's easy and good. For plain muffins, try this recipe:

1¾ cups all-purpose flour	1 egg
3 teaspoons baking powder	1 cup milk
½ teaspoon salt	¼ cup oil or melted butter
¼ cup sugar	

Sift the flour, baking powder, salt, and sugar into a large bowl. Beat the egg with the milk and oil. Pour the egg mixture over the flour mixture and stir only until the flour is dampened. Do not try to remove all of the lumps. Too much stirring ruins the muffins. Spoon into paper muffin cups or buttered muffin tins and bake in a 400° F. oven for about 15 minutes. Serve the children and wrap the adults' muffins in foil, to be reheated just before serving.

To vary: Use bacon fat instead of oil and add about 3 tablespoons of crumbled bacon to the dough. Add sliced, pitted dates or raisins to the dough.

Desserts

A food editor of a major magazine tells me that she gets more recipe requests for desserts than for any other type of food. I assume that this is because most women particularly enjoy making desserts—certainly they are apt to be most appreciated by their families. This chapter contains suggestions for quick desserts, some of my favorites, which I hope will be new to you, and ideas for changing mixes and prepared desserts into something a bit different.

FRUIT DESSERTS

Fruit makes a wonderfully refreshing dessert after a heavy meal and is good from a nutritional point of view. Serve fruit only once during a meal. In other words, do not serve a fruit dessert if you are also serving a fruit salad or a main dish that contains fruit.

Fresh fruits are especially appealing, but many of the canned and frozen fruits are magnificent, too.

Fruit cups are particularly attractive and can be prepared in advance and refrigerated until serving time. Following are some suggestions for serving combinations of fruit:

1. Drain fruit cocktail or a combination of canned fruits—pineapple tidbits, pear slices, and mandarin oranges, for example. If convenient, add fresh fruit—sliced or diced banana, seeded or seedless grapes, orange sections, unpared apple or pear slices, or melon balls. Place all of the fruits in a bowl mixing well so that the banana, pear, or apple will not darken. Open a small container of frozen strawberries or raspberries. Place on top of the fruits and refrigerate. Stir again before serving to the children. Return to the refrigerator and serve the rest to the adults. This is especially good if the berries are still slightly icy at serving time.

[201]

2. Prepare a combination of fruits or fruit cocktail. Refrigerate and serve the children. Then add 2 tablespoons of sherry or rum to the fruit and continue to refrigerate until the adults are ready for dessert.

3. Top drained and chilled fruit cocktail or a combination of fruits with small scoops of fruit-flavored sherbet just before serving.

4. Top fruits with sour cream sprinkled with brown sugar, chopped candied ginger, or nuts.

5. Make a topping for fruit by combining ½ cup cream, whipped, with ½ cup cream-style cottage cheese.

6. Pour grenadine over a mixture of diced fruits.

7. Drain pear halves. Make a sauce by combining ¼ cup mint jelly with 2 tablespoons pear syrup. Bring to a boil and set aside. Just before serving, spoon lemon sherbet into dessert dishes. Top with pear halves and spoon mint sauce over the top.

8. Cut melons into serving-size wedges. Put a scoop of pineapple sherbet on each wedge. Top with blueberries, with the mint sauce given above, or with crème de menthe.

9. Drain canned peach halves. Make a sauce by combining red raspberry jam and water and heating until smooth. Put a scoop of vanilla ice cream in each peach half and top with sauce.

10. Top drained pear halves or sliced bananas with vanilla ice cream and chocolate sauce.

11. Heat canned apricot or peach halves with just a little of their syrup. Spoon sour cream on the fruit and top with a little brown sugar or finely chopped candied ginger.

12. Slice bananas. Top with thawed frozen raspberries, whipped cream, and crushed macaroons.

DESSERT SALAD I

1 cup cooked white rice
11-ounce can mandarin oranges, drained
8-ounce can pineapple tidbits, drained
8-ounce can sliced pears, drained
¼ cup halved maraschino cherries
1 cup miniature marshmallows
½ cup sour cream

In a large bowl combine all of the ingredients above. Mix well and refrigerate overnight. Serve on lettuce leaves for a salad or in sherbet dishes for dessert. This makes an especially nice late-evening snack served with fancy breads.

DESSERT SALAD II

1-pound can fruit cocktail
3-ounce package lemon-flavored
  gelatin
½ cup heavy cream, whipped

½ cup mayonnaise
½ cup miniature marshmallows
2 bananas, sliced
6 maraschino cherries, halved

Drain fruit cocktail well, adding water to the juice to make 1 cup. Bring the juice and water to a boil and add the gelatin, stirring until dissolved. Cool. Add the whipped cream and mayonnaise, stirring to combine well. Add fruit and marshmallows. Be sure the bananas are well coated with the gelatin and cream. Refrigerate at least 3 hours before serving on lettuce leaves or in sherbet dishes.

MERRY BERRY

8-ounce package frozen raspberries
  or strawberries
1 cup liquid
3-ounce package raspberry- or
  strawberry-flavored gelatin

2 cups (1 pint) vanilla or
  strawberry ice cream
Whipped cream, or whipped
  cream substitute (optional)

Thaw and drain berries. Pour berry juice into measuring cup and add enough water to make 1 cup. Bring to a boil, remove from heat, and stir in gelatin. When gelatin is dissolved, add ice cream, stirring until smooth. Add drained berries and blend. Pour into parfait glasses or dessert dishes and chill in refrigerator—*not* the freezer. Top with whipped cream just before serving if you like.

This is a perfect party dessert because it is good, unusually pretty, and can be made a day in advance. It also makes a delicious pie. When you have prepared the mixture, pour into a baked or crumb pie shell. Top with whipped cream just before serving.

1 pint blueberries	2 tablespoons cornstarch
¾ cup sugar	¾ cup water
¼ teaspoon cinnamon	1 tablespoon lemon juice

Wash and pick over the blueberries. Combine sugar, cinnamon, cornstarch, water, and 1 cup of the blueberries in a saucepan. Place over a low heat, stirring constantly, until the mixture boils and thickens. Add the rest of the blueberries and the lemon juice. Stir well, remove from the heat, cover, cool, and refrigerate. The first cup of berries will make a delicious sauce. The second addition of berries will remain whole and delicious.

This is a magnificent sauce for anything from ice cream to pancakes. It's the almost-raw berries that make it so good. You can serve it over a plain cake and top with ice cream for a blueberry shortcake, with ice cream in parfait glasses, in small tart shells, or thin it down with water and serve it over pancakes or waffles.

CHERRY BRANDY GELATIN

1-pound can pitted sweet cherries	¼ cup brandy
Water	Slivered almonds (optional)
1 envelope dark cherry gelatin	

Early in the day drain cherries. Add water to the juice to make 1½ cups. Heat to the boiling point and stir in the gelatin. When dissolved, add the cherries. Cool and pour into 4 dishes. Add 2 tablespoons water to each of the children's dishes and 2 tablespoons brandy to each of the adults' dishes. Stir. Add a few slivered almonds to each dish and stir again as the gelatin begins to set.

PUDDING DESSERTS

Pudding mixes are a godsend for busy mothers. I prefer the ones that require a few minutes of cooking, but you may substitute instant-type puddings. Following are a few festive variations on the pudding theme. You can probably think of many more.

I have nice heavy parfait glasses which seem to be almost indestructable. If you have delicate "wedding present" glasses or sherbets, be very, very careful to cool puddings before you put them in the glasses; I don't want your broken crystal on my conscience. If you sprinkle a little sugar on the top of the pudding while it cools, it will cut down on the scum, or you can put plastic wrap right down on the pudding while it cools.

COCO MOCHO

1 tablespoon instant coffee powder
1 package vanilla pudding mix
Milk
1 package chocolate pudding mix

Walnuts or pecans
Whipped cream or whipped
  cream substitute

Stir the coffee powder into the vanilla mix, add the milk, and prepare according to package directions. Prepare the chocolate pudding according to directions. Cool, if necessary to prevent breaking your glassware. Put a spoonful of chocolate pudding into each of 6–8 parfait glasses, depending on size, and top with a few nuts broken into large pieces. Add a spoonful of coffee pudding and more nuts. Continue adding alternate layers of the puddings and nuts until all of the pudding is used up. Put a piece of plastic wrap on top of each glass to prevent a "skin" from forming, and refrigerate. If you do not have parfait glasses, substitute small water goblets, fruit juice glasses, custard cups, or sherbet dishes. Just before serving, top with whipped cream or substitute if you like.

APRICOT-VANILLA DELIGHT

1 package vanilla pudding mix,
  prepared according to package
  directions

Drained canned apricots
Apricot jam

Put about 2 tablespoons of pudding in the bottom of each of 4 parfait glasses, top with an apricot half and 1 teaspoon apricot jam. Continue to add layers of pudding, apricots, and jam until the glasses are filled. Chill. Make this the day you intend to serve it.

TIPSY APRICOT DELIGHTS—FOR ADULTS ONLY

Follow the recipe above but substitute apricot brandy for the apricot jam.

[205]

STRAWBERRY-VANILLA DELIGHT

1 package vanilla pudding mix,   Strawberry jam or preserves
  prepared according to package
  directions (cooled, if necessary)

Layer pudding and strawberry jam in parfait glasses, or stir jam into pudding to give a marble effect, and pour into dessert dishes. Chill.

ICE CREAM

We all scream for ice cream but it's nice to offer it in new guises. Even dieters can substitute ice milk for ice cream to end their meals on a happy note.

Sundaes and parfaits are interesting and glamorous. For this purpose it pays to keep several different sauces, syrups, and toppings on hand—either the kind you make yourself or ones that you buy.

Chocolate sauce. One of the easiest can be prepared by melting a 6-ounce package of semisweet chocolate pieces with 1 tablespoon butter and 1/4 cup milk or cream.

Fruit sauces can be made by heating fruit jam with a little water and stirring until smooth, or by cooking a package of frozen fruit with 1 teaspoon cornstarch mixed with 1 tablespoon cold water.

Maple syrup is a delicious ice cream topping. Heat it slightly and top with chopped nuts. Or combine with crunchy peanut butter and heat.

Crispy sugared cereals are child-pleasing ice cream toppings.

Liquors or liqueurs are delightful toppings for adults only.

Combining ice cream and sherbet will add interest to the dessert course. Try chocolate ice cream and orange sherbet or vanilla ice cream and raspberry sherbet.

Following are suggestions for other interesting combinations:

Chocolate or vanilla ice cream sprinkled with freshly grated nutmeg.

Nut ice cream with maple syrup or honey.

Vanilla ice cream with water-thinned cherry pie filling. Flavor with cinnamon, if you like.

Peach ice cream with brandy or light rum.

Coffee ice cream with chocolate sauce or Crème de Cacao.

Vanilla ice cream or lemon or pineapple sherbet with green or white crème de menthe or any of the several orange-flavored liqueurs. Thin mint jelly with a little water and heat, stirring until smooth for the children.

Vanilla ice cream with crushed fruit, to which kirsch or a fruit-flavored brandy may be added.

Vanilla ice cream with prepared mincemeat, to which a few drops of rum may be added.

Now it's your turn. Quickly, think of 5 more tempting combinations!

GLAMOROUS DESSERTS

Two especially glamorous desserts are cherries jubilee and baked Alaska. Both are surprisingly simple to make.

CHERRIES JUBILEE

For 2 adults—the children can have chocolate ice cream at their earlier dinner—drain the liquid from an 8-ounce can of pitted black cherries into an attractive skillet or chafing dish. Add 1 tablespoon sugar and 1 teaspoon cornstarch. Whisk together well and cook until the juice begins to thicken slightly. Add the cherries. When they are warm, pour 3 tablespoons warmed brandy or kirsch over the cherries. Light with a match and spoon the sauce over the cherries, using rather grand, sweeping gestures. This should be done at the table for maximum effect. When the flames die down, serve over vanilla ice cream.

Ice cream
Cake, 1 inch thick
Whites of 3 large or 4 medium-size
  eggs

⅛ teaspoon cream of tartar
Few grains salt
6 tablespoons sugar
½ teaspoon vanilla

Any time during the afternoon, remove the ice cream from the freezer so that it will soften a bit. As soon as you have done that, start to work on the cake. If your cake is too thick, split it. It must be 1 inch thick. It is important to have a cake that's flat on top so that the ice cream won't slide off. Cut the cake into 3- or 4-inch squares or into circles, using an inverted 8-ounce custard cup as a guide. Place 2 squares or circles of cake on each of 2 inverted cake pans or any other flat metal surface.

Beat the egg whites, cream of tartar, and salt until the mixture holds stiff peaks. Then beat in the sugar and vanilla.

Spoon the ice cream onto the cake, rounding it in the middle. Completely cover the ice cream and cake with the meringue. For this purpose, it is easier to use a colored ice cream than to use vanilla, so that you can see at a glance that no ice cream remains uncovered. The meringue and cake insulate the ice cream and prevent it from melting. Place, uncovered, in the freezer.

Five minutes before serving time, set the frozen desserts in a preheated 450° F. oven and brown lightly. This will take about 4 minutes. Using a broad spatula, transfer to dessert plates. Bow modestly and serve. Pass a sauce if you like.

There is no limit to the kinds of baked Alaskas you can prepare. Following are a few suggestions:

Use chocolate cake or brownies and coffee, peppermint, vanilla, or butternut ice cream. Top with chocolate sauce if you like.

Use angel food cake and top with vanilla or strawberry ice cream and pass strawberry sauce.

Use almost any fruit-flavored sherbet on any white or yellow cake. Pass a fruit or mint sauce.

Put nut or vanilla ice cream on spice cake and pass butterscotch sauce.

MERINGUES

2 egg whites
2/3 cup sugar
1 teaspoon cornstarch

1 teaspoon vinegar
1/2 teaspoon vanilla

Consult the weatherman before you decide to make meringue. That's no joke. If the weather is humid, you may—you probably will—have trouble. So select a nice dry day and then go to it.

Preheat the oven to 450° F. Place 2 thicknesses of brown paper—a cut-up grocery bag will be fine—on a cookie sheet. Beat the egg whites until they stand in soft peaks. Combine the sugar and cornstarch and add 2 tablespoons of this mixture at a time to the egg whites, beating after each addition. Add the vinegar with the third addition of sugar and the vanilla with the fourth. Using a pastry tube or a teaspoon, arrange the egg-white mixture on the brown paper in 4 large rings. Put the meringues in the oven, close the door, and turn off the heat. Leave them in the oven for at least 3 hours or overnight.

Serve the meringues with fruit, ice cream, sherbet, or a combination of these. Strawberry ice cream and fresh strawberries are particularly good. See the fruit and ice cream sections of this chapter for other ideas.

ICE CREAM PIE

6-ounce package semisweet
    chocolate pieces
3 tablespoons butter or margarine
2 1/2 cups Rice Krispies

1 quart coffee, mint, or butter
    pecan ice cream
Bitter chocolate

Melt the chocolate pieces and butter. Stir in the cereal. Press into the bottom and sides of a 9-inch pie plate. Refrigerate an hour or so. Remove the ice cream from the freezer to allow to soften a bit. Spoon into the cooled pie shell, pressing down with the back of the spoon. Dip the spoon in hot water and smooth out the top of the pie. Grate bitter chocolate over the top of the pie. Cut with a sharp knife into 6 pieces. Freeze. Remove the pieces 15 minutes before you expect to serve them. (This may be kept several weeks at 0° F.)

¾ cup boiling water

⅛ teaspoon salt

6 tablespoons butter or margarine

3 eggs, at room temperature

¾ cup all-purpose flour

If you've never made cream puffs, you're in for a delightful surprise: they're easy to make.

Pour the boiling water over the butter in a saucepan. Heat until the butter melts, stirring occasionally. In the meantime, measure out the flour and put the salt on top. When the butter is melted, add the flour and salt all at once and stir vigorously over the heat until the dough leaves the sides of the pan and forms a mass around the spoon. This takes only a minute. Remove from the heat and let stand for 4–5 minutes. Break an egg into the dough and beat with a spoon until the mixture is smooth. Add the other two eggs one at a time, beating well after each addition. Continue to beat until the mixture is stiff enough to mound. Then spoon 4 mounds of dough onto a well-greased cookie sheet. The dough will expand, so place the mounds at least 3 inches apart. Put into a preheated 400° F. oven for 15 minutes. Reduce the heat to 325° F. and continue to bake another 25 minutes. Turn off the oven and open the door slightly. Leave the cream puffs in the oven until cool.

With a sharp knife, cut off the tops. Pull out and discard any sticky dough and fill with one of the following:

Vanilla pudding mix, cooked with 1¼ cups milk. Return the tops and spoon chocolate sauce (made by melting ½ cup semisweet chocolate pieces, 1 tablespoon butter, and 1 tablespoon milk) over the puffs.

Whipped cream. Dust puffs with confectioners' sugar.

Ice cream, added just before serving. Top with chocolate or butterscotch sauce.

CAKE, COOKIES, AND BARS

Cake is one item that separates the duty cooks from the dedicated cooks. The duty cook takes her money to the bakery and buys the cake she serves. The dedicated cook spurns all shortcuts and mixes. She measures and sifts and beats and creates magnificent cakes, which are the envy of her friends.

Neither of these types has any need of this section of this book. The duty cook doesn't want cake recipes and the dedicated cook doesn't need them.

For the rest of us, we who vacillate between the two extremes, I am including suggestions which may be helpful in providing interesting desserts with very little effort.

I personally think that cake mixes are a godsend. If you follow the directions on the box faithfully, the results just have to be delicious. However, don't think that you can add an extra egg or a half cup of butter or cream and produce *richer* and *better* cakes. If you tamper with the ingredients you are more apt to produce flat flops.

The number of different cakes available in mix form is constantly growing. Now, too, you can buy mixes for big 2-layer cakes or smaller mixes for 1-layer cakes. If you have the freezer space, you may find that it is most convenient to prepare and bake the large mixes, planning to freeze part of the cake. You could, for example, put part of the batter in a well-greased 9-inch square pan and the rest in an 8-inch round pan or in muffin tins for cupcakes. Or, you could bake it all in a large flat pan and then cut off part of the cake and freeze it. You can cut a single layer in half and stack one half on top of the other to make half of a layer cake suitable for a small family. Whatever you do, don't fill the pan more than ⅔ full of batter. Cakes can be frozen either frosted or plain. Just wrap them well. A frosted cake will wrap easier if you put it in the freezer uncovered for a few hours and then take it out and wrap it.

Frosting mixes are also helpful, and the variety is growing. Both frosting and cake mix are packed together by some manufacturers. Following is a recipe for simple confectioners' sugar frosting which is just as easy to make and quite a bit less expensive than a mix.

¼ cup butter or margarine   1 teaspoon vanilla
¼ cup milk or cream   Confectioners' sugar
Few grains salt

Melt the butter and stir in the milk, salt, and vanilla. Beat in powdered sugar, a little at a time, until the mixture is thick but spreadable. If it becomes too thick, add a few drops of milk. This will frost the tops of 2 layers. To do the sides, too, increase the butter and milk to ⅓ cup each.

Chocolate Frosting. Add ¼ cup cocoa to the butter and cream or melt 1 or 2 ounces baking chocolate with the butter. Try spreading this on graham crackers. Children love it.

Maple Frosting, which is delicious on spice cake, can be made by substituting maple syrup for the milk.

Penuche Frosting is made by adding ½ cup brown sugar to the butter. Top with nuts if you like.

Orange or Lemon Frosting may be made by substituting juice for the milk and grating a little peel into the mixture. Omit the vanilla.

Mocha Frosting. Add ¼ cup cocoa to the butter and substitute very strong brewed coffee for the milk.

Those are all suggestions for varying the same frosting recipe. Following are more cake suggestions.

Bake a yellow, white, or chocolate cake from a mix. When the cake is done, place flat *chocolate mints* on the top of the cake and return to the oven for about 2 minutes or until the chocolate begins to melt. Remove from the oven and swirl the mints over the cake with a knife to make a delightful and attractive frosting.

Crush or grind *peanut brittle* or *peppermint sticks.* Fold into whipped cream or whipped cream substitute and spoon onto wedges of angel food or sponge cake.

Mix a jar of *apricot puree*—baby food—with whipped cream and spoon onto cake wedges.

For adults only, soak cubes of plain, unfrosted cake at least two days old in *sherry*. Serve with a soft custard which may be made from thinned vanilla pudding mix. Add an extra ½ to 1 cup of milk to the 2 cups called for on the package.

UPSIDE DOWN CAKE

¼ cup butter
½ cup brown sugar
Canned peach or apricot halves or
    pineapple slices, well drained

Maraschino cherries (optional)
Walnuts or pecans (optional)
Yellow or white cake mix batter

Melt butter in the bottom of an 8-inch cake pan. Sprinkle brown sugar over the butter and lay fruit close together on the sugar. You may also want to tuck cherries and nuts among the fruit. Gently pour the batter over the fruit and bake according to package directions. Be sure that the pan is no more than ⅔ full. If you have extra batter, make cupcakes. Cool 10 minutes in the pan and turn out on a plate. Serve warm or cold, plain or with whipped cream or ice cream.

Orange Upside Down Cake can be made by substituting ½ cup orange marmalade for the brown sugar and using well-drained mandarin oranges and nuts.

EASY BOSTON CREAM PIE

9-inch layer yellow cake
1 package vanilla pudding and pie
    filling mix

Milk
½ cup semisweet chocolate pieces

Split cake crosswise. If you have baked it yourself, be sure it's cool. Mix pudding mix with 1½ cups milk and bring to a boil according to package directions. Notice that you will be using less milk than package directions call for. Cool the pudding and spoon on the bottom half layer. Put the other half on top. Melt the chocolate pieces and stir in 2 tablespoons milk until smooth. While the chocolate is still hot, pour over the top of the cake, spreading with a spatula. Cool and refrigerate.

You may, of course, use a cake that is smaller than 9 inches, in which case you will probably have a little pudding left over. The icing could be reduced by using ⅓ cup chocolate pieces and *4 teaspoons* milk.

To vary: Use spice cake, butterscotch pudding, and butterscotch pieces.

GRANDMA'S CRACKER DESSERT

3 egg whites
1 cup sugar
1 cup coarsely chopped English
   walnuts

16 saltines, crushed
½ teaspoon vanilla
Whipped cream

My grandmother used to make this dessert, which is chewy and delicious.

Beat egg whites until stiff. Stir in the sugar, walnuts, saltines, and vanilla. Spread in a well-buttered 9-inch-square baking pan and bake 20 minutes in a 350° F. oven until the top is crusty and lightly browned. Cool and cut in squares. Serve with whipped cream. Makes 8 servings.

GINGERBREAD TREATS

The regular-size box of gingerbread mix makes too much for my family to eat in one sitting. Perhaps you have a similar problem, so here are ideas for serving gingerbread on two occasions in two different guises.

GINGER-LEMON TREATS

1 package gingerbread mix,
   prepared according to package
   directions and baked in a
   9-inch-square pan
1 package lemon pie filling mix

2 egg yolks
⅓ cup sugar
2¾ cups water
2 egg whites

While the gingerbread is in the oven, combine the lemon mix with the egg yolks, sugar, and water. Cook, stirring constantly, until the mixture boils and thickens and the capsule in the mix breaks. Beat the egg whites until stiff and fold in the lemon mixture. Cut the gingerbread in half and then cut one of the halves into square or oblong serving-size pieces. Save the other half for the Ginger-Banana Treats below. Just before serving, spoon the mixture over the gingerbread squares. This may be served either warm or cool.

GINGER-BANANA TREATS

Half of 9-inch-square baked
  gingerbread (see recipe above)
1 large or 2 small bananas

½ cup heavy cream, whipped with
  1 teaspoon vanilla (or use
  dessert topping mix)

Split gingerbread in half to make 2 layers. Spread half of the whipped cream on the bottom layer. Top with banana slices. Put top layer on bottom layer and spread rest of whipped cream on the top. Refrigerate. Slice just before serving. For variety, sprinkle with chopped salted peanuts before serving.

LAZY DAISY CAKE

Your mother and grandmother probably made this. In case you've forgotten the ingredients, here they are:

¼ cup melted butter
¼ cup brown sugar
3 tablespoons cream or milk

¾ cup chopped nuts or coconut,
  or a combination of the two
1 plain yellow cake layer, 8- or
  9-inch round or 8-inch square

Combine the butter, brown sugar, cream, and nuts or coconut, and spread over the top of the cake. Put under the broiler until lightly browned. Watch carefully as the topping will burn in an incredibly short time. Serve plain or with scoops of ice cream.

COTTAGE PUDDING

¼ cup sugar
1½ teaspoons cornstarch
½ cup water
¼ teaspoon grated lemon peel
2 tablespoons butter

1 tablespoon lemon juice
Shake nutmeg
Few grains salt
Squares or wedges of plain yellow
  cake

Combine sugar and cornstarch. Add water and lemon peel and beat over heat with a wire whisk. Boil until mixture thickens. Remove from heat and add butter, lemon juice, nutmeg, and salt. Serve warm or cold over the cake.

9-ounce box condensed mincemeat	Water
½ cup apple juice or apple cider	2 eggs
1-pound 2-ounce box yellow cake mix	

Break up mincemeat in a small saucepan. Add the apple juice or cider and bring to a boil according to directions on the mincemeat box. Allow to cool while you prepare the cake mix using only ⅔ cup of water and 2 eggs. Beat according to package directions. Add 2 cups of the cake batter to the mincemeat and combine well. Pour into a well-greased 9-inch-square pan and bake in a 350° F. oven for about 40 minutes, until the cake tests done. Serve warm or cold. It may be cut in large squares and served with whipped cream or a vanilla-sherry sauce, or it may be cut into small bars and served as cookies.

Add another ⅓ cup water to the cake batter that remains. Beat to combine well and pour into a greased 8-inch-square or 9-inch round cake pan. Bake according to package directions. This cake may be frozen to be served later with one of the icings or toppings suggested in this chapter.

Vanilla-sherry sauce may be made by cooking 1 package vanilla pudding and pie filling mix with 2 cups milk, according to package directions. Remove 1½ cups of the pudding, to be served later. Add ¼ cup milk and ¼ cup sherry, or ½ cup milk, to the pudding that remains in the pan. Return to a boil and cool.

FRUIT CRISP

1 can apple, cherry, blueberry, strawberry, or peach pie filling	½ cup flour
¼ cup butter	½ cup quick-cooking oatmeal
½ cup brown sugar	¼ teaspoon cinnamon

Empty pie filling into a greased 8- or 9-inch pie plate. Melt butter and combine with the rest of the ingredients. Sprinkle over the pie filling. Bake 30 minutes in a 350° F. oven. Serve warm or cold with ice cream, whipped cream, or whipped-cream substitute. May be reheated in the oven if desired.

FRUIT COBBLER

1 can peach, cherry, or blueberry
  pie filling
Grated peel of ½ lemon

1 small (about 7-ounce) box yellow
  or white cake mix
¼ cup melted butter
¼ cup lemon juice

Empty pie filling into greased 1–1½-quart casserole. Sprinkle lemon peel over the pie filling. Sprinkle with dry cake mix just as it comes from the box. Combine butter and lemon juice and spoon evenly over the cake mix. Bake 40 minutes in 350° F. oven until top is lightly browned. Serve warm or cold with cream or ice cream. Cobbler may be reheated in the oven if desired.

CEREAL CRUNCH COOKIES

1 cup vegetable shortening
1 cup white sugar
1 cup dark brown sugar, packed
2 eggs
2 teaspoons vanilla
2 cups sifted all-purpose flour

1 teaspoon baking soda
1 teaspoon baking powder
¾ teaspoon salt
2 cups quick-cooking rolled oats
2 cups Rice Krispies
1 cup Grape-Nuts

Preheat oven to 350° F. Cream shortening and sugar. Add eggs and vanilla. Add flour, which has been sifted with soda, baking powder, and salt. Mix. Add cereals. Drop the stiff dough by heaped teaspoons onto greased cookie sheets, leaving 2 inches between cookies. Flatten a little. Bake for 10 minutes or until golden. Makes about 75 large cookies. Store in airtight containers.

For an appealing variation, add a 6-ounce package of chocolate bits to part or all of the dough.

If you don't wish to bake so many cookies all at one time, you can form the dough into long rolls, 2 inches in diameter, wrap in foil, and freeze. When ready to bake, remove from the freezer and cut into 1-inch-thick slices. Cut each slice into quarters and proceed as for dropped cookies.

These are cookies with so many good nutrients you could serve them to the children for breakfast, with an eggnog and fresh fruit. Speaking of breakfast, have you thought of serving ice cream on cereal or cold baked custard with fruit? They're nutritious, so why not?

6-ounce package chocolate bits   3 cups Chinese noodles or rice
cereal, or a combination of
the two

Melt chocolate in the top of a double boiler over water. Stir in
noodles or cereal. Mix well and press into a buttered 9-inch-square pan.
Refrigerate and cut into squares.

PIES

Pie crust is like homemade bread; either you can and do make it
or you can't and don't. Also like bread, making it sometimes seems to
be a waste of time when there are so many good mixes and prepared
pie shells on the market.

Once you get the knack, however, pie crust is easy to make. Following are two recipes. One is for a 2-crust pie made by the long-estab-
lished method. The secret for success with this crust is speed. Work
quickly and handle the dough as little as possible. The second recipe is
for a crust that has some unusual ingredients but tastes like any other
good pastry crust. It is foolproof. This recipe, which cannot be reduced, will make 2 9-inch double-crust pies and a single shell. Remember that pie-crust dough may be stored in the refrigerator for up to 3
days or in the freezer for up to 6 months.

TRADITIONAL PIE CRUST

1¾ cups all-purpose flour   ⅔ cup shortening
1 teaspoon salt   ⅓ cup very cold water

For 1 double-crust pie or 2 single-crust pies. Sift the flour and salt
into a bowl. Add the shortening. I use one of the vegetable shortenings
that come in a can, but lard or a combination of butter and vegetable
shortening or lard can also be used. Don't try to use margarine. Break
up the shortening into the flour. You may use a pastry blender, but I
prefer to press the mixture between my thumb and first two fingers.
When the shortening is *fairly well* broken up and mixed with the flour,
stop. Sprinkle most of the water over the top of the flour and mix with
a fork until most of the flour is sticky. Pick up as much of the flour mixture as you can and mold in your hand. Sprinkle the rest of the water
on the flour that remains in the bottom of the bowl. Add that to the

dough in your hand. You may still have a little flour in the bowl. Sprinkle a few more drops of water onto the flour and add it to the dough ball. When you have all of the dough picked up, divide it into 2 balls. Wrap each one in wax paper or plastic wrap and chill in the refrigerator for an hour—or for a day or two. If you are in a hurry, you may skip the chilling process.

FOOLPROOF PIE CRUST

3¾ cups all-purpose flour
1 tablespoon sugar
1 teaspoon salt
1¾ cups shortening

1 tablespoon vinegar
1 egg
½ cup water

For 2 double-crust pies plus 1 single-crust shell. Sift flour, sugar, and salt together. Add the shortening and mix with a fork, pastry blender, or your fingers. In a separate dish, beat together the vinegar, egg, and water. Combine the two mixtures and stir with a fork. Pick up as much dough as possible and mold into a ball. You may have a little dry flour left in the bottom of the bowl. If so, moisten it with a few drops of water and add it to the ball. Wrap or cover the dough and refrigerate for at least 30 minutes. Break off the amount you need for the pie or pies you wish to make, and store the rest of the dough for up to 3 days in the refrigerator or up to 6 months in the freezer.

To roll out pie-crust dough, sift a little flour on a pastry cloth, bread board, or a slab of marble. I use marble. Put dough for one crust onto the floured surface. Turn it once so that both sides are lightly coated with flour. Too much flour, like too much water, makes a tough crust. If the dough has been chilled, bang it a few times with your rolling pin. Then roll the dough into a circle larger than your pie pan. To be sure it's big enough, invert your pie pan on the dough. You should have at least a 1-inch margin of dough all around the top of the pan. When the dough is rolled, fold it in half, pick it up and put it in one half of the pie pan, and unfold it to fill the other half of the pan.

If you are making a 2-crust pie and the crust is to be baked with the filling, fill the pie shell. Then roll out another circle of dough. With a sharp knife, cut a few slits in the top half of the crust. Fold it in half. Lay it on half of the pie and unfold to cover the other half. You can press the edges of the crust together on the edge of the plate with a fork that has been dipped in water or you can turn under about ½ inch of the dough that hangs over the edge of the pan and make it stand upright. Press this edge with your fingers to make a fluted edge. Trim off any excess dough. Bake pie on center rack in oven, following recipe for specific filling.

To make a 1-crust pie, just roll half of the dough and put in the pan and crimp the edges. If you want to bake the crust before filling it, prick it all over with the tines of a fork to prevent the crust from puffing up and shrinking. Bake in a 450° F. oven until browned, about 10 minutes.

If you are still not interested in making your own crusts, you can buy prepared crusts, pie-crust mix, or sticks of pie-crust dough. You can buy bakery or frozen pies, for that matter.

CRUMB CRUSTS

As for crumb crusts, those that come ready made in sturdy aluminum pans are very satisfactory. You can also make your own using graham crackers, cornflakes, zwieback, ginger snaps, crisp chocolate cookies, or vanilla wafers. You can buy prepared crumbs or you can make your own in an electric blender or by rolling the crackers or cookies between sheets of waxed paper or in a plastic bag.

For a 9-inch pie, melt ½ cup butter or margarine. Add 1½ cups crumbs. If you like, you may also add up to ½ cup sugar, although I find that the cookies and crackers are usually sweet enough without adding any sugar. Mix well. If you want to sprinkle crumbs on top of the pie, set aside about ⅓ cup of the crumbs. Press the rest against the sides and bottom of the pie plate and chill in the refrigerator for about 1 hour, or bake in a 375° F. oven for about 8 minutes. The sweeter crumb crusts have a tendency to burn, so watch them carefully.

Coffee pie. For a spectacular pie put ¼ cup water in a small saucepan. Sprinkle 1 envelope unflavored gelatin over the water and, when it is softened, dissolve over heat. In the meantime, beat 2 cups (1 pint) heavy cream with 3 tablespoons instant coffee powder, ½ cup confectioners' sugar, and a few grains of salt. When the cream is whipped, add the gelatin and ½ teaspoon vanilla and mix well. Turn into a chocolate-cookie crumb crust and sprinkle a few crumbs on top. Chill. This is very rich but very good.

Apple pie is surely the universal favorite. It seems useful to include a recipe here since apples are available all year round and are relatively inexpensive. Line a pie pan with pastry. Peel, core, and slice enough apples to fill the pan, heaping them in the center. The best pie apples are very tart and crisp. If your apples seem bland, grate a little lemon peel over them. Mix together about ½ cup brown or white sugar—a little more if the apples are particularly tart—¼ teaspoon salt, 1 tablespoon flour, ½ teaspoon cinnamon, or ¼ teaspoon cinnamon and ¼ teaspoon nutmeg. Sprinkle this mixture over the apples. Dot with about 1 tablespoon butter. Cover with the upper crust and bake in a 400° F. oven until the apples are tender and the crust is lightly browned, about 1 hour.

A raw apple or two may also be added to give a homemade flavor to a jar or can of apple-pie filling or to prepared mincemeat.

Which brings us to the subject of *prepared fruit fillings.* Many of these are delicious and can be seasoned to your taste. If you like tart pies you may want to add a little lemon juice to apple, cherry, or berry pies. You can add cinnamon to apple-, peach-, or cherry-pie filling. You may also combine two or more of the fillings—blueberry and peach, strawberry and rhubarb, etc. Most of these cans and jars actually fill an 8-inch pie properly. Use in a 9-inch pan if you want an "affectionate" pie—one with the crusts close together.

Now for the *packaged pudding and pie filling mixes.* These mixes have excellent directions and variation suggestions on the labels.

Lemon-pie filling is delicious. I like to add a little grated lemon peel to the cooked filling.

Banana cream pie. Prepare a package of vanilla pie filling mix according to package directions. Put a little of the cooked and cooled filling in the bottom of a graham-cracker, ginger-snap, or chocolate-cookie crumb crust. Slice bananas over the pie filling and top with the rest of the filling. Sprinkle extra crumbs, shredded coconut, or chopped peanuts on the top, and chill and serve.

Two-layer cream pie may be made by preparing a box of vanilla pie filling mix. While still hot, remove 1 cup of the mix and add 1 ounce pre-melted cooking chocolate. Stir to blend well and put in a baked or crumb crust. Spoon the vanilla pudding on top and chill well. Serve with whipped cream or whipped cream substitute.

Coconut cream pie. Add shredded coconut to vanilla pie filling mix and sprinkle more coconut on the top, or use coconut flavored pudding mix.

See the section on puddings for more combinations which may appeal to you and your family.

Index